New York
at
Mid-Century

Recent Titles in
Contributions in American History

New York
at
Mid-Century

The Impellitteri Years

Salvatore J. LaGumina

Contributions in American History, Number 147
Jon L. Wakelyn, Series Editor

Greenwood Press
Westport, Connecticut • London

Library of Congress Cataloging-in-Publication Data

LaGumina, Salvatore John.
  New York at mid-century : the Impellitteri years / Salvatore J.
LaGumina.
    p.   cm.—(Contributions in American history, ISSN 0084-9219
; no. 147)
  Includes bibliographical references and index.
  ISBN 0-313-27205-0
  1. New York (N.Y.)—Politics and government—1898-1951. 2. New
York (N.Y.)—Politics and government—1951- 3. Impellitteri,
Vincent R. (Vincent Richard), 1900-1987. I. Title. II. Series.
  F128.5.L19   1992
  974.7'104—dc20   92-8844

British Library Cataloguing in Publication Data is available.

Library of Congress Catalog Card Number: 92-8844
ISBN: 0-313-27205-0
ISSN: 0084-9219

First published in 1992

Greenwood Press, 88 Post Road West, Westport, CT 06881
An imprint of Greenwood Publishing Group, Inc.

Printed in the United States of America

The paper used in this book complies with the
Permanent Paper Standard issued by the National
Information Standards Organization (Z39.48-1984).

10 9 8 7 6 5 4 3 2 1

Copyright Acknowledgments

Every reasonable effort has been made to trace the owners of copyright materials in this book, but in some instances this has proven impossible. The author and publisher will be glad to receive information leading to more complete acknowledgments in subsequent printings of the book and in the meantime extend their apologies for any omissions.

Excerpts from the Edward Corsi Papers, George Arents Research Library for Special Collections at Syracuse University.

Excerpts from the *New York Times*, December 22, 1941 and June 10, 1951. Copyright © 1941, 1951 by The New York Times Company. Reprinted by permission.

Excerpts from the oral history interviews with Luther Gulick and George S. Combs, Columbia University Oral History Research Office Collection, Columbia University.

Excerpts from the following letters: C. T. Crain to Vincent R. Impellitteri (12/22/33); Sidney Hillman to Vincent R. Impellitteri (7/2/31); William C. Dodge to Vincent R. Impellitteri (1/31/36); Joe Louis to Vincent R. Impellitteri; Robert Moses to Lazarus Joseph (8/9/51); Daniel Kornblum to the Editor of the *New York Times* (8/27/53); Howard McSpedon to Vincent R. Impellitteri (9/2/53); Bill McMenamin to Ed Carr (7/2/52); Ed Carr to Jack Tierney (4/25/52); and Abraham Beame to Vincent R. Impellitteri (8/31/53). Vincent R. Impellitteri Papers, Municipal Archives, Department of Records and Information Services, City of New York.

Contents

Acknowledgments

I wish to acknowledge the help rendered via discussions, suggestions and selective readings by a number of colleagues such as Frank Cavaioli, Joseph Varacalli and Jerome Krase. My thanks are extended to the librarians of the New York City Municipal Archives, Nassau Community College, Columbia University Oral History Research Center and Syracuse University Library for their valuable assistance. I am also in debt to members of the Impellitteri family, especially Rose Impellitteri Comcowich, and other acquaintances whose interviews provided a humane dimension. My indebtedness goes to Nassau Community College for extending a sabbatical that enabled me to conduct intensive and uninterrupted research and writing.

I wish to take this opportunity to express my deep love and gratitude to my wife Julie for her continued encouragement and my thanks to my children Frank, Mary, John and Christine for their constant reassurance.

Introduction

To recall life in New York City during the
Impellitteri years is to evoke memories of an era
when the impossible happened. It was an incredible
moment in the city's history. It was a time when a
Sicilian immigrant with scant political experience,
one whose credentials for presiding over the
nation's largest and most important city were at
best modest, surprised observers by challenging and
defeating a powerful political machine. To cite
Harry Golden, "only in America" could such an
extraordinary phenomenon occur: Vincent
Impellitteri was the only man to be elected mayor
of modern New York City as an independent candidate
supported by none of the major political parties.
Possessing neither personal family wealth nor
strong connections with city power brokers, his
victory against immense odds served as a cause of
inspiration for the little guy, the common man at
mid-century.

Born in 1900 in Isnello, Sicily, Vincent was
brought to America in 1901. After a short stay in
New York City the Impellitteri family moved to
Ansonia, a small industrial town in Connecticut,
which provided the prosaic setting in which Vincent
spent his childhood, went to school and mixed with
the working population of several nationalities.
Like other youngsters of his ethnic background,
early in life he gained experience in various,
proletarian activities--lathering customers for
shaves in his brother's barbershop, stocking fruits
and vegetables in another brother's store, earning
ten cents an hour during the night shift as a
wire-spooler in a local factory.

Demonstrating a rather rapid pattern of

assimilation, the recently graduated high school student joined the United States Navy at the outbreak of the First World War, a move which not only enabled him to see combat action, but that also marked the end of his residence in Ansonia. After the war he moved to New York City, obtained a law degree at Fordham University and began his entry into the city political whirligig as a lower echelon functionary in the Democratic party. Throughout the 1920's and 1930's, during which time he practiced law with distinction both in the public and private spheres, he also reinforced his political ties especially as a leader of New York's Italian American Democratic bloc. In consequence of his toil within the ethnic political vineyards, he was rewarded with appointments as Assistant District Attorney in Manhattan and as secretary to two New York State Supreme Court judges. This training propelled him to a primary municipal rank as Democratic party candidate for President of the City Council. It was clear that because the Republicans had previously turned Italian ethnicity to political advantage by electing Fiorello LaGuardia mayor, the Democrats would have to follow suit to attract the growing Italian-American bloc of voters. By name, inclination and experience, Impellitteri proved to be an excellent choice. With William O'Dwyer leading the ticket for mayor and Impellitteri for City Council President, the Democrats won the city elections in 1945 and 1949. Indeed in the latter election Impellitteri's vote total exceeded all others and thereby served as preparation for the unusual mayoral election of 1950 necessitated by Mayor O'Dwyer's resignation. Each of the three principal candidates: Impellitteri, Ferdinand Pecora and Edward Corsi were of Italian birth and all maintained significant ties with the ethnic community. Such a phenomenon affecting the Italian American community had not occurred previously, and it would seem safe to say would never happen again. But the uniqueness of the election was also inherent in the fact of Impellitteri's victory on an independent ticket over the major parties. Clearly Impellitteri's success was an historic political achievement.

Because the 1950 election was a special vote to choose a mayor to complete O'Dwyer's second term of office, it would be an abbreviated tenure of three years. Nevertheless, the 1950-53 period were years of immense significance for the nation and the city with their new statuses requiring huge adjustments as the world's preeminent national power and the leading municipality. The confrontation occasioned by the Cold War and pressures on city governments to make up for years of postponed projects and salary increases, rendered this an extraordinary transitional period. These were years also of serious scandals for the city then undergoing significant demographic changes as many left the metropolis for the suburbs while newcomers filled the consequent void.

In the few works that touch on the subject, assessments of Impellitteri as mayor of the great metropolis, are on balance, less than laudatory. This evaluation can be attributed to an appalling paucity of indepth research and consideration. Opting for seemingly more appealing mayoralties and for the more magnetic personalities such as LaGuardia, these studies are largely deficient in their failure to consult the extensive public papers of Impellitteri's mayoralty. By contrast, I have spent considerable time examining the public papers of his administration as well as his family papers in addition to surveying numerous relevant primary and secondary material and consequently conclude that the Impellitteri mayoralty possessed much that commends itself to the objective reviewer. Indeed, compared to many city administrations both prior to and subsequent to his own, Impellitteri accomplished an impressive record in the areas of sound and equitable labor policies, school and hospital construction, constructive appointments to administrative positions, commercial development and environmental concerns. Although incomplete, he did take some meaningful steps designed to effect a more efficient administrative structure. Of no small importance and in sharp contrast with so many other city administrations, is the virtual absence of scandals while Impellitteri presided. While critics can point to shortcomings, it must be remembered that Impellitteri had to deal with a fractious predominant political party and with many high members of his own administration actively trying to replace him. Simply put, critics have tended to overlook his work in behalf of the city: his exhausting personal efforts to exact more state aid, his estimable espousal of a more democratic form of city government designed to give greater voice to the City Council, his singular impact on national legislation such as that which led to a successful bid to obtain a desperately needed housing program for the nation's cities. Ignored too is the extremely vital role he played in behalf of United States foreign policy. In 1951 he undertook a lengthy good will tour of Italy at the direct behest of President Truman in a successful bid to stem the possibility of a Communist electoral triumph in that country. No other American representative to Italy--not even the famous LaGuardia--was to be as enthusiastically received in the land of his birth as was the Sicilian-born mayor. In sum, the short tenure of the Impellitteri administration is worthy of study.

It may be asserted that it is difficult to truly get to know the inner man in the absence of extensive writings. This important reflective method was not a part of Impellitteri's adult life, although interesting enough, he was a diarist in his youth. While Impellitteri left no memoirs of his public years, there exists an impressive body of material such as letters, speeches, notes, articles, and so forth written by him or about him that provide considerable insight into his personality and outlook. Moreover, as a visible public figure holding what some consider the second most prominent public office in the country, he received very extensive newspaper coverage. I have also examined at length the body of this material.

New York
at
Mid-Century

1

At the Creation of the Century

The major molders of public opinion greeted the new
century with unbounded optimism, if the New York
Times editorial of January 1, 1900 is to be taken
as typical it recalled highlights of the past year
as "wonders," but it further predicted that "the
distinction of highest records must presently pass
to the year 1900 . . . . The outlook on the
threshold of the new year is extremely bright."
This hopeful attitude reflected the perspective of
American newcomers who, although destined for the
most part to live humble proletarian lives, imbibed
the prevailing optimism.

The ebullient boosterism that characterized the
nation as it entered the new century had particular
meaning for New York City, which had just recently
positioned itself for years of unbounded growth and
prosperity. The incorporation of Greater New York
City in 1898 consolidated the previously separate
cities of Brooklyn and Manhattan together with the
counties of Richmond, Queens and the Bronx and
thereby propelled the already great metropolis to
preeminence as the nation's largest city and one of
the world's great urban centers. At nearly three
and a half million people it more than outmatched
its nearest rival, Chicago, whose population stood
at 1,698,000. Enjoying this premier status as it
commenced the new century, New York City was
preordained to continue to bask in the glow of
supremacy as the wealthiest, most influential and
most ethnically heterogenous municipality. So
pronounced was its eminence that it controlled the
destinies not only of residents within its borders,
but also of people within the entire metropolitan
area. For suburbanites within its orbit it was

sufficient to refer to "the city" without fear of
being misunderstood. The sheer size, diversity and
wealth of the metropolis assured its predominance
as the "First City" in the United States, first in
economic power, cultural pursuits and ethnic
representations. Given its favorable geographic
position, its vast and excellent port facilities at
the turn of the century, which was a time of
industrial acceleration and immigration influx, it
was guaranteed a mammoth share of sustained
economic activity and population growth. Its total
population would jump to 4,766,883 in 1910 and
finally 7,891,957 in 1950, its peak year.

Boasting of extraordinary affluence as typified
by the concentration of economic power on Wall
Street and the luxurious private mansions on Fifth,
Madison and Park Avenues, the city also had its
poor. A city of extremes, it was the home of some
of the world's richest and poorest folks often
living incongruously side by side. While John
Pierpont Morgan, chief of the mightiest banking
house in the world, enjoyed his invaluable
paintings, rare books and priceless manuscripts in
his mahogany-paneled library in mid-Manhattan, tens
of thousands of New Yorkers lived amidst incredible
poverty, filth and wretchedness only a few blocks
away. There was also a substantial middle class,
which, however, did not attract as much attention,
as did the extremes.

New York was America's classic cosmopolitan
city. Daily numerous vessels steamed into its giant
port carrying people from all over the globe who
were attracted by promises of a better future.
Along its wharves one could hear the speech and
slang of speakers of dozens of tongues hastening
along their converging ways, with a significant
number remaining as dwellers in the great
metropolis where they were determined to make their
"fortunes." By becoming a port for all the world,
it seemed that New York was merely fulfilling its
providential mission--its manifest destiny, as one
observer put it. Blessed by Mother Nature with an
abundant shoreline adjoining deep waters, its
evolution to a premier depot for newcomers was a
natural consequence.

Although statistics could easily be adduced to
demonstrate the enormous range of nationalities,
races and religions that made up the great city

population mix--a greater mixture than anywhere
else in the world--no statistical analysis could
depict the complexity of the human element that
peopled New York. The scores of foreign language
publications, the dozens of ethnic neighborhoods
and the hundreds of nationality restaurants that
dotted the metropolis readily underscored its
polyglot nature. By 1900 the numerically
preponderant nationalities were the Austrians,
English, German, Hungarians, Irish, Polish,
Russians and Italians. First and second places were
held by the Germans and Irish, however, after 1900
Russian Jews and Italians replaced them, but both
would suffer in the estimation of native Americans
and those who had arrived earlier. For the Jews it
was their supposed private mannerism and their
reputation for greed that were held against them,
while for the Italians the concern was a
tendentiousness toward violence and involvement in
criminal activities that formed the bases for
unfavorable evaluations.

Pervasive anti Italian prejudice actually
preceded mass immigration so that even before
Italians entered the country in significant
numbers, Americans could read about their asocial
traits: a penchant for begging, gross ignorance and
illiteracy, deplorable religious customs
approximating superstition, weak and even deformed
physiques and most glaring of all, their
inclination toward criminality. Readers of city
newspapers were regularly regaled with accounts of
private vendettas in Italian city neighborhoods in
which ear-biting, knife-wielding and organized
gangster activities seemed to be the daily staples
of life. Even when writers were not bent on
depicting immigrants at their worst, the results
were similarly negative. Accordingly, in a
description of a boat arrival scene of a cargo of
lemons from Italy, Italian longshoremen were
pictured as "cheerful, undersized men . . . can
carry prodigious loads from sunrise to nightfall,
and then shuffle homeward in their much too large
coats and picturesque hats . . . chattering for all
the world as if they were just going to their
labors."[1]

Immigration was essential to the growth of the
United States, of course. It was also especially
critical for the emergence of New York City. Until

the 1880's the newcomers were so-called "Old
Immigrants" who came from northwestern European
countries. However, from the 1880's on, "New
Immigrants" constituted the preponderance of new
arrivals. Coming from southern and eastern Europe,
the latter arrivals with their unique language,
hearty foods, strange religions, curious dress,
alien customs and exotic cultures, stood in sharp
contrast to the prevailing groups in the nation. As
such they frequently drew unwelcome attention to
themselves, yet even though they experienced
discrimination, they continued to emigrate. Between
1880 and 1910, 8.4 million arrived with over 1
million entering in 1907, the peak immigration
year. Italians constituted the largest single
nationality of the "New Immigration" influx.

Italian mass immigration stands as one of the
great migrations of any people in recorded history.
In size, multiplicity of destinations and
complexity of forces that created the movement, it
was almost without parallel in modern history.
Between 1900 and 1910 over two million Italians
entered the United States, mostly through New York
City. It is estimated that over four million came
between 1891 and 1920, with southern Italians
forming the largest portion of the exodus. The full
significance of the movement is best understood by
examining the social and historical environment
from which it developed.

Among the factors that prompted movement out of
Italy were an assortment of social and cultural
determinants, but clearly economics was the
overriding reason. For years southern Italy had
been a land that time had forgotten, a place of
hunger and backbreaking toil, an area afflicted by
the ravages of deforestation and malaria, a locale
of peasants tilling the soil of indifferent
absentee landlords. It was a land that had also
experienced a significant population increase with
decreasing opportunities for offspring. The
economy, moreover, had recently been buffeted by
the biological destruction of wine-making, one of
its major agricultural industries and by stiff
foreign competition in the form of citrus fruit
production. As word of better economic
opportunities seeped into Italy's towns and
villages, poor but determined people decided to
make their move.

Settling for the most part in large cities on the eastern seaboard of the United States, New York became home for more Italian immigrants than any other city in the Western Hemisphere. The influx produced many "Little Italies," beginning with Manhattan's legendary "Mulberry Bend" and subsequently East Harlem. The neighborhoods were characteristic slums; indeed Mulberry Bend, with its old buildings, fetid rooms and foul air served as residence for successive waves of the city's impoverished inhabitants. Many an ethnic people endured life in this environment until fortune, which frequently came in the form of a new successor underclass, enabled the former residents to escape. Hordes of southern Italian immigrants lived in these slums under conditions as terrible as those reputed to beset inhabitants of the world's most notorious neighborhoods. The famous Danish-born muckraker Jacob Riis, a long-time Mulberry Bend observer, left us an indelible description of how the other half lived.

I have in mind one Italian "flat" among many, a half underground hole . . . reached by odd passageways through a tumble down tenement that was always full of bad smells and scooting rats . . . where five children slept with their elders. How many of those there were I never knew. There were those big family beds, and they nearly filled the rooms, leaving only patches of the mud floor visible. The walls were absolutely black with age and smoke.The plaster had fallen off in patches and there was green mold on the ceiling and yet, with it all, with the swarm of squirming youngsters that were as black as the floor they rolled upon, there were evidences of a desperate, if hopeless, grasping after order, even neatness.[2]

Not surprisingly, the casualty rate for inhabitants of these dark, dank, airless and over congested quarters was enormous, exacting a high toll of infants whose mortality rate became one of the most staggering in the city. Nor were other children and adults spared from the debilitating effects of slum diseases. Thus survival of tenement life proved to be an early grim testing ground for the immigrant masses. Notwithstanding the undesirability of the dwellings, the city Italian population grew, as illustrated in the following tables.

Italian Foreign Stock Living in New York by Decade*
(First and Second Generation)

YEAR	POPULATION
1900	219,597
1910	545,178
1920	807,048
1930	1,070,355
1940	1,095,000
1950	1,028,980
1960	858,601
1970	682,613

* Since foreign stock only included first and second generations, when additional generations are added statistics are significantly affected.

Population of Italian Americans of All Generations Living in New York City by Decade

YEAR	POPULATION (estimated, x 100)
1900	219.0
1910	862.0
1920	1,274.7
1930	1,511.8
1940	1,587.5
1950	1,716.9
1960	1,951.3
1970	1.739.7

Source: Edward J. Miranda and Ino Rossi, New York City's Italians (New York: Italian American Center For Urban Affairs Inc., 1976), 118.

For countless Italian immigrants these city neighborhoods became permanent destinations. There they lived out their lives, and there their children and grandchildren would seek their destinies. For others, these initial Italian enclaves were only temporary way stations before they moved to other parts of the expanding city as they helped establish newer "Little Italies," such as Williamsburgh and Bensonhurst in Brooklyn, Long Island City and Astoria in Queens, Belmont and Williamsbridge in the Bronx and Rosebank and Dongan Hills in Richmond. And so the new century saw the city Italian population assume tidal proportions. Together with their offspring, they were destined to become the largest single nationality in the city.

Of course New York City's Italian Americans were only one of dozens of ethnic groups with whom they interacted and competed. Frequently the Italians settled in areas previously inhabited by other ethnic clusters such as Germans, Irish and Jews. Italians uneasily shared houses of worship with Catholics from disparate countries and mixed with them in the workplace. At school their children came into contact with youngsters called by unfamiliar names, who belonged to strange religions and were often of different skin color. In short, the city's Italian Americans entered into a pluralistic society even while they resided within the protective environment of their distinctive neighborhoods.

How did Italian immigrants and their progeny fare in the early decades of the new century? With over half a million Italians living as city residents in 1910, it is not surprising to learn that they occupied many walks of life. They were an emerging force in trade and industry, attaining dominance in the artificial flower manufacturing and retail fruit businesses. Italian hotels and restaurants were attracting customers beyond the immigrant neighborhoods, and a sizeable number of Italians had created "banks" doing legitimate transactions. It was in this period also that they began to appear in the professions as doctors, lawyers, artists, and so on. The formation of the Italian Chamber of Commerce in 1887 attests to the growing importance of their participation in the city's economic affairs.

These examples of a rising immigrant people must be kept in perspective, however, because clearly the overwhelming majority of Italians were unskilled workers earning low pay for arduous labor. Along with other immigrants of agricultural, peasant background, life for the city's Italians was an unending struggle to make ends meet, earning their bread in the construction and needle trades and other forms of manual labor. While they were thereby laying the foundation for their children and their grandchildren's successes, first generation immigrants were primarily a proletarian people who were destined to witness upward mobility at a very slow rate.

Life's hardships were rendered more palatable by the warmth, love and succor of their nuclear and extended families. They could count on the support of their own institutions, such as the church and mutual aid societies. In addition, they were beginning to gain influence through participation in labor organizations and politics, although in the latter regard, progress did not come easily. The city contained numerous neighborhoods that possessed unique characteristics reflecting common national, ethnic, social and economic backgrounds. Notwithstanding that these little worlds afforded newcomers sites of acceptance amid the gregariousness of a people with familiar cultural patterns, no group could be entirely unaware of others. Furthermore, no neighborhood remained static; changes could be detected within one's lifetime as ethnic group replaced ethnic group in community after community. No group could avoid interaction with others.

Those charged with political leadership were, perforce, required to master ethnic politics, that is to be aware of and sensitive to the competing needs of various groups within the body politic. They were also required to deal with the issues of inclusion and absorption. The observation of de Tocqueville, made more than a century and a half earlier, that Americans tended to form associations for every purpose, found its validation in the city's myriad ethnic/national associations attempting to exert influence on public officials. While much attention has been paid to the pathological consequences of ethnic group conflicts, it is significant to note that the pluralistic nature of society manifested itself in ethnic group politics as a normal means of functioning. This is, in essence, a recognition of the absence of a homogenous society and a further acknowledgment of ethnic ties as critical influences in intergroup associations. Ethnic groups served the immigrant city population in two ways: that of self-identification and that of self-interest. As important as these considerations were, they by no means preempted the total experience of city inhabitants as other associations, devoid of ethnic heritage also came into play. Thus, to function satisfactorily in a pluralistic society, it would not be uncommon to harbor multiple identifications, a development that necessitated considerable flexibility.

   In the fabled gilded age of the late nineteenth
and early twentieth centuries political power was
linked to economic power as the wealthy exerted
major influence largely through the Republican
party. Republican ascendancy had not gone
unchallenged, however, as the Democrats, led by
Tammany Hall leaders of Irish extraction, emerged
as powers in their own right. From the latter part
of the nineteenth century until the midtwentieth
century, Irish Americans dominated the city's
Democratic party.
   It has been asserted that to understand
municipal governance, it is necessary to realize
that the political machine, an organization created
for the election of officials and the passage of
legislation it desires, is at the heart of the
matter. The machine is composed of professional
politicians who serve on committees and hold
various party positions; these functionaries
represent the organization to the party and the
public. Because it is implied that the organization
places its interests before those of the general
public, the term "machine" has a derogatory
connotation. Rank and file party workers can
exercise their own influence, however, real power
traditionally has been in the hands of party
officers headed by the boss, who might or might not
hold elective office. The city machine has provided
a ladder whereby participants, particularly those
of lower and middle-class background, often
immigrants, have been able to improve their
circumstances. Bereft of the advantages of
inherited wealth or family connections enjoyed by
old stock Americans, these party leaders achieved
power by commanding large numbers of voters.
   In New York City the Tammany machine found its
expression within the Democratic party even before
the Civil War, and it continued to hold forth as it
entered the twentieth century, stymied occasionally
by reform groups both within and without the party.
The history of the Tammany successes over reformers
prompted the cynical but realistic observation of
wily George Washington Plunkitt.

I've seen more than one hundred "Democracies" rise and fall in
New York City in the last quarter of a century. At least a
half a dozen so-called Democratic organizations are formed
every year. All of them go in to down Tammany and take its

place, but they seldom last more than a year or two, while
Tammany's like the everlasting rocks, the eternal hills and
the blockades on the "L" road-it goes on forever.[3]

When Greater New York was incorporated in 1898,
Manhattan-based Tammany was required to accommodate
other county Democratic organizations that now
formed segments of the big city party. Thus the
powerful Brooklyn Democratic party headed by Hugh
McLaughlin was a force with which to reckon.
Nevertheless, by virtue of its control over large
numbers of new immigrants, its affinity with
influential money sources, and its long political
tradition, Manhattan's Tammany retained its
dominance. At the time of incorporation, Irish-born
Richard Croker was helping to shape the classic
machine structure. The organization hierarchy
consisted of the overall Tammany boss, assembly
district (ward) leaders, precinct captains and
party workers. District leaders and others were
elected to a General or County Committee that
deferred to an Executive Committee that, in turn,
chose the overall chief. Major and minor bosses
exercised varying degrees of political power, the
latter within distinctive, cohesive neighborhoods
and ethnic enclaves, always conscious of the
specific needs of those who lived in them: jobs,
apartments, averting legal restrictions, and so on.
So long as these party functionaries delivered, the
masses reciprocated with their votes.
In this fashion it can be said that politics
characteristically reflected the presence of ethnic
groups, some of which became effective voting
blocs. Party allegiances accordingly, were
encouraged along ethnic lines and thereby exercised
considerable continuity over time. However, it was
impossible in the pluralistic environment, for one
group to secure power over the city indefinitely, a
realization that led to the development of
alliances that transcended ethnic divisions. New
York's Democratic party machinery was in the hands
of the Irish, but they in turn depended on working
arrangements with the Germans, Jews and Italians.
Far from perfect, these arrangements sometimes
broke down and resulted in conflicts in which one
group sought to assert itself over the others.
Much to the dismay of Progressive leaders who
were primarily of "Old Stock" Protestant heritage

and who were consequently alarmed at Catholic Irish
political prowess, the Democrats were regarded as
self-serving, and unenlightened, if not outright
corrupt. Surely the tainted career of the Scotch-
Irish Tammany Boss William Marcy Tweed was
considered proof of how sullied New York City
politics could become. Tweed, who ironically was
not Catholic, earned a place of ignominy in
American political history by his control of
Tammany Hall which enabled him to retire a
millionaire, although he never held more than a
modest job. Progressive cartoonist Thomas Nast's
caricature of a big, corpulent, gluttonous man left
an indelible impression on the American mind of
Tweed as the epitome of "boss" politics at its
worst. And now, after Tweed's demise, it was his
Irish successors, Honest John Kelly, Richard Croker
and George Washington Plunkitt, who emulated him by
becoming leeches and enriching themselves at the
trough of the city treasury as they exploited the
newly arrived immigrants. In the process, the Irish
leaders rooted Tammany Hall even more firmly among
rank and file Democrats, an achievement unmatched
by other political clubs of the day.
    In denouncing this state of affairs,
Progressives employed selective criteria (namely
their own standards of political and moral
deportment) to render judgments. Beyond their own
ken, however, there were other considerations of
meaning to the immigrants such as jobs or favors,
that were of more immediate import when compared to
the nebulous intangible Progressive ideals.
Furthermore, Progressives readily overlooked the
contributions rendered by such products of Tammany
Hall as Robert Wagner and Alfred E. Smith, whose
outstanding careers commended themselves to the
body politic. The widespread perception that
Tammany "owned" city hall is an exaggeration as the
scholars Sayre and Kaufman have so ably
demonstrated.

If Tammany is taken in its precise meaning as a pejorative
synonym for the New York County Democratic Party organization,
then it can be said to have exercised dominant supervision
over the city's Mayors for less than a fourth of the sixty
year period since 1897.[4]

Nevertheless, it was the negative, narrow

perception that preoccupied the public mind rather
than a broader definition of New York politics in
which mayoral domination has eluded Tammany Hall.
Consequently it appeared that the city was
impervious to the Progressive impulse in an age of
reform.

The phenomenal growth of the city was the result
of two movements. One could be attributed to a
fecund overflow of the American countryside moving
into urban centers, while the other movement was
the massive migration from Europe. American rural
areas bemoaned the loss of its farmers lured to the
city by its unparalleled economic opportunities and
its overall verve and excitement. The city also
presented an inviting prospect to men and women
abroad who were willing to mingle with others of
sundry races, nationalities and religions bound for
the promised land. It was the advent and political
involvement of the newly arrived immigrants that
proved particularly irksome to Progressive
reformers who, as representatives of old Yankee
stock, found themselves outnumbered and
overwhelmed. The number of the foreign born and
their progeny left old stock Americans with a siege
mentality wherein they were forced into their own
ghetto, albeit a well-to-do one. Moreover, by
breeding and inclination Progressives were poorly
disposed to cultivate and develop meaningful
rapport with the newcomers who were destined to
become voters. The Democratic Irish leadership, by
contrast, welcomed the opportunity to work with the
immigrants within the context of their own culture
and in the process succeeded in consolidating
political power.

Progressive hostility toward the immigrants
voiced concern over the deleterious effect on the
American labor movement because the newcomers were
willing to accept lower wages and to be used as
strikebreakers. Immigrants were also said to be
illiterate, unhygienic, prone to criminality and
alcoholic. In sum, they were dangerous to the
American democratic experiment. Hostility to the
foreigners was, in essence, a reflection of the
difference in background and outlook on the part of
the archetypal Progressive vis-à-vis the typical
immigrant. Whereas the foreign born still operated
within the parameters of cultural baggage of his
European heritage, the Progressive measured

acceptance, assimilation and desirability with the rapidity with which one learned and adopted American ways and sheared off one's European identity. The response of the masses of immigrants to this was to turn to the political boss who accepted them as they were without demeaning their cultures nor coercing deep changes.

The diversity and variety of New York's population guaranteed that whatever else the city had to offer, watching government in action was bound to be fascinating. As such it could confirm the observation of novelist Frank O'Connor in <u>The Last Hurrah</u>, that politics, or the deployment of people in the political arena, was the nation's greatest spectator sport, the activity in which more Americans participated than any other. Surely no other city in the nation provided so classic a laboratory experiential test for ethnic politics as did New York.

First generation, pre-World War I Italian Americans engaged in an entering phase of New York political life, wherein they exercised limited and peripheral influence. Their minimalist role could be attributed to a lack of political experience in the old world compounded by unfamiliarity with American political practices, high rates of illiteracy and difficulties with the English language, their preoccupation with economic welfare, an absence of substantial funding and unity within the group, as well as an inclination toward temporariness because most expected to return to Italy. More so than any other large immigrant group, Italian repatriation was a major phenomenon of the migration experience. Because jobs in America frequently were of the outdoor type with consequent diminishment during winter, the opportunity was thereby provided for immigrants to revert to their Italian homes where they remained until warmer spring temperatures lured them back once again to the land of opportunity. These immigration patterns earned them the critical sobriquet "birds of passage" from native Americans who did not appreciate foreign exploitation of job possibilities by those who presumably took their savings out of this country for investment abroad. This was, of course, an exaggeration and an overly simplistic explanation of a more complicated situation that frequently resulted in reinvesting

such monies in activities that redounded to the
welfare of the nation. Accordingly, much of the
funds were used to pay passages for other members
of the family to journey from Italy to America; in
addition, substantial amounts were invested in
their adopted land.

Italian unification completed in the 1860's and
1870's notwithstanding, provincialism continued to
mark relationships not only in Italy but among her
sojourners in America. Accordingly, Antonio
Mangano, who wrote extensively about New York
Italian immigrants in the early part of the
century, explained that the common conception of
the large body of Italians as a compact body
sharing a unity of purpose and identity was wrong.
Because they came from every nook and corner of the
peninsula, with strong attachments to their
provincial and regional subcultures, which were
little altered by the recent unification of Italy,
Italians were far from united. "This means that the
Italian colony is divided into almost as many
groups as there are sections of Italy
represented."[5] Even had the situation been
otherwise, there is the impression of an apolitical
people. Describing the transplantation of 200
families from Cinisi, Sicily to Manhattan, one
observer noted the almost total disinterest in
American politics in 1920.

In the Cinisi colony there are no political parties. The group
has not been interested in citizenship. Of 250, one or two
were citizens before the war and now all those who returned
from the war are also citizens. These young men sell their
votes for favors.[6]

A young Edward Corsi, who was destined to become a
major participant in New York City politics, made a
similar observation.

The Italian, by the way, is not much of a politician. He is
too poetic for the "game". He prefers loftier pastimes. While
the Irishman is organizing the ward and the Jew listens
attentively to the platitudes of the soap-box orator on
"Trotsky Square" (the Hyde Park of the neighborhood) the
Italian is at home, enjoying the rapturous strains of "O Sole
Mio".[7]

The political culture from which the Italians
sprang was one in which the ruling establishment:

the nobility, the Church and outside conquerors exercised ruling exclusivity. Against this background Southern Italian peasants equated government with an endemic exploitation unmitigated by the nineteenth-century Risorgimento and national unification. Reliance on family rather than political structures was the heritage against which emigrating Italians confronted the urban political system. It is no surprise, therefore, to learn that there were only 15,000 Italian voters among the half million Italians in New York City in 1911.

To understand the minor role Italian Americans played in New York City politics during the first two decades of the century one must also consider resistance on the part of those in control--largely the Irish in the Democratic party--to relinquish power. It was, after all, through the wielding of political power that the Irish Americans had obtained meaningful social and economic positions in this country. Irish politicians, furthermore, were skillful at co-opting ambitious Italians, allowing them to exercise some semblance of neighborhood power in order to keep their countrymen in line.

These factors notwithstanding, the potential for an important political role to be played in the city by Americans of Italian descent was present and some farsighted individuals and political parties were already beginning to position themselves to absorb the group. The Democratic party had gained renown for its cultivation of the immigrant vote, and indeed the first New York City area Italian American to attain a prestigious political position was Democrat Francis B. Spinola. Born in Stony Brook, Long Island in 1821, as a young man Spinola moved to Brooklyn, then a separate city, where he became active in politics, first as a Whig, then as a staunch Democrat. Elected to the New York State Assembly in 1855 and then to the State Senate, he served as a general during the Civil War. At the conclusion of the conflict he moved to Manhattan where he was elected to the State Assembly, wining reelection repeatedly until 1886 when he won a seat to the United States Congress, the first of his nationality to reach that political pinnacle. Although Spinola demonstrated concern for incoming immigrants and publicly acknowledged pride in his ethnic

background, he could not be considered an authentic
Italian American politician in the sense of
reflecting the needs and aspirations of a distinct
minority struggling for survival and acceptance.
Nor does one find evidence of an obligation to the
Italian ethnic community for his success or
verification that the ethnic group looked to him
for leadership; in fairness to Spinola, the Italian
ethnic community was not numerically significant
during his political career. Likewise New York
Judge Charles Rapallo, who in 1870 became the first
of his nationality to serve in the New York
judiciary, also reached prominence in the era
preceding the large influx of Italian immigrants
and accordingly was not representative of Italian
American political life, however exemplary his
career.

With the onset of mass Italian immigration, the
Republican party emulated its opposition by
cultivating the Italian bloc vote. In 1894 it
boasted that with the nomination of Andrea F.
Sbarboro, the party was the first to put forth an
Italian American for the State Assembly. While
inaccurate in the light of Spinola's career and
notwithstanding Sbarboro's loss, the incident is
interesting in that it reveals an obvious and
undisguised effort to tap the ethnic Italian vote.
The Republican nomination of F. L. Frugone,
publisher of <u>Bolletino de la Sera</u>, for Congress
that same year further attests to the deliberate
effort to garner the ethnic vote. The first of his
heritage to be nominated for that position by the
Republican party, Frugone was not destined to win,
however. The party nevertheless, continued to name
city Italian Americans for public offices, finally
gaining a victory in 1906 when A. C. Astarita won
election as alderman.

One of the more interesting examples of
Republicans linking themselves with the New York
City Italian bloc at the turn of the century was
that of the remarkable James E. March. Born Antonio
Michelino Maggio in Lucca, Italy, he emigrated
first to upstate New York, Lewis County where he
acquired the name James E. March, an appellation
purportedly descriptive of his penchant for
strolling with a distinctive military bearing.
Despite the name change he remained deeply
identified with Italians. March was in fact an

influential Italian padrone whose middleman status rendered him an effective intermediary between Italian laborers and American businesses. A self-styled leader, the picaresque March, also known as "The Mayor of Lafayette Street," demonstrated his usefulness to the two groups even while he exercised opportunities to exploit labor. For example, through the skillful deployment of his gifted tongue and by offering valuable promises, he assembled 1,000 men to work in construction gangs for the construction of the Erie Railroad--not failing to exact a substantial fee from the laborers for his efforts. Successful in commerce, he opened a financial institution in New York City and gained election as district leader in a predominantly Italian neighborhood that boasted that it possessed more registered Italian American voters than any other district in the city. Governor Theodore Roosevelt rewarded him by appointing him warden of the Port of New York, whereupon the Italian political leader responded by founding the James E. March Club, one of the first Italian American political organizations in New York. In 1904 he won a seat to the Electoral College and became a fast friend of Theodore Roosevelt who was assiduously cultivating the Italian vote.

The campaign strategy of Republican President Roosevelt offers a revealing insight into how political leaders of this caliber campaigned for the immigrant vote. Roosevelt was on the one hand a strong nationalist whose chauvinistic comments have been cited frequently for their insensitivity to hyphenated Americans. After all it was during his administration that Congress created the Dillingham Committee that denigrated "New Immigrants." Such an association understandably leads to the conclusion that Roosevelt was unsympathetic to newcomers. On the other hand Roosevelt was an astute politician who, parenthetically, did extend himself toward Italians with an unusual receptivity, precipitated undoubtedly by political reasons intermingled with personal leanings. Perhaps this was a function of empathy with the Mulberry Street dwellers elicited by leading muckrakers and augmented by his own visits to the area. In addition, one cannot discount the influence of his experience through intimate acquaintance with Italian immigrants who

were, in effect, his neighbors because so many of
them had settled in Oyster Bay, his Long Island
home. He also was very cognizant of their growing
importance in New York City. Accordingly, when
Bishop Giovanni Scalabrini, a major champion of
Italian immigrants, visited the United States in
1907, the president honored him with a well-
publicized audience. In 1912, a few years after his
presidency was over, when Roosevelt attempted a
comeback for the nation's highest office under the
Bull Moose label, he once again engaged in ethnic
campaigning by enlisting the aid of Italian
speaking journalists who spoke before New York City
Italian American voters. There was, however, a
significant difference in the way professional
politicians and Vincent Caso, a pro-Roosevelt
reporter for <u>Il Progresso Italo-Americano</u>,
endeavored to attract the Italian ethnic vote.
Discarding prepared brochures provided to him by
Bull Moose advisors, which dutifully detailed
Roosevelt's platform and which Caso concluded would
have little meaning for Italian immigrants, Caso
decided to remind his co-nationals of Roosevelt's
endorsement of half a million dollars in aid for
Italian earthquake victims in 1909, surely a much
more concretized and tangible message.[8]

The Democrat party was, on the whole more,
successful in reaching out to New York City's
Italian American community. Shrewdly sensing the
importance of intraethnic organizations like the
Italian Chamber of Commerce, whose leadership
sought political prominence along with economic
gain, as key influences within the nationality
group, the senior party linked its political
fortunes with the businessmens' organization. In
1897, Italian Chamber of Commerce President Antonio
Zucca, a Democrat, was elected coroner for Greater
New York in what was probably the first example of
an Italian American political base functioning as
the decisive factor in the election of an Italian
American New Yorker. In 1904 Democrat Pietro
Acritelli succeeded Zucca as both president of the
Italian Chamber of Commerce and coroner. It was in
that same year, 1904, that Charles H. Francisco of
Bushwick, Brooklyn, was elected to the New York
Assembly. In 1911, John J. Freschi and Louis L.
Valente were elected city judges, probably the
first of their nationalities to attain such

positions in the city. Albeit that these were relatively minor political offices, the incipient Italian American community would have to be satisfied with these peripheral positions during the entry stage of political involvement. Although far from the pinnacle of local power, the acquisition of such offices nevertheless provided an uplift to the ethnic community that lost no occasion to acknowledge and celebrate its modest advancement. When contractor Michael Rofrano was rewarded by Tammany Hall for his success in attracting recently settled Italians to the Democratic party by being chosen first deputy police commissioner in 1914, he was hailed "as one of the best Italians in New York," before more than 300 of his fellow ethnics who rendered him homage with a dinner testimonial. Thus, although this was a relatively subordinate post, its attainment by one of its own resonated within the New York City Italian community. Of some consideration is the realization that Rofrano's elevation was in the police department, a fact not lost on the ethnic community so desirous of achieving a more positive image in law enforcement. It was also a measure of their total absence in the higher echelons of city political power positions at the time that even a semiprestigious office could excite such intraethnic excitement. "Your new and honorable post will give you the opportunity not only to serve New York, but through clean politics to fittingly represent the great Italian people who are the hope of the future of our city," was the comment of a proud community leader at the dinner occasion. For his part Rofrano accepted his elevated political position as "the duty of those of us who through luck or ability, have advanced a little beyond our countrymen, to help those countrymen and not exploit them."

In the wake of mass immigration to New York City prior to 1914, those born in Italy became a populace living and working on the fringes of the city's social, economic, cultural and political life. There were, to be sure, some Americans whose knowledge and understanding of higher Italian culture predisposed them to acknowledge their contributions to Western civilization. Thus, patrons of the arts and connoisseurs of music were positively inclined to an expansion of Italian

higher gentility, of which the world of opera is a
case in point. Although Italian music was heard in
New York from colonial times, its increase in
popularity coincided with the growth of the Italian
immigrant population by the end of the nineteenth
century and its continued acceleration in the early
twentieth century. The careers of two musical
luminaries of the era illustrate the point.
Accordingly from his spectacular New York City
debut in 1903 to his death in 1921, Enrico Caruso
was the most celebrated tenor in the world.
Likewise the appointment of Guilio Gatti-Casassa as
general manager of the Metropolitan Opera House, a
post in which he was held in the highest esteem
until his retirement in 1934, brought added
prestige to Italian names and New York opera. The
impact of opera had special meaning for first and
second generation Italian Americans in the city who
eagerly sought out live performances or settled for
listening to their radio sets for familiar arias.
It appeared that the good fortune of the musical
form was being translated into a positive sign that
the lowly immigrants were now gaining
respectability and acceptance.

Appreciation for this rarified cultural form did
not, however, have the desired effect of causing
good will to trickle down to the ordinary Italian
American city resident. The same consumers of high
culture also denigrated the typical immigrant as
coarse, unlettered and boorish. Italian immigrants
in this early phase were, in the main,
proletarians. Their immediate world and the near
future were those of humble destinies, worlds in
which they could anticipate unending, arduous labor
and in which they could expect to occupy
insignificant positions in city affairs. It was,
nevertheless, a beginning, a start that provided
the hope of upward mobility. Although otherwise
attainers of puny political rewards in city
government and public affairs in general, they were
on the threshold of greater participation and could
now begin to dream of achieving enhanced political
influence.

The Great War, which began in September 1914,
could serve as a convenient line of demarcation
from the turn of the century era of immigration to
a second era that would extend into the 1920's and
the 1930's. Like most Americans, New Yorkers met

the events of the late summer of 1914 that precipitated the conflict with a certain sense of detachment. In other words the concomitant results of the causes of war: militarism, secret alliances, imperialism and nationalism, were of little concern to an American people that had prided itself on the good fortune of having stayed out of European embroilments. Although it was inaccurate to depict the United States as "isolated" from European affairs, the country was in fact a neutral nation determined not to succumb to a bellicose spirit. President Woodrow Wilson's admonition to remain neutral in word, action and thought seemed to be sage advice that comported well with the prevailing mood. It was, however, not so simple an admonition to carry out in the light of a number of cultural, political, economic and military considerations.

NOTES

1. George Buchanan Fife, "A Port for All the World," Harpers' Magazine 107 (June 1903): 188-195.

2. Jacob Riis, How The Other Half Lives: Studies Among the Tenements of New York (New York: Charles Scribner's & Sons, 1890), 134-135.

3. William L. Riordan, Plunkitt of Tammany Hall (New York: E.P. Dutton & Co., Inc., 1963), 57.

4. Wallace S. Sayre and Herbert Kaufman, Governing New York City (New York: W. W. Norton Inc., 1965), 688.

5. Antonio Mangano, "The Associated Life of Italians in New York City," in The Italian in America: The Progressive View, ed. Lydio F. Tomasi (Staten Island: Center For Migration Studies, 1978), 154.

6. Gaspare Cusumano, "A Sicilian Colony in Manhattan," in A Documentary History of the Italian American, ed. Wayne Moquin (New York: Praeger Publishers, 1974), 345.

7. Edward Corsi, "My Neighborhood," in A Documentary History of the Italian in America, ed. Wayne Moquin, 360.

8. Interview, Vincent Caso, August 19, 1963.

2

When New York Was Italian

The unique dilemma confronting Italians in America at the outbreak of the First World War was one of ambiguity owing to Italy's antebellum pact with the Central Powers that was in sharp contrast with United States sympathy with the Allies. The resultant uneasiness was mitigated, however, in 1915 when Italy abandoned her earlier ties and entered into agreements to join the Allies. During the 1915-1917 period, while the United States maintained a posture of neutrality, a number of Italian Americans made the momentous decision to return to their homeland and don military uniforms for Italy's defense. For an even larger number of the ethnic group America's entry into the war in April 1917 was the turning point that found them poised to assume more meaningful leadership positions in society, albeit by the sometimes questionable adornment of an unsavory mantle.

Paul Vaccarelli (also known as Paul Kelly), for example, found himself on the periphery of influence during the late war years as a result of his role as fifth vice president of the International Longshoreman's Association, one of the most powerful unions in New York City. It was said that because he refused to tie up the Port of New York with a strike and thereby paralyze port activities at a critical time during the war, he had earned the gratitude of President Wilson. An earlier gangster career notwithstanding, Vaccarelli had so reformed that by this time he had become an adept handler of organized labor and thereby commanded the loyalty of tens of thousands of Italian American dock workers who had long resented Irish dominance in the trade. This mode of interethnic rivalry was to characterize the generation between the two world wars. Thus, while Vaccarelli never held a publicly elected office, he was the acknowledged leader of 15,000 men who went

out on strike in a 1919 action that elevated him to
a position of power among the city's Italian
element. By launching the strike in defiance of
Irish union leadership, Vaccarelli was presenting
an audacious, if blunt challenge to command from
the Sons of Erin. Little-known outside of close
contemporaries, Vaccarelli deserves some credit
as a minor yet indispensable behind-the-scenes
figure in the political emergence of New York
City's Italian Americans. The observant Edward
Corsi, then a young journalist, left a concise
description of his own impressions that underscores
this observation; he also provides fascinating
information that despite Vaccarelli's opposition to
Irish political factors, he married a woman of that
background.

> Paul was a tough little fellow who operated in a sort of
> gray area between legitimate trade union activities and
> brawlish east side gangster operations closely allied with the
> Tammany Machine of his days. Many people regarded him as an
> outright gangster but he appeared to me as a conventional
> Robin Hood in the days when the Italians and the Irish were
> fighting for supremacy on the east side of New York. The
> fighting, naturally, often bordered on outright lawlessness
> and violence.
> He was a smart, rather charming little man, tough as nails.
> He bolted his party in 1918 when he supported Fiorello
> LaGuardia for the presidency of the New York Board of
> Alderman.
> In his later years he operated as a conservative and
> respected real estate man and made every effort to live down
> the reputation of his earlier years. He was reputed to be
> wealthy at the time of his death but I doubt that he left his
> Irish widow more than a few dollars to keep her   from charity
> during the remainder of her life.[1]

Simultaneously and much more important was the
role to be played by New York's Fiorello H.
LaGuardia. One of only a handful of congressmen to
leave the safety of the national legislature,
LaGuardia served as a United States Army airman in
Italy. Whatever reservations Americans harbored
about these immigrants in their midst previously,
now underwent sufficient dissipation after seeing
the newcomers fighting side by side and shedding
their blood with those whose ancestry was of longer
standing. And so it was that New Yorkers were
prepared to witness the Italian Americans making a
meaningful transition from the entry stage to the
assertive stage in politics.

Although the entry phase was characterized by faltering and uncertain striving for politically important positions, there were some exceptions. Nationally the pre-World War I period witnessed the ascension to politically prominent positions on the part of individuals such as Andrew H. Longino, governor of Mississippi, 1900-1904; John Phinizy, mayor of Augusta, Georgia, in 1837; Constantine L. Lavretta, mayor of Mobile, Alabama, 1892-1898; Francis B. Spinola, Congressman from New York 1887-1891; Anthony Caminetti, Congressman from California 1891-1895; and Fiorello H. LaGuardia, Congressman from New York 1917-1920 and 1923-1933. Of the above-mentioned only Caminetti and LaGuardia can be considered Italian-American political figures in the sense that they represented aspirations of rising Italian enclaves from which they sprang.

A growing trend toward greater participation in the American political enterprise was discernible in the late 1910's and the early 1920's. Whereas Italian Americans previously did not readily obtain citizenship because of an ardent desire to return to their mother country, prolonged residence in the United States, stimulated by activist political parties and patriotic organizations, expanded the newcomers' interest in naturalization. Keen observers, such as Robert Foerster, writing in 1924, noted that although Italian immigrants were initially attracted to the Republican party, undoubtedly because of its name, in large cities such as New York, the Democratic party made greater inroads. "We have even had the spectacle of an Irish politician reading to an Italian throng a speech rendered in Italian. Undoubtedly the naturalized Italians are . . . often volatile and easily confer their support where eloquence is greatest or latest." Pragmatism rather than idealism seemed to characterize the primary Italian American political trait. "Partly it is the Italian sense of the practical and the expedient which determine his attitude."[2] Despite a dubious sense of national Italian patriotism because of Italy's divisive history abetted by strong regionalism and exaggerated provincialism, a degree of national pride was emerging in the New York Italian colony.

In iterating the politicization of Italian Americans, attention must be given to the development of certain neighborhood institutions such as the saloon. Long a fixture in Irish American neighborhoods, these places of business became unofficial "social centers" for innumerable poor workers; they also promoted proprietors to significant positions of influence. Less well known but playing a similar role were the saloons of Italian neighborhoods as, for example, on the lower east side of Manhattan. It was there that Potenza-born Michael Santangelo became a saloon keeper of an establishment where many local Italians congregated to socialize and exchange ideas about religion, economics and politics. As a community fixture Santangelo promoted American patriotism during the First World War by sponsoring parades and encouraging his followers to buy Liberty Bonds. He also functioned as an "Italian banker," wherein he performed various services such as transferring monies to Italy, arranging for the purchase of transportation from the old country and holding deposits. In addition, he was a builder of many homes in the community. Regarded as an honest man and a natural leader, it was only after he stood up to and physically defied the local dominant Irish bosses, who patronized his establishment but refused to pay for their goods, that he gained the latter's respect. After the burly six foot four inch Santangelo engaged them in a physical fight, the Irish fully accepted him as a leader of the Italian element.

By the First World War Santangelo was regarded as so influential a figure among the Italian American electorate that he attracted the attention of and collaborated with Tammany Hall chieftan Christopher Sullivan. Michael's close bond of friendship with the famous Alfred E. Smith was underscored by the decision of the Italian immigrant leader to name one of his sons after him Alfred E. Santangelo who subsequently launched a meaningful political career as a New York State Senator and a United States Congressman from Italian East Harlem. Robert V. Santangelo, another of Michael's sons, became an assistant district attorney in Manhattan and a judge. And Paul, still another son, combined an unlikely career as a medical doctor and district Democratic leader on the lower east side.[3]

One barometer of political maturity in New York City was the frequency with which ethnic groups created political clubs. Often of a social, service and cultural nature, these associations came to dot the political landscape of city neighborhoods as they represented local centers of power and influence. The clubs were sought out by many an individual anxious to ingratiate himself with neighborhood power brokers in return for the granting of desirable favors. For decades this had been the accepted and proven vehicle that launched Irish Americans into active political careers, particularly through the Democratic organizations that, accordingly, provided them with power bases of enormous clout.

New York City Italian Americans had, by the 1920's, cultivated the skill of forming such organizations to such a degree that they commanded the attention of astute students of the subject. Roy Peel, for example, in describing the development of Italian and German clubs in New York City in the 1930's found that they "have gone further, however, in regularizing and synthesizing their instruments of cohesion." One explanation regarding the herding motivation is traceable to Old World culture, that is, the tendency towards male association so characteristic of small town and village life in Italy as a normal, daily form of socialization. This propensity has been discussed by many an observer of the Italian American community such as William F. Whyte, who in his classic sociological work, Street Corner Society, describes the importance of social clubs in the typical Italian American milieu of eastern cities and further traces their frequent evolution into political organizations.[4]

Perhaps the earliest of these clubs were the Italian Democratic Club of Brooklyn, with Anthony Cafiero as president, and the James E. March (Maggio) Republican Club with James March, president, which came into being in the late nineteenth century. In meetings the Italian language was often used, lively Old World songs were heard and familiar ethnic customs and folkways suffused the atmosphere. By engaging in numerous community activities including sponsoring sports teams for youngsters, supplying food for the needy and other favors for local inhabitants, these clubs succeeded in building a posture of loyalty and gratitude among cohesive groups of Italian

Americans. The holiday parties, dances and other social functions organized by the clubs served to cement bonds of solidarity while recognizing the accomplishments of those of their nationality. "The Italians are always honoring judges and other high officials of their own nationality . . . " was the way this activity was described.[5] So extensive was the growth of political clubs among New York's Italian Americans that by the 1930's they composed the largest number of such associations throughout the city. Clearly the ascendancy of the political star of the gifted LaGuardia served as a spur to foster growth. "Hundreds of Italian political clubs sprang up all over the metropolis--some in open revolt against old-time incumbent leaders, others affecting a bland loyalty to party principles," so that even while underrepresented in the party machinery, it was predicted that they were on the threshold of attainment of greater political power.

In some instances Italians Americans supplanted other nationalities in extant organizations. Thus, failing to obtain their just share of party power, in 1931 Italian Americans supported Albert Marinelli's seizure of power from Irish Democratic leaders in the Second Assembly District on the east side of Manhattan. This was followed by former Justice Francis X. Mancuso's action in 1933 to oust from the leadership of the eighteenth assembly district in East Harlem, H. Warren Hubbard, Commissioner of public works, and a close associate of Tammany Hall leaders. Stubbornly refusing to relinquish his post, Hubbard attempted to deflect Italian American resentment, by nominating ethnic group members for office, as in the case of naming Pasquale J. Fiorilla for alderman in 1933. But it was to no avail as local Democratic Italians finally chose Mancuso, despite a previous indictment. Known as "the Indian" because of his ruddy complexion and beaklike nose, Mancuso was to use the East Harlem bailiwick as a position of influence in Tammany Hall for years to come. Meanwhile a similar scenario transpired in Brooklyn's Nineteenth Assembly District as Jerome Ambro replaced German American Henry Hasenflug in 1932, thereby providing Ambro with his own power base.

For Ambro the struggle for recognition within the Democratic Party forced him to firmly entrench himself within the local clubhouse power base. In 1925, at the age of 26, the young Brooklynite lawyer won election to the New York State Assembly (Nineteenth assembly district), retaining that seat until 1933. In that year he attempted to become the first Democratic Italian American mayoral candidate. Although he commanded much support in the Italian neighborhoods of Brooklyn, he lost the primary race to John P. O'Brien, who as the official Democratic candidate, subsequently lost the general election in a three-way race for mayor to LaGuardia. Ambro's penetration of the political arena also embraced the social and familial when his son, Jerome Ambro Jr., married the daughter of Judge John H. McCooey, scion of the powerful Brooklyn Democratic leader. In time the younger Ambro went on to a distinguished career of his own, gaining election to United States Congress where he served for six years.

Closely linked to the Democratic party in the city during this period was Generoso Pope, who, although departing from Italy for America as a poorly educated eleven year old, quickly advanced within the ranks of business, journalism and politics. A wealthy sand mining contractor, he was also publisher of Il Progresso Italo-Americano, the largest Italian language daily newspaper in the United States. Increasingly the senior political party sought to influence New York's Italian American community by cultivating him, and Pope, of course, relished the opportunity to serve as a power broker within the ethnic group because it enabled him to become a mover of city affairs. Enjoying his public notoriety, Pope nevertheless was genuinely interested in promoting the political cause of members of his nationality who, he averred, were under-represented in public office. Thus, early in 1933 one could read numerous editorials in his daily newspapers in which he inveighed heavily against political leaders' disregard of the numerical and moral strength of the city's Italian American population. Skillfully he sought to influence political power brokers that practical politics alone warranted greater inclusion of Italian Americans because their rate of citizenship in recent years propelled them to the largest bloc of naturalized aliens. Pope was especially indignant over the fact that 120,000 of

400,000 Brooklyn residents were of Italian descent yet no member of the ethnic group occupied an important public office. Although other leaders within the Italian American community censured the notion of political preference based solely on ethnic grounds, for more observers the indisputable fact was that of gross underrepresentation.

That Italian Americans felt underrepresented in the political arena was a deeply held conviction of many of the keener observers of the ethnic community. A discerning analysis of the rosters of the state and county officials in the three states with the largest Italian American populations, concluded that even "the most enthusiastic advocate and supporter of Italian American politicians [finds] that politics is one field in which the sons of Italy do not excel." To the writer, the phenomenon was attributed to "the easy going, friendly Italian disposition" that was repelled by the pugnacious nature of American politics as it habitually resorted to ridicule and sarcasm against Italian American candidates.[6] Another commentary uttered a similar conclusion thereby fairly accurately reflecting a widely held view within the ethnic group. "Whichever way you look at it, the fact remains that the Italian-Americans, as a class are not represented politically in proportion to their numerical and moral strength."[7]

Nor was this merely a blatant display of plaintive ethnic chauvinism because statistics were adduced that emphatically strengthened the argument for an increased role for Italian Americans in public life, a fact that was further bolstered by the 1930 census tabulations that showed that there were an astonishing one million or more Italians in New York City, that is one sixth of the city population. Edward F. Corsi, then a census official, further observed that population shifts among Italians saw large numbers moving out of Manhattan to the other four boroughs. This development was taken to mean that Italian Americans had progressed economically to a point where they could now purchase their own homes in outlying sections.

Could the increased visibility be translated into effective political gain? It seemed to ethnic enthusiasts of the early 1930's that with such a large number of Italian American city residents, the time was ripe for major political strides. The hope was that those of Italian ancestry with the temerity to enter the political arena could become the recipients of group coalescence. Accordingly, among the more chauvinistic nationality organizations a clarion call commenced for blanket endorsement of Italian American candidates for public office regardless of party affiliation. In the general election of 1932, for example, the journal of one such organization, while proclaiming neutrality when two Brooklyn Italian Americans, Sicilian-born Victor Anfuso and Jerome Ambro, vied for Democratic leadership of the nineteenth assembly district, unabashedly supported the primary aspirations of Francis D. Saitta because his opponent for the Democratic nomination for Congress was not Italian.[8] Indeed, the Italian organization deemed it an "obligation" to vote for Saitta because in a predominantly Democratic area his nomination would be tantamount to victory and would thereby present Italian Americans with their first Brooklyn congressman. The call for unity, for bloc voting on ethnic grounds, proved a dismal failure. Not only was there an absence of coalescence on behalf of Saitta, but there also was a lack of support for Republicans Nicholas Pinto and Alexander Pisciotta, who were unsuccessful in their attempts to gain nominations to Congress and county judge, respectively. The latter examples underscored the simple fact that party loyalties were more powerful than ethnic ones. Thus, regardless of the fact that in the aggregate Italian Americans were potentially a formidable bloc, they rarely united behind a single candidate, even when presented with capable choices. Virtually all of the above-named candidates, for instance, went on to illustrious political careers: Anfuso became a congressman, Ambro an assemblyman, while Pinto, Pisciotta and Saitta enjoyed careers either in law or on the bench. This point is made effectively by a recent study of Italian Americans in Brooklyn politics that shows that notwithstanding the evidence that Italian Americans comprised approximately 25 percent of that borough's population in the 1920 to 1940 period, it was totally un-reflected in their election to public office. In 1920, of 49 elected positions including state assembly, state senate, United

States Congress, city council, borough president
and district attorney, only one was held by an
Italian American. The figure jumped to six in 1935,
and seven in 1945.[9] It would seem that only in the
presence of the most brilliant of their political
practitioners were Italian Americans prepared truly
to unite, a phenomenon that became unmistakable in
the career of Fiorello H. LaGuardia.

Easily the most visible public personality of
Italian descent, LaGuardia possessed an unorthodox
background. Born in New York City of an Italian
Jewish mother and an Italian father, he spent his
childhood in the unlikely environment of western
American army camps where his father served as
military bandmaster. In his twenties LaGuardia
worked as a staff member in the American consulate
in Austria-Hungary rising subsequently to consular
agent in Fiume in 1904. On his return to New York
City he became an interpreter at Ellis Island while
attending New York University's Law School from
which he obtained a law degree in 1910. Fiorello
served a short period as deputy attorney general of
New York when in 1916 he was elected a Republican
member of the House of Representatives for the
fourteenth congressional district. LaGuardia's
election to Congress was indeed a turning point for
New York City's Italian Americans. Unlike Spinola
who had preceded him, LaGuardia was a product of
the Italian American hubris, one whose every fiber
resonated with an Italianita. His Italianess was
not of the transparent kind that was manufactured
merely to obtain votes from those of his ethnic
background, although as a shrewd politician he was
aware of the dividends to be reaped by organizing
Italian Americans into a cohesive and potent
political force. He genuinely enjoyed his ethnic
heritage and was involved in numerous ethnic causes
designed to promote the advantages of his group.
His election from a distinctive Italian
neighborhood could be considered a reflection of
the onset of Italians coming of age in New York
City.

LaGuardia served two consecutive terms in the
fourteenth congressional district, sandwiching in
an illustrative army career as an aviator during
the hostilities of Great War. In 1922 he was
elected president of the Board of Aldermen in New
York City, however, in that same year he returned

to Congress, this time to represent the twentieth congressional district in East Harlem, Manhattan, then emerging as the largest Italian enclave in the city. For ten years he served with distinction as a progressive leader and a champion of the "little man." In 1932, in the wake of the New Deal landslide, he was defeated for reelection, a setback that proved to be temporary, however, and in retrospect, providential because he could now concentrate on the more important goal of being elected mayor of New York City. In actuality LaGuardia's mayoral ambitions were of long standing; indeed he was the Republican candidate for mayor in 1929, losing badly to the popular, Democratic incumbent, dapper Jimmy Walker. Nevertheless by 1933 the discredited Democratic organization was in disarray thereby enabling LaGuardia to win as a Republican-Fusion party candidate, thereby ushering in an era of exceptional municipal government. It is generally conceded that LaGuardia's mayoralty marked the high-water mark for New York City in the twentieth century. His outstanding, no-nonsense performance earned public accolade as the electorate rewarded him with victories in 1933, 1937 and 1941.

Notwithstanding LaGuardia's career and its association with Italian Americans, he was in many respects more than just a typical ethnic politician because his appeal transcended that of his own ethnic group. LaGuardia was to a large context atypical. In the words of his biographer Arthur Mann, LaGuardia was a hybrid politician.

> His hybridism derived from an extraordinary mobility. Born in Greenwich Village but raised on western army posts and growing to maturity in the Balkans . . . He was a true cosmopolitan, which is to say that he was at home nearly everywhere, but without the roots that bind a true insider to the group and the place in which he was born.
> His parentage foreordained that he would be what sociologists call a marginal man . . . . But his being Protestant set him apart from his ethnic group, which was, of course, overwhelmingly Catholic.[10]

For more typical New York City Italian American political careers during the assertive stage that emerged after World War I, we must turn to some other individuals who perhaps are less well known but are far more representative. One of the best

illustrations is that of Salvatore Cotillo, an
urban liberal and Tammany Hall candidate whose
career furnishes a useful perspective on the
connection between ethno cultural concerns and the
city's population of Italian ancestry. As a ten
year old in 1896, Naples-born Cotillo immigrated to
New York City where he lived with his family in the
emerging Little Italy of East Harlem, which was
destined to become the largest Italian American
center outside of Italy. He attended the local
Catholic Church and public schools, Manhattan
College and Fordham Law School. Although basically
a Progressive, his original foray into elective
politics was a reflection of pure ethnic influence.
Simply put, the growing Italian element in the
twenty-eighth assembly district urged his candidacy
on a reluctant Democratic party leadership. In 1912
he was elected to the New York State Assembly, the
first of his nationality to be sent to that body
from an Italian ghetto. In the course of Cotillo's
legislative career he battled, among other things,
for immigrant rights and protection, as well as
women's suffrage and child welfare reform. For
example, in 1923 and 1924 he served as chairman of
New York State's Joint Legislative Committee that
launched a major investigation into the subject of
immigrant exploitation in New York. Under his
direction the committee uncovered numerous
instances of harm done to poor immigrants who,
because of English language difficulties, unwisely
commissioned questionable private "immigrant"
banks, operated by members of their nationality,
that tended to impose excessive charges for
services such as foreign money exchanges, money
transmissions to other countries and sale of
steamship tickets. Of importance to the entire
range of immigrants, this matter was extremely
important to the New York Italian American
community that numerically, was most seriously
affected by these abuses.[11] The end result of the
investigation was the submission of bills devised
to curb the excesses and carefully regulate
enterprises engaged in such businesses. In short,
the robust immigrant legislator evinced such a
consistent progressive record that by the early
1920's he was clearly one of the most respected
public figures in New York's Italian American
community. In 1923 he reached the pinnacle of his

public career when he was elected a judge of the New York Supreme Court, which he held until his death in 1939.

Obtaining a niche in the powerful Manhattan Democratic organization as a springboard for future judiciary careers was the road followed by others like Paul Rao who immigrated to this country as a five year old in 1904. Admitted to the bar in 1924, he traversed a path to a high level federal judgeship through such traditional Democratic patronage jobs as assistant district attorney for Manhattan in the mid-1920's and an assistant United States Attorney General in the Franklin D. Roosevelt administration. The positions were, in essence, rewards for his political stewardship as a stalwart Tammany Hall functionary with considerable influence among the city's Italian Americans and veterans groups. In 1948 he reached the goal of many politician lawyers--judgeship--when he was appointed a customs court judge and subsequently became chief judge of the customs court.

For a smaller but generally brighter group of Italian Americans, political assertion came through the Republican party. LaGuardia was a case in point, as was Vito Marcantonio who fashioned a career as one of the most brilliant if controversial political leaders produced by the ethnic community during the 1920's and 1930's. An inveterate radical, an accomplished iconoclast and a fiery exponent of socialism, the diminutive, dark-haired Marcantonio might on the one hand appear to have been least influenced by purely ethnic considerations. Nevertheless, the overwhelming evidence is that he was a genuine champion of Italian American rights and ringing proof of ethnic influence in American political life. The son of an immigrant mother, who was raised in the most Italian neighborhood in the United States, who spoke Italian, ate Italian food and regaled in Italian customs, he evinced an early predisposition to Italianita. His precocious political acuity quickly arrested the attention of the astute LaGuardia who, in the 1920's, selected the youthful East Harlemite high-school student as his campaign manager. Throughout the remainder of LaGuardia's congressional career, Marcantonio served in that capacity and as LaGuardia's "eyes and ears" in East Harlem. In 1934 Marcantonio

himself was elected to a congressional seat and
with the exception of one term, represented East
Harlem in the national legislature until 1950,
becoming a leader of the new left-wing American
Labor party in the process. It was the virtuously
unanimous support of Italian Americans that was
responsible for his long congressional tenure
wherein he espoused many controversial causes,
always remaining, however, a reliable defender of
the rights of Italian Americans, repeatedly and
effectively arguing on their behalf whether they
were American citizens or aliens. More than any
other Italian American congressman of his time, he
had national impact.

A committed left-winger, Marcantonio was not
above urging political preference on the basis of
ethnic descent. In 1943, for example, as the leader
of the nascent but potentially powerful American
Labor party, he suspended ideology in support of
the candidacy of Judge Thomas Aurelio for state
supreme court primarily because of his belief that
the post should go to an Italian American.
Marcantonio's liberalism notwithstanding, when
running for mayor of New York City in 1949, he
protested to the Roxy Theater for its showing of
the Hollywood production "House of Strangers"
because the film stereotyped good Italian
Americans.

In the end Marcantonio's espousal of Socialist
and Communist programs produced a growing
alienation with the masses of New Yorkers. Some
media sources even adopted a policy of blocking out
his activities during the mayoral race. His
complaint of such treatment to the Brooklyn Eagle,
elicited the offensive ethnic riposte, "It couldn't
happen to a nicer fish peddler." He was also
opposed by Il Progresso Italo-Americano's Generoso
Pope and other influential elements of the city's
Italian American establishment. Nevertheless,
Marcantonio was expected to garner a sizeable, if
losing vote in the 1949 mayoralty race against
Democrat William O'Dwyer and Republican Newbold
Morris. In other words there was some fear among
Democratic chieftains that he might be regarded as
a "favorite son" candidate among the city's large
Italian American electorate, a prospect that
prompted the O'Dwyer forces to change their
strategy in the final weeks of the campaign in

order to concentrate on the ethnic group. Accordingly, City Council President Vincent Impellitteri was pressed into major electioneering service. Although denying that he was engaging in red-baiting, Democrat Impellitteri vociferously denounced Marcantonio during a 1949 radio address, for being a false friend of Italians because he had remonstrated against the Marshall Plan "that had saved Italy's life and today is helping to make Italy strong." Impellitteri reminded fellow Italian American New Yorkers of Mayor O'Dwyer's wartime humanitarian work in Italy in urging his reelection. Once again New York politics proved the viability of the Democratic process as O'Dwyer won by a wide margin and Marcantonio's 356,000 votes earned him a distant third place finish. In the smothering nationalist atmosphere of the emerging Cold War, the demise of the American Labor party was inevitable, as was Marcantonio's hold on public office.

Just as the Manhattan political organizations began to accommodate the Italian element in the 1940's, so too did their counterparts in Brooklyn, especially the Democratic party. In this most populous county, which then harbored what would become the largest concentration of Italian Americans in the city, the emergence of the ethnic group in Democratic partisan politics was a notable event. It can be seen in the career of Anthony Jordan (Giordano) who was appointed liaison between the ethnic group and the James Madison Democratic Club.[12] Club founder John H. McCooey, second only to Tammany Hall as wielder of important partisan political power, wisely recognized the importance of co-opting the support of the borough's constantly increasing Italian population. Although Italian Americans simultaneously entered leadership ranks in the Republican party, in Brooklyn it was the Democratic party that really counted and thus inclusion in the latter's deliberations was of great moment.

Jordan's bilingual abilities and his connections within the ethnic community as well as with the politically influential, rendered him an effective factor. Accordingly, over the years he was instrumental in enlisting support within the Italian neighborhood for the candidacies of people like Stanley Steingut and Abraham Beame who were to

become speaker of the New York State Assembly and
mayor of New York City, respectively. This, in
effect, meant access to high places in state and
city government. Jordan was the typical ethnic
machine figure, one who assiduously cultivated the
Italian vote which responded by supporting
Democrats and thereby opening doors for
neighborhood Italian Americans to obtain numerous
political patronage jobs. In a perfect example of
traditional ethnic politics, Jordan's efforts
earned rewards for himself and for his family.
Anthony's son Joseph, for instance, was
subsequently appointed by the Democratic
organization to run for a judgeship, which was
tantamount to election in that heavily Democratic
section of New York.

By the mid-1930's it could be said that the sons
and daughters of Italy had acquired a love of the
city and a keen sense of civic responsibility.
Having resolved the issue of permanent residence
largely in favor of their adopted country, Italian
immigrants and their numerous progeny formed a
plethora of ethnic benevolent, philanthropic,
medical, cultural, educational, sports and business
associations. The process of Americanization of the
previous quarter of a century had, with increasing
rapidity, performed its task of accommodation and
acculturation to a point where Italian Americans
were now confronted with an entirely new political
process. Because many came from rural Italian
villages in which the franchise and civil rights
were either absent, imperfect or of such recent
vintage as to be unfamiliar, they were required to
make quick and major adjustments to the American
setting. Their original apathy towards politics,
which marked their stay earlier in the century,
gradually gave way to the inexorable American
environment and pressures of assimilation so that
by the 1930's they were recognized as composing
"one of the most active and politically conscious
groups among New York's citizenry."[13]

The notion of bloc voting among New York City's
Italian Americans was said not to have been a
feature of political life in the earlier stage,
later, however, the idea of ethnic coalescence to
win political concessions for the Italian community
began to gain credence. A powerful chain of
political clubs known as the Italian American

Federation of Democratic Clubs sponsored by Generoso Pope, publisher of <u>Il Progresso Italo-Americano</u>, claimed an impressive membership of 150,000. By the mid-1930's this umbrella organization was expertly used by emerging Italian American political figures. Matthew T. Abruzzo is a case in point. Of Italian immigrant parents, Brooklyn-born Matthew (b. 1889) graduated from Brooklyn Law School in 1910. After service as judiciary clerk Abruzzo joined the Henry Hesterberg twenty-first assembly district Democratic organization where he soon surfaced as a rising Italian American political star. In a relatively short time he became a borough wide force among Italian Americans as he organized voters for the Democratic ticket thereby helping candidates roll up heavy pluralities. He was, furthermore, spokesman for the ethnic group which by the 1930's, found itself the unhappy recipient of the stings of popular prejudice due to an alarming growth of stereotyping in the media, especially in the movies. Whereas Hollywood film stereotypes of Italian Americans in the "silent screen" era emphasized buffoonery and the excitability of Latin-speaking Europeans, the advent of talking pictures saw the film industry fix on the connection between criminality and Italian heritage. The 1931 film "Little Caesar," in which Edward G. Robinson played the role of an aspiring Italian American hoodlum, ushered in a veritable Hollywood preoccupation with such criminal themes in numerous instances in which Italian Americans were portrayed on the screen. As spokesman for the ethnic community, Abruzzo sponsored a resolution before the New York Federation of Italian American Democratic Organizations condemning the frequent presentation of Italian Americans as gunmen and gangsters in screen and stage plays. "It is unfair to that vast majority, working and striving to be real Americans, and bringing up their children to be real Americans,"[14] was his emphatic rebuke of ethnic prejudice. In 1936 President Franklin D. Roosevelt appointed Abruzzo a federal judge.

It was during the 1930's that Americans of Italian origin challenged and succeeded in breaking through the Irish hegemony within the Democratic party structure in places like Greenwich Village. In making this breakthrough Italian immigrants

evinced an evolutionary path that saw them overcome
a degree of apathy by taking machine politics more
seriously. They desired the jobs and the other
perquisites that accrued to the group that
exercised political power. Accordingly, the
elevation of Albert Marinelli to the Democratic
leadership of Greenwich Village in 1931, ushered in
a new era of Italian American participation in
partisan decision making. Marinelli, a second
generation Italian American, got into politics in
the pre-World War years as a minion of surly "Big
Tim" Sullivan who exercised obdurate political
dominance over the local ward. Throughout the
1920's Marinelli expanded his power base, abetted
by Italian American underworld elements. As a
result of association with known hoodlums that
understandably tainted his career and after serving
only an abbreviated tenure as party chieftan,
Marinelli was forced to relinquish his leadership
post to Louis DeSalvio, another American of Italian
descent.

That Greenwich Village Italian Americans were
climbing the political ladder was also evident in
the career of Carmine DeSapio. Born of immigrant
parents in the heavily Italian neighborhood,
DeSapio decided on a career in politics, becoming a
youthful but faithful errand runner for the local
Huron Democratic Club, then firmly in Irish hands.
By 1937 DeSapio made a trial run for club
leadership. Temporarily set back, he organized his
own Democratic clubhouse, challenged and won the
district leadership in a primary contest, only to
be denied the post by Irish Tammany leader
Christopher Sullivan. But it would only be a matter
of time, just a few years, before DeSapio emerged
as unchallenged district leader and member of the
Tammany executive committee. It was one of the most
powerful intraparty positions yet attained by
Italian Americans.

It was also during the interwar years that the
three principals in the New York City 1950 election
were emerging as political factors and achieving
degrees of success that would bring them to the
attention of the wider public. Ferdinand Pecora,
the oldest of the three was born in 1882 in
Nicosia, a mountain town in eastern Sicily. The
third of four children, in 1886 he immigrated to
New York with his parents Louis and Rose who became

parents of three more children. Louis Pecora, like
his father before him, eked out a living as a
shoemaker. The family lived in a small basement
apartment in a non-Italian neighborhood. As an
octogenarian Ferdinand remembered "we probably were
perhaps the only family that spoke Italian for
miles around, and I was probably the only boy in
school that spoke Italian for which I received peer
derision with epithets as 'dago' and 'wop'."
Isolation from city Italian communities was
undoubtedly a deliberate choice on the part of
Ferdinand's father, who was also known as a strong-
willed, stubborn individualist, in emulation of
Giuseppe Garibaldi, whom he admired. Residence
outside of traditional Italian ethnic neighborhoods
proved to be significant in shaping his son
Ferdinand's views regarding ethnic enclaves. Simply
put Ferdinand regarded them as obstacles to
assimilation: "it is unfortunate that immigrants
have gathered largely in segregated groups in
various parts of New York . . . cut off from the
influences of an American nature and making their
assimilation difficult."[15] Residential locus also
colored Ferdinand's opinions about ethnic
societies, which he thought beneficial primarily to
the personal interests and advancement of leaders
or organizers. Ferdinand's father's individualism
manifested itself in critical decisions that had a
bearing on the upbringing of the children, as, for
example, resentment over being denied the means of
a formal education, apparently in deference to
reserving that important commodity for another
brother who became a priest, an action that led
Louis to abandon the Catholic Church in favor
Protestantism. The deed was acceded to by Louis's
wife Rose, who also left the church as a result,
but she returned to the Catholic faith. The
father's religious decision led to ostracism and
suffering for the Pecora family and obviously
affected the choice of a residence. The religious
decision was, furthermore, to have profound
influence on young Ferdinand who was brought to
local Protestant Episcopal Church services presided
over by Italian-speaking clergy.

As they were for so many recent immigrants, the
early years were difficult ones for the Pecora
family, constantly beset by seemingly overwhelming
economic problems. As a lad Ferdinand attempted to

help by earning a few dollars a week via milk and
newspaper deliveries. During summer vacations he
joined his father at work in a shoe factory where
he acquired firsthand experience in the hazards of
an impersonal industrial system and where he became
concerned with the absence of enlightened factory
laws. Throughout these years, Ferdinand continued
his formal education, in which he excelled,
graduating as valedictorian at the head of his
public school class in 1895. Because secondary
schools were rare at the time and because of
limited funds, he applied instead directly to City
College of New York. Because he was then only
thirteen and thus below the minimum admission age
of fourteen, he was required to wait for a year. In
the interim the clergy at St. Peter's Episcopal
Church on 120th Street persuaded him to study for
the ministry. As a seminarian he proceeded to study
at St. Steven's College, remaining there until he
was fifteen, when his father's industrial accident
necessitated Ferdinand's return home to assume the
role as the main family breadwinner. He obtained a
junior clerkship with a New York City law firm
while his mother combined her childrearing with
full-time work in a garment sweatshop. In time the
family's position improved and it was able to move
to better quarters. Both parents offered strong
encouragement to all their children to continue
with their education with the result that two of
Ferdinand's sisters became teachers and a brother
became an attorney.

An intelligent young man, Ferdinand studied law
at the New York Law School, and he graduated in
1904. He later became a member of the board of
trustees of that institution. In 1918 Ferdinand was
sworn in as assistant district attorney in New
York, thus beginning his long public career. From
1922 to 1930 he was the chief assistant and acting
district attorney of New York County. (He also ran
and lost a race to become Manhattan district
attorney.) In January 1933 he was appointed counsel
to the United States Senate Committee on Banking
and Currency, and for seventeen months thereafter,
conducted its investigation into the New York stock
exchange as well as the banking practices involved
in the issuances and sale of securities. The
investigation was regarded as one of the most
extraordinary inquiries on the subject produced in

a Washington committee room and led to a revealing dissection of the seamy side of American financial life. A string of financiers, their lawyers and briefcase-toting aides were called to the witness stand by the inexorable, diminutive Sicilian-born counsel. The bronzed and swarthy-faced, cigar-smoking prosecutor with a square and solidly set jaw, made an indelible impression on the nation as he extracted from chastened witnesses the sad story of stock manipulation by greedy millionaires at the expense of small investors. For example, the president of the National City Bank of New York was found to have received over three million dollars in bonuses, yet he was legally exempt from paying income taxes because of his ability to claim a loss on the sale of bank stock to family members, which he later repurchased.

The Senate Investigating Committee headed by Pecora produced evidence that resulted in Congressional enactment of various laws designed to eliminate several evils and violations of fiduciary responsibilities by stock brokers and their exchanges as well as by commercial banks and investment bankers. One of the laws created the Securities and Exchange Commission, which came into existence in 1934. President Franklin D. Roosevelt appointed Pecora to the five member commission. Although Pecora's original effort to translate his national reputation to the conspicuously visible electoral post of Manhattan district attorney ended in failure, he nevertheless achieved prominence when in January 1935, New York Governor Herbert H. Lehman appointed him to fill a vacancy as a justice of the New York Supreme Court. On at least one occasion he rendered a decision that was fraught with long-range partisan political implications when he ruled a mistrial of Manhattan District Attorney Thomas E. Dewey's prosecution of Tammany leader James J. Hines, thus frustrating Dewey's intention of becoming the Republican candidate for governor of the state in 1938. Subsequently Pecora was elected for a full-term to the Supreme court and in 1949, in a further affirmation of support for his judicial performance, he was re-elected as candidate of the Democratic, Republican and Liberal parties.

Edward Corsi, was the bearer of an illustrious name when he immigrated with his family in 1907.

Born in 1896, in Capestrano, in the Abruzzi region,
Edward was the son of Filippo Corsi, an Italian
deputy, agrarian reformer, union organizer, editor
and disciple of Giuseppe Mazzini. As a youngster
Edward accompanied his father into exile, along
with the fiery radical Carlo Tresca, who himself
was to become famous among New York's Italians.
Circumstances and conviction, however, precluded
any tendency on Edward's part to rest on the
laurels of a family name. Filippo's death at an
early age required sacrifices of all members of the
newly arrived Corsi family. The first years in
their new country were years of unusual hardship
and adversity. Work was a necessity for young
Edward whose first jobs here were as a lamplighter
in the preschool hours, and subsequently, as a
messenger and clerk in a telegraph office. Further
tragedy afflicted the family in the wake of the
1907 depression when while rummaging through the
New York Central Railroad freight yards for coal,
Edward's brother was in an accident that cost him
an arm. The shock of the accident killed his
mother. Edward would overcome these adversities and
even as a teenager, he showed promise, becoming
leader of a local debating team. He was also
sensitive to the political temper of the country
with Theodore Roosevelt surfacing as his idol
especially because Corsi witnessed the Republican
president addressing a crowd in Italian.

After working his way through St. Francis Xavier
College, Edward earned a law degree in 1922. For
years he combined a career in the social work field
with journalism and politics. Thus, he became
director of the Haarlem House on 116th St. in East
Harlem, then the center of a vibrant Italian
neighborhood. His work and residency in this social
settlement house brought him into intimate contact
with progressive-minded politicians Fiorello
LaGuardia and Vito Marcantonio and the area's
esteemed educator and avuncular community leader
Leonard Covello. These individuals were intelligent
and brilliant exponents of progressive action as
well as unflinching proponents for the emergence of
Italian Americans as factors in civic affairs.
Accordingly, although most in the area joined the
local Tammany club, Corsi joined the Republican
club along with the "less practical, more
idealistic," young men like LaGuardia and

Marcantonio. As he recalled it,

> In my own case, it was the influence of Theodore Roosevelt
> that led me to spurn the conventional Tammany advances. Also,
> I did not particularly like the shady characters and
> overweight politicians who hung around the Tammany table in my
> district. I had a little of the reformer in my blood, I
> confess, and I could not deny it at a decisive moment.[16]

That Corsi was proud of his heritage is evident in
the forward he wrote for the 1938 WPA-sponsored
work, The Italians of New York, which stands as a
valuable font of information on the entire group in
city affairs into the late 1930s. "I could not help
but exult in the pageant of contributions and
achievements of New York's Italian, for I too am
Italian," he wrote as he rhapsodized about the
immigrant yearnings that he observed in those
passing through Ellis Island "into the promised
land as I did."[17] A busy young man Corsi had
worked as a reporter for several serious American
journals of opinion such as The Outlook and
Reader's Digest, and also became a founder and
publisher of La Settimana, a weekly illustrated
bilingual magazine that lasted for several years.
By the 1930's Corsi's multiple talents had elicited
the attention of President Herbert Hoover, who
appointed him United States Commissioner of
Immigration. In making the appointment Hoover may
also have been influenced by the realization that
Corsi was instrumental in organizing the Columbian
Republican League, an ethnic political group that
was intended to promote Republican candidates among
New York's Italian Americans. In 1929, against what
seemed to be an ethnic Democratic preference, Corsi
pointed out that although Democrats controlled
state government, that party failed to recognize
Italian Americans, citing their absence in worthy
positions in Governor Franklin D. Roosevelt's
administration and their virtual absence in the
state senate since the lone Italian member was a
Republican as were three of the five Italians in
the New York assembly. Corsi's performance as
immigration commissioner was so extraordinary that
he was retained in the post even by Democratic
President Franklin D. Roosevelt. Whether or not
Roosevelt did this to ingratiate himself with New
York's Italian Americans, in view of Corsi's

earlier insinuations is unknown, however, one can
plausibly conjecture that the shrewd Roosevelt was
indeed   anxious   to   cultivate   progressive
Republicans.

In 1934, as immigration diminished to a trickle,
Corsi resigned the federal post to become director
of home relief in New York City and in 1935 he was
named second deputy commissioner of Public Welfare.
A warm, personal friend of LaGuardia, he was quite
effective in marshalling ethnic group support on
behalf of his friend during his mayoral campaigns.
As successful as were his sundry activities, his
own   efforts   at   gaining   elective   office   were
frustrated. He lost a bid to become a Republican
city councilman in 1937 and in 1938, was the
unsuccessful Republican nominee for United States
Senate for New York. He also played a major role in
revising the New York State Constitution in 1938.
Thus he had already accumulated valuable political
experience.

Isnello,   a   gray,   impoverished,   nearly
inaccessible little town of 3,000 in the Madonie
Mountains   in   north   central   Sicily,   was   the
birthplace of Vincent Impellitteri in 1900. In
1901, the entire Impellitteri family departed for
America where it settled in the "Little Italy" on
Elizabeth Street in Manhattan. For five years
Vincent's exclusively Italian-speaking father tried
to eke out a living by conducting his inherited
shoemaking trade, however, limited success and the
lure of other relatives already living there,
induced the Impellitteris to move to Ansonia,
Connecticut. There, in this midsized industrial
town in the central part of the state that was home
to various immigrant groups, young Vincent spent
his remaining childhood and teenage years, and it
was in that locus that he acquired Polish, Jewish
and Irish friends. For his first year of formal
schooling, the future mayor attended the Catholic
parochial school a block away from his home,
however, the twenty-five cents weekly tuition
proved to be a hardship for the poor family,
prompting it to send Vincent to the Elm Street
Public School and then to the Lincoln School and
Ansonia High School.

The Impellitteri family consisted of mother,
father, six brothers and a sister, all of whom were
born in Sicily except the youngest, Rose. The roots

planted in the Connecticut town proved to be a lifetime attachment for the family. Vincent's mother and father lived there for the rest of their lives and most of the children remained there or in its immediate vicinity as adults. Typical of Italian families, ties between family members were close especially during childhood and adolescent years. Vincent always remembered his father as a "wonderful man but a tough disciplinarian," an attitude that can be illustrated by the following example: Indulging in a bit of mischievousness as an elementary school youngster, Vincent feigned sickness to play "hookey" one day. Unfortunately for him his teacher happened to stop by his father's cobbler shop and, thinking his absence was due to illness, innocently asked his father how "Jimmy" was feeling. The father reserved his wrath for home. "When I came home with my books, I took one look at his eyes. I made for the door quickly. He took a little hammer, threw it after me, just missed me." That was the abrupt end of a short-lived and dubious hookey-playing career. Vincent's mother, by contrast, was known for her patient and calm disposition and her religiosity. A daily church-goer, she made certain that her large family attended mass regularly and remained faithful to the Catholic Church. As a youngster Vincent served as an altar boy. Apparently no one in the family manifested an interest in politics. Even if one had shown such an attraction to political activities, turn-of-the-century Ansonia would have provided little opportunity because it was firmly controlled first by the native WASP element, and then by Irish Americans who came to dominate the local Democratic party.

Vincent, or "Jimmy" as many Italian Americans bearing his first name were called, was considered a good but not an academically superior student. He took the contemporary array of high school academic courses including science, math, English, social studies and foreign languages, namely Latin and German. Whether or not Italian language was offered at the school then is unknown, however, later in life he expressed regrets for not having studied the language of his forefathers as it would have served him well in his political career. His biggest difficulties were with science and math (by failing the math portion of the qualifying

examination, this weakness attributed to his
rejection from the naval academy in Annapolis). On
the other hand he excelled in high school athletics
in which he received As, won a letter in football
and demonstrated organizing and managerial
tendencies through his role as manager for the high
school baseball and basketball teams, which
accounted for more As. He also was member of the
debating team, fife and drum corps and the
temperance and benevolent association. In short, he
was a joiner. The formative high school years, both
from the perspective of academic preparation and
interscholastic activities, would have important
impact in his professional career. As he described
it, "It was such experiences at school that helped
me later in carving out my future."[18]
Prophetically, the class prognostication for
Impellitteri asserted that he was destined to be a
lawyer.

Summer vacations were spent working for low wages
in local factories where he intermingled with the
proletarian element of several nationalities. One
season included a twelve hour nightshift for which
he received ten cents an hour operating a copper
wire-spooling machine. Another summer saw him doing
duty as a foundry coreman's helper. During the
school year he worked afternoons in one of his
brothers' businesses. Samuel Impellitteri owned a
fruit and vegetable store and later operated one of
the largest restaurants in town, while Gaetano
operated a barber shop where Vincent lathered
customers before their shaves. In 1917, in
conjunction with a special school program to aid
the war effort by increasing food production,
Vincent took a summer job on a farm. Thus, the
early, impressionable years were filled with the
realities of hard work among the immigrant masses,
not unimportant preparation for the future when he
would preside over the nation's classic immigrant
city.

Financial straits prevented the Impellitteri
family from satisfying Vincent's desire to attend
college. Moreover, the entry of the United States
into the First World War in April 1917 caused many
to change their plans. Upon completion of high
school in June 1917, Vincent joined the United
States Navy. Like many a romantic young man
attracted by the blandishments of a national

propaganda to enlist in the armed services in order
join in the noble crusade to make the world safe
for democracy, he responded affirmatively to the
multicolored posters indicating that the navy was
seeking young high school graduates for radio
school training. He quickly enlisted, soon
realizing that the transition from civilian to
military life was not so simple. Moreover, as a
seventeen year old, 135 pound enlistee assigned as
a coal passer to the battleship Arkansas, he found
the work arduous. Fortunately he was soon
transferred to duty as a radio operator on the
destroyer Stockton, which was assigned to overseas
missions. In the course of its convoy duty the
Stockton saw a great deal of military action with
German U-boats. The military service career proved
to be a rich, rewarding experience that served as a
turning point in his life; now he was on his own
without the support of family and it offered an
opportunity to intermingle with older men from all
over the country. Furthermore, his military service
enabled him to visit different parts of the world
such as England and Ireland. A diarist in those
days, he wrote with eagerness of his interest in
the sights and people he now saw in person. He was
especially impressed with Ireland and Irish women,
and thus it was not surprising to learn that he
later married one of Irish ancestry and that he
always possessed a warm spot for the Emerald Isle.
Many years later, while acting mayor, he would
recall this background in a greeting to a visiting
Gaelic Athletic Association Hurling Team, during
which he indulged in a rare personal revelation.

I had the privilege of visiting many parts of Ireland, when I
was stationed there in the service of the United States Navy
during the First World War. All the youthful dreams born of
friendly talk with Irish exiles here came true when I was in
Ireland. The old nation was at that time waging her epic fight
for freedom; the war that brought independence to five-sixths
of a territory which of right is, and always was, indivisible.
The realism as well as the romance of this ancient people were
brightly revealed to me in those stirring days. The spell of
Ireland has greatly influenced my life. I may add, that the
girl I chose as my life-time partner bore the famous clan name
of McLaughlin.[19]

In January 1919, soon after the armistice that
ended hostilities was signed, Vincent received an

honorable military discharge.

The nineteen-year-old exserviceman now made the momentous decision to eschew a return to the safe family home base in Connecticut, opting to settle in dynamic New York City instead. The perception was that the great metropolis contained more opportunities than Ansonia; it also housed many fine law schools. And thus it was that he entered Fordham Law School. He lived in school dormitories and supplemented his income by working as a bell boy and night clerk at the city's landmark beaux arts Ansonia Hotel, famed as the residence of celebrities such as composer Gustav Mahler and opera great Enrico Caruso. Matriculation at Fordham was an enriching experience not only because of the excellence of faculty and staff, but also because of the interaction with law students, many of whom possessed strong political motivations and connections. One was Thomas Curran, a future powerful Republican leader in New York. Most students, such as Alfred E. Smith, Jr., son of the famous governor and future presidential candidate, were like their parents in closely identifying with the Tammany Hall-oriented Democratic party. In a word Impellitteri got his feet wet politically during the "roaring twenties," the colorful, exciting, wicked period during which Tammany Hall products, for better or for worse, dominated the political scene. During this period the capable Charles J. Murphy, arguably the most astute leader the organization had yet produced, presided over Tammany Hall and served as mentor not only for Smith but also for Robert F. Wagner, outstanding United States senator and John A. Foley, the most respected surrogate judge in the nation. Murphy also launched the career of Jimmy Walker, whose flamboyance, frolicking and philandering as mayor of New York City rendered him the beloved symbol of the naughty decade.

It was then that Tammany Hall skillfully launched the careers of outstanding progressives, as well as scoundrels, which introduced Impellitteri into serious politics. The Hall, which exercised its customary influence over the political destinies of the great municipality, was under Hibernian control. It was becoming aware, however, of the rising aspirations of newer waves of immigrants, such as the Jews and Italians. Impellitteri was

attracted to the Democrats because of the influence
of fellow law students and also because of the
realization that the organization would inevitably
accede to the granting of recognition to the more
recently arrived immigrants. Moreover, he regarded
Republicans as of a different economic strata;
namely the province of big business and the old,
sturdy, native stock Americans therefore not a
party in which he could feel comfortable.

Upon graduation from law school in 1924,
Impellitteri joined the Griggs, Baldwin and Baldwin
Law Firm. Ironically Griggs was a prominent New
Jersey Republican who had served under President
William McKinley, whereas Arthur J. Baldwin was
personal counsel to Charles J. Murphy. In 1929,
while Pecora still served as one of a number of
Manhattan assistant district attorneys,
Impellitteri was named to the same office. From
1929 to 1938 Impellitteri served as Assistant
District Attorney of New York, and then returned to
private practice as an associate with the noted
criminal attorney Samuel Leibowitz. Throughout this
time, Impellitteri remained active in Democratic
politics, albeit in somewhat obscure roles. In 1941
he became law secretary to Justice Peter Schmuck of
the New York State Supreme Court, and in 1943 he
filled a similar position for Supreme Court Justice
Joseph Gavagan. Thus he entered the 1940's as a
long-time, active but virtually unknown Democrat.

The growing specter of fascism that engulfed
Europe, was a movement that originated and
triumphed in Italy and that also impinged on the
life of Italian American communities and political
leaders. Some like Generoso Pope, who had succumbed
to assiduous cultivation of ethnic loyalty on the
part of the Mussolini government, were lavish in
their praise of the undemocratic ideology even in
the face of aggression perpetrated by the Italians,
such as that of Italy's invasion of Ethiopia in
1935. While many Italian American radicals like
Carlo Tresca and labor leaders like Luigi Antonini,
were outspoken in their denunciation of this act of
infamy, other left-wing and progressive Italian
American politicians became very circumspect.
Loathsome as fascism undoubtedly was to men like
LaGuardia and Marcantonio, they exercised great
care not to get too far out in front on the issue.
As residents of the large Italian colony of East

Harlem, they were conscious of the tensions
developing in their home base where there were
reports that African Americans intimidated Italian
owners of local businesses. The Italian victory in
the African country was followed by a riot in East
Harlem in which 400 Blacks raided Italian stores
and battled police. While not endorsing Italy's
military actions LaGuardia did support an Italian
Red Cross rally at Madison Square Garden, despite
charges that it was a cover-up for war
contributions to Italy. Whatever the division
within the Italian American community during the
1930's, the heyday of fascism would come to an end
with the outbreak of the Second World War and
America's entry on the Allied side.

NOTES

1. Letter from Edward Corsi to Giovanni Schiavo, November
9, 1965, Box 27, Edward Corsi Papers George Arents Research
Library for Special Collections at Syracuse University.
2. Robert Foerster, The Italian Emigration of Our Times
(Cambridge: Harvard University Press, 1919), 400.
3. William F. Whyte, Street Corner Society (Chicago: The
University of Chicago Press, 1955).
4. William F. Whyte, Street Corner Society, (Chicago: The
University of Chicago Press, 1955).
5. Roy V. Peel, Political Clubs of New York City (Port
Washington, New York: I.J. Friedman Publishing Co., 1935),
186.
6. Evelyn M. Bacigalupi, "The Italian Americans in the
Political Arena," Atlantica (August 1933): 155-156.
7. _____, Atlantica (February 1933): 216.
8. L'Independente IV (September 4 and December 1932): 8.
9. Jerome Krase, "The Missed Step," Italians and Irish in
America, ed. Francis X. Femminella, (Staten Island: American
Italian Historical Association, 1985): 184-187.
10. Arthur Mann, LaGuardia Comes To Power (Philadelphia:
J.B. Lippincott, 1965), 24-25.
11. State of New York, Report on the Joint Legislative
Committee on the Exploitation of Immigrants (Albany, 1924).
12. Jerome Krase and Charles LaCerra, Ethnicity and Machine
Politics (New York: University Press of America, 1991): 39-41.
13. Federal Writers' Project, Italians of New York (New
York: Random House, 1938): 97.
14. New York Times, May 30, 1971.
15. Dominick Lamonica, "The Man Behind the Headlines,"
Atlantica (August 1933): 157-158.
16. Corsi, "Speech to Young Republican Club," (January 25,
1946) :ECP.

17. <u>The Italians of New York</u>, vii.

18. <u>The Evening Sentinel</u> (Ansonia: December 18, 1950).

19. Vincent R. Impellitteri, Speech, (September 21, 1950), Box 51, <u>Vincent R. Impellitteri Papers</u>, New York Municipal Archives.

3

Transition from War to Peace

By the end of the 1930's the collective security envisaged by post-World War I idealists was already succumbing to uninhibited aggression perpetrated by Germany, Japan and Italy. Chastened by the bitter memories of costly participation in the Great War, most Americans agreed that however outrageous the behavior of these countries, the United States resolutely should stay out of the conflict. So strong was isolationist sentiment that for a time the otherwise intervention minded President Franklin D. Roosevelt refrained from actions that could foster violent dissension among Americans. Understandable caution notwithstanding, United States sympathy for Allied nations was so strong that by 1940 the country had committed itself to aid its friends by all means "short of war." Nevertheless, it took the Japanese attack on Pearl Harbor on December 7, 1941 to terminate division in public opinion as virtually all elements of the population endorsed America's entry into the war.

New York City newspapers were unanimous in urging the population to exert itself to the utmost to bring about an Allied victory. Even Il Progresso Italo-Americano, publisher, Generoso Pope, who previously had been conspicuous for his support of the Mussolini regime, now joined in the patriotic chorus exhorting his co-nationals to an unrelenting affirmative response to the American cause. Significantly, he now was featured regularly in his newspaper as the leader of the New York City Italian citizenry, who periodically proudly announced that the ethnic community had purchased millions of dollars in Il Progresso Italo-Americano sponsored war bond drives. The change in Pope's status in political circles was remarkable. Previously dismissed by critics as an un-regenerate fascist, others saw him as epitomizing the uneasy status of the Italian American prominenti or

demiprominenti (that is, acculturated but
unassimilated self-made men), and therefore
vulnerable.[1] To the Treasury Department Pope had
now become a valuable asset in raising large sums
of money and to the Office of War Information, now
favoring a united front of all Italian Americans
behind the war effort, he was a force to be
cultivated in order to mold favorable public
opinion among Americans of Italian descent--a task
he now pursued vigorously. Some elements within the
Italian American community such as the anti-Fascist
Mazzini Society and the radical Carlo Tresca, while
in favor of the United States effort to defeat
fascism, nevertheless refused to cooperate with
Pope. Notwithstanding the latter's reluctance, it
was evident that the larger number of Italian
American political leaders were willing to accept
Pope's metamorphosis from Fascist sympathizer to
American patriot. So successful was he in this
transformation that liberal and left of center
Italian American political figures such as
Marcantonio now began writing him friendly notes
while others like LaGuardia, Pecora and Antonini
felt obliged to make public appearances with him in
promoting fund-raising activities.[2] In reality
Mussolini's reckless foreign policy already had
lost the support of Italian Americans as well as
others by 1941.

The outbreak of the war drastically affected life
in the city as it did throughout the land. Frenetic
concern over military defense and internal security
surveillance inevitably led to restrictions on
civil liberties and also resulted in fostering
suspicions. City residents expressed horror at
being informed that upwards of a half a million
aliens, including a substantial number from "enemy"
nations, lived in their midst. Although the war
hysteria that gripped the West Coast and led to the
disheartening internment of over 100,000 Japanese
Americans never afflicted the East Coast, some
zealots were intent on seeking out scapegoats by
rounding up numbers of German and Italian aliens.
In some instances, fervent neighbors reported
"suspect" Italian immigrants to the Federal Bureau
of Investigation, that proceeded to probe the
individuals. Even though a truly negligible number
of Italian Americans were incarcerated, it clearly
was a testing time for the group, many of whom

advisedly assumed a lower profile. In such circumstances a degree of prejudice against Italians was rather pervasive and could be seen in some of the serious war movies of the day. The Noel Coward film, "Proudly We Serve," is a case in point. In this tense high seas drama there is a scene which depicts two British sailors engaged in a discussion as they watch enemy sailors jumping overboard from their recently-torpedoed craft. Speculation as to the nationality of the fleeing enemy served as a backdrop for the following dialogue:

First British sailor: "I lay you ten to one they're all Germans. Never get the macaronis to tackle dangerous jobs like that, not for love nor money." Second British sailor: "Go on the Eyetalians will do anything for money." First British sailor: "Oh anything but fight, that's why they were so lousy in the last war. That's on account of their warm, languorous, southern temperament.[3]

For some the pressures were more than could be sustained. In one extreme case a young Italian American attempted suicide because of his inability to endure harassment and ridicule that depicted Italians as inferior, cowardly fighters.[4] Such examples fortunately were few as many saner American minds warned against overreacting. Nonetheless, Italian language broadcasting stations in New York and elsewhere were banned and alien Italians in New York City were required to disconnect short-wave radio receivers lest they become unwitting subjects of propaganda emanating from enemy nations. The vast majority of Italian Americans, however, demonstrated unflagging loyalty privately and publicly. On December 20, 1941, over 1,000 of them attended a rally at Cooper Union College during which they pledged their lives to the cause of freedom. A few days later city Italian American Protestant clergymen met to denounce dictators, especially Mussolini, and simultaneously pledged loyalty to the United States. These manifestations of patriotism elicited positive reaction from the New York _Times_, which praised Italian Americans for their devotion and loyalty.

American citizens of Italian origin were among the first to proclaim their loyalty to this country when war was declared. They are among the first, as a group, to organize formal

demonstrations of support of the war efforts and war aims of
the United States . . . . representatives of 110,000 Italian-
American trade unionists in the New York area set up a
permanent organization, the nucleus of a nation-wide movement,
to spur Italian participation in all phases of the war program
. . . . the great majority of Italian-Americans are
wholeheartedly united with all Americans in the struggle to
defeat the Axis powers . . . . They have a double reason to
back the war effort. In fighting for American victory they are
also fighting for the future of their motherland.[5]

The change in Italy's status from enemy to
cobelligerent presaged a further improvement in
relations between native Americans and those of
Italian heritage. This change, furthermore, was
reflected in the attitudes towards Italian
prisoners of war stationed in the United States.
Taking advantage of the urgent need for manpower,
large numbers of prisoners volunteered to work in
American industrial enterprises in the realization
that such service on behalf of the United States
contained numerous advantages including the
opportunity to obtain leave from their bases and,
under escort, to participate in social activities
in nearby communities. Accordingly a number of them
could be seen in Italian neighborhoods of New York
City where they generally received a positive
welcome in contradistinction to criticism and even
hostility that attended visits to other areas. More
than a few of these prisoners of war made contact
with relatives in the city and were entertained by
Italian organizations and Italian parishes.[6]

City residents soon became aware of the war's
impact. They learned how to cope with ration books
and live with the tension of air raid drills,
blackouts and brownouts. They took advantage of the
unprecedented favorable work opportunities
presented--opportunities that found jobs for
virtually every able-bodied person. With supply and
demand principles now working on their behalf, city
dwellers frequently confronted the unaccustomed
problems of scarcity of goods to purchase and the
totally unfamiliar restriction of possessing only
circumscribed time in which to spend their inflated
incomes due to their excessively heavy work
schedules. The necessity of rationing found people
queuing in lines at butcher shops and women rushing
for silk stockings when knowledge or rumor located
them at a particular store, a practice paralleled

by men whose rush to buy remaining stocks of golf balls compelled merchants to institute their own rationing system of recreation items. The events that brought about these developments also brought about a change in what had been a standing reproach against New Yorkers: a lack of neighborliness. Observers of the New York scene remarked that a sense of solidarity brought on by the war rendered a large part of the populace more disposed to be of assistance to one another, a development not without blemish, however, as an ugly incidence of racial violence that left six people dead in Harlem in August 1943 attested. This disturbance was, in effect, a repercussion of the worst wartime race riot in Detroit in June of that year which cost thirty-four people their lives. On balance, however, the city's cold-hearted reputation was mitigated.

Manifesting a profound sense of resignation regarding the gravity of the ambiguous situation of their adopted country (the United States) being officially at war with the land of their forebears, New York Italian Americans came to terms with stressful wartime conditions. Noncitizens were required to register as "enemy aliens," a designation that was ironic because the children of those so derisively labeled were even then performing admirably via service in the American armed forces (indeed one estimate was that over 70,000 Italian American servicemen were sons of "enemy aliens"). Accordingly many were destined to suffer various indignities including denial of jobs in war plants, and other inconveniences, actions that Italian American political leaders, frequently led by New Yorkers, vigorously condemned. Thus, East Harlem's Congressman Vito Marcantonio chided Congress for calling into question Italian American loyalty when in fact they were so conspicuous in the armed forces. One estimate put their number at one and a half million or ten percent of the total of all the military servicemen-- a figure, therefore, well out of proportion to their percentage of the population. It was an indication of aggrieved feelings to note that an assortment of Italian American organizations normally opposed to Marcantonio's political agenda, nevertheless, were unanimous in endorsing his demands for better treatment of wartime Italy, especially with respect

to food and medical treatment. Emerging as a
consistent spokesman for the Italian ethnic group,
Marcantonio brought to light the heartening
response of the ethnic community to war bond
drives, their dedicated work in war industries,
even while they continued to exhibit an Italian
accent, and most telling of all, that they were
parents of masses of Italian Americans in the army,
navy and marines.

For Italian American New Yorkers, political life
in a wartime atmosphere became a complex tapestry
of design and texture. If attributes such as
access, motivation, money, unity, leadership,
resources, skills, numbers, location, timing and
opposition are regarded as necessary for the
exercise of power, Italian Americans can be said to
have possessed many, but not all, of these
attributes as they sought to exercise more
political clout. One sage analysis perceived that
while by 1941 New York Italians were setting the
pace for all American Italian communities in
business, the professions, arts, and so forth, they
also struggled against certain disadvantages.

As against the assets of their collective life, the Italians
of New York have many liabilities. They have the largest
number of unemployed in the city, with the exception of the
Negroes and the Puerto Ricans. They are one of the largest
elements on relief. They are still the leading inhabitants of
sub-standard housing areas in the city. They have the largest
number of aliens of any nationality group in the city.[7]

Largely Democrats in the city, they were faced
with a complicated situation that saw them veer
away from their traditional political base in the
presidential election of 1940 because of President
Roosevelt's pejorative characterization of Italy's
attack on France as a "stab in the back." Wishing
to rid themselves of a negative stereotype which
had plagued them for years, they reacted against
Roosevelt who, nevertheless, won his third term
although with a reduced margin. City Italians
furthermore, split into various political and labor
factions, with Marcantonio heading the left-wing
American Labor party (ALP) and Antonini, a
principal leader of the anti-Communists within the
ALP, breaking away to form the Liberal party.
Notwithstanding this factionalism that might
otherwise be considered a source of impotency,

nevertheless, all elements within the Italian community were united in demanding assistance and better treatment of Italy. An issue that struck a responsive chord with Americans of Italian descent, it was soon recognized as an important electoral issue by the political parties. Republicans were quick to remind the ethnic electorate that it was the Democrat, Roosevelt who was responsible for sanctions against Italy, while Democrats wooed Italians by having Italy declared a cobelligerent against Germany thereby enabling Italy to receive generous amounts of American economic aid.[8] It was this point that the ever pragmatic President Roosevelt seized on as he prepared for his fourth term election in 1944. Realizing that the election hinged on the support he could obtain in the major urban centers, particularly New York, he carefully cultivated the city Italian vote by deftly maintaining ties with the various hues of the political spectrum. For example, he courted the support of Judge Ferdinand Pecora, chairman of the American Committee For Italian Democracy, an unsuccessful anti-Fascist effort to unify Italian American war efforts. By such steps Roosevelt aspired to offset his opponent, Governor Thomas E. Dewey of New York, who shrewdly used the influential Edward Corsi in a move to attract the "Italian vote" to the Republican side. The President responded by using his wartime authority and appealing to the Italian Americans via a series of executive decrees aimed at alleviating dire conditions in Italy. In sum, he "fully recognized the power of the Italian-American vote and willingly courted it. And the Italian-Americans willingly gave it in the presidential election of 1944."[9]

The war years corresponded with Mayor LaGuardia's third consecutive term in office. Widely regarded as the mayor who gave New York the finest administration ever seen in City Hall, it was also acknowledged that by 1945 his initial luster had begun to fade and that he was losing support from some of his earlier staunch supporters. Some believed that his failing health was the reason for the negative appraisal, while others attributed the turning of the tide to LaGuardia's dismissal of reform members of the administration in order to ingratiate himself with Tammany Hall political

power brokers like Edward Flynn of the Bronx. Still
others point out that LaGuardia declined in
popularity because of his assumption of national
wartime duties since he served as the national
director of the Office of Civil Defense (OCD).
Desirous of playing a major role during the war,
specifically aspiring to become a general,
LaGuardia had to settle instead for the OCD post.
One biographer concludes that wearing too many hats
did neither him nor the city any good and that the
assumption of national responsibilities served to
divert attention from municipal affairs. Perhaps
the best explanation comes from LaGuardia's
biographer, the perceptive Thomas Kessner, who
concludes that the mayor, was tired of municipal
administrative responsibilities and was no longer
animated by the crusading spirit of his first two
terms.[10] Even President Roosevelt, who in an
unusual display of nonpartisanship in 1941,
supported Republican LaGuardia's candidacy against
Democrat William O'Dwyer, had by 1945 come to the
conclusion that LaGuardia's political star had
begun to decline.[11] Whatever the real story, the
critical point was that LaGuardia chose not to run
for reelection in 1945, thus ending a significant
era in city politics, yet ushering in a new phase
of Italian American political participation, the
emergence of elected Democratic politicians to
premier positions in city government; this
transition culminated in Vincent R. Impellitteri's
1945 election to city council president, which was
second only to the mayor in the hierarchy of
municipal power.

The announcement of Victory in Europe (V-E Day)
on May 8, brought joy and jubilation to the city
that had been in mourning over President
Roosevelt's death in April. Eagerly anticipated for
weeks, Germany's surrender marked the official
termination of a major phase of hostilities, and
despite Japan's strenuous, even suicidal,
persistence in continuing the war, common consensus
concurred that it was merely a matter of time
before the costliest war in history would be over.
Hardly had the fighting in Europe ceased when the
trek of United States troops back from European
combat zones began. New York City ports were
bursting at the seams with the influx of returning
veterans who, in their anxiety to come back, were

willing to take any transportation including poorly equipped western-bound cargo ships. Speed rather than suitable accommodations was the key. The large welcome mat New York City offered these veterans was a sign of the desire to return to a peacetime atmosphere. The sharp fall-off of the Seventh War Loan Drive then underway was another portent of the prevailing mood.

In one respect August, 15, 1945 was a typical hot, sultry, humid dog day of summer that found New Yorkers simply hoping to endure, to survive. But in another respect this was an extraordinary day, because it was Victory in Japan (V-J Day) which signalled Japan's unconditional surrender and saw, finally, the cessation of the deadly war. New York City joined with the entire American people in greeting the event with a carnival-like outburst of unprecedented joy. While every hamlet and community in the nation celebrated V-J Day, New York's response was unmatched as exuberant crowds poured through city streets laughing and singing; sailors in their navy whites and soldiers and Marines in their khakis danced in the streets with young girls and more sedate matronly women as a supremely happy atmosphere pervaded a Times Square jammed as never before with 2,000,000 jubilant revelers. For months both before and after V-J Day returning servicemen were confronted with huge "Welcome Home" signs and the embrace of enthusiastic families, friends and even strangers. Virtually every city neighborhood witnessed uncanny, joyful scenes amid a cacophonous symphony of blaring car horns, train whistles, trumpets and other loud instruments. In Italian neighborhoods, old-timers with calloused hands and sun-burnt skins that attested to their outdoor employment, proudly surfaced from their cool cellars with their best home-made wines and, in a gesture of thankfulness, interlaced with phrases of broken English, offered it to any passerby. Volunteers prepared to supply ample basic food, drink, fireworks and other gastronomic delicacies for community celebrations, were plentiful. Moreover, for the next couple of years, similar, although reduced versions of these observances could be found in scattered city neighborhoods on the anniversary of V-J Day.

During the immediate postwar years the nation was fundamentally complacent about the nature of its

own society. There were, to be sure, significant
problems revolving around urban decay, festering
race relations, health care costs for the poor, and
inadequate infrastructures, however, it appeared
that for the time being they could be ignored.
After all, the prevailing view was that Americans
were riding a crest of affluence and were now in a
position to consume goods previously accessible
only in dreams. Beneficiaries of expanded incomes,
they now saw themselves increasingly as middle
class. They wanted to spend and to enjoy; they
wanted to secure a comfortable life; they were not
in the mood for radicalism. Such was the mood as
New York City prepared to resume its place as the
premier city of attraction in the land. It exuded a
buoyant sense of confidence that it was entering a
splendid fulfillment as the supreme, symbolic
American city, indeed the foremost city of the
Western world if not the entire globe. A 1945
Gallup Poll found that 90 percent of New Yorkers
considered themselves happy. In a word, the
atmosphere was suffused with feelings of energy and
excitement, and a remarkable mixture of innocence
and sophistication.

Newcomers to the city, whether from other parts
of the country or abroad, continued to be
fascinated by the great metropolis that boasted of
an array of breathtaking sights ranging from the
wide expanse of New York Bay to the exalted towers
of shiny, glimmering skyscrapers. They could
enthuse over the bright neon signs that, while
muted during the war, now showered Broadway, Times
Square and other city streets with their colorful
luminescences. They could be dazzled by the smart
shops on Madison or Fifth Avenues or the gaudy
movie houses and cheap entertainment shops of honky
tonk 42nd Street. Not all was glitter and glamour,
of course, for the city possessed its share of
defects, but these too could be bypassed in so far
as they did not constitute a priority for a people
who wanted a surcease of the sacrifice that had
been exacted from them both by a protracted
economic depression and a terrible war. They wanted
to return to normal, as it were, in a slightly more
affluent fashion.

In reality it would be difficult if not
impossible to revert to former times for extensive
fundamental alterations had taken place. One

important change was in the very makeup of the
city's population. In defiance of the myth of the
"melting pot" thesis which prescribed that whatever
their ethnic backgrounds immigrants were intent on
quickly shedding the cultural baggage of their past
and becoming "American," a truer picture of New
York was that it was a city of neighborhoods in
which ethnicity was the key factor. Enclaves
existed for virtually every European nationality
group rendering New York City the most foreign city
in the nation. Irish, Jews and Italians
predominated, but by the end of the 1940's Puerto
Ricans and African-Americans had increased
significantly so as to be in a position to begin to
challenge the other ethnic groups as major elements
of the city's population.

The face of city politics had undergone a
significant change as well for with the exiting of
the LaGuardia administration came an end to the
dynamism of political life that had throbbed along
ideological lines since the early 1930's.
"Politically the city had been numbed or pacified
by the war and its prosperity," wrote Jan Morris in
describing the ebbing of passion that now attended
political debate.[12]

For Italian Americans participation in the war
had wrought a change as well, promoting the feeling
that the sacrifices involved should finally have
resolved all issues of dubious loyalty. They felt
they had been redeemed by their wartime role and by
the change of status accorded Italy during the war.
The land of their forebears had made the transition
from the status of an enemy nation to that of a
cobelligerent or nearly of an ally. That Italian
Americans had performed honorably during the war,
of that there could be no question. They purchased
war bonds to help finance the war, worked in war
plants to churn out the equipment necessary to win
the war, and they wore American colors in combat.
There was a heavy sprinkling of Italian names in
the American Armed Forces that advanced under enemy
shelling and kept vigil in forsaken locations. By
shedding their blood heroically, (more than a few
like Marine Sergeant John Basilone won the nation's
highest medal for extraordinary bravery in action),
they had earned the respect of their fellow
Americans for their ethnic group as a whole.

In New York City during the immediate postwar

years, Italian Americans were increasingly
conspicuous and accepted. One indication of their
acceptance was the prominence of Italian names
among the city's sports heroes. Thus, in pugilism
Rocky Graziano, Jake LaMotta, Willi Pep and Joey
Maxim, who served as world champions of various
weight classes during the 1948-1952 period, were
virtually household bywords. Most significant of
all was their growing prominence in baseball, which
was more than just the national sport pastime, it
"more than almost anything else, seemed to
symbolize normalcy and a return to life in America
as it had been before Pearl Harbor." A sport that
singularly mesmerized the American people, baseball
had special meaning for immigrants and their
children. "It was also the embodiment of the
melting pot theory, or at least the white melting
pot theory, of America."[13] Reflecting the view of
many Italian Americans who were sensitive to their
tenuous place in society, Judge Michael A.
Musmanno, just returning from a tour of duty as a
member of the International War Crimes Tribunal in
Germany, fondly recalled his exaltation in
observing the status enjoyed by New York City
Italian Americans.

Returning to America in the summer of 1948 I had ample reason
to be happy about the status of Italians both in their home
country and in the United States . . . . It was the happiest
day of my life when I disembarked in New York . . . . we
motored out to Yankee Stadium to watch the mighty Yanks
perform. Here my yearning to see Americans of Italian lineage
recognized for demonstrated merit obtained thrilling
realization. Four of the redoubtable Bronx Bombers were full-
blooded sons of parents hailing from the Italian peninsula:
Joe DiMaggio, center fielder; Phil Rizzuto, shortstop; Yogi
Berra, catcher; Vic Raschi, pitcher.[14]

Rizzuto and Berra won most valuable player awards
in 1950 and 1951, respectively, while DiMaggio, who
won his third most valuable player award in 1947,
was deemed the greatest ball player of his time.
The adulation accorded DiMaggio was unique: On the
one hand he was the subject of typical ethnic
stereotyping in 1939 when Life Magazine, found him
surprisingly groomed for one who was not a WASP.
"Instead of olive oil or smelly bear grease, he
keeps his hair slick with water. He never reeks of
garlic and prefers chicken chow mein to

spaghetti."[15] On the other hand by 1950 he had come to approximate the "all-American" hero status, one whose flawless performance on the ball field was characterized as approaching "royal elegance." Meanwhile another city baseball team, the feisty, colorful Brooklyn Dodgers, also featured Italian American heroes: Al Gionfriddo, a center fielder who in 1947 electrified fans by plucking a "sure" DiMaggio home run ball from the stands; Harold "Cookie" Lavagetto, who in 1948 broke up a no-hitter in the ninth inning and helped the Dodgers win the game; Dolf Camilli, solid first baseman; Carl Furillo, rifle-arm right fielder; and Ralph Branca, stand-out pitcher. And finally, on the New York Giants roster were better-than-average players like Joe LaFata, Sal Yvars, Sal Maglie and Danny Gardella.

Postwar New York City was geared to experience the interplay of politics amid an aura of optimism, a background of a city and a country that enjoyed a sense of satisfaction as well as security in that the United States had emerged from the war as the unquestioned world power. It was content that the period of sacrifice and deprivation had happily ended and that all the wartime trappings had either terminated or were on their way to being phased out. It was perceived, mistakenly in view of the surfacing of the Cold War in 1946, as a period of lessened international tension thereby providing a unique opportunity to return to the pursuits of peace. For city residents, 1945 saw the conclusion of the outstanding LaGuardia era, which indeed was admittedly highly regarded, however, there was no expectation of imminent decline for the candidates for the major municipal offices seemed to proffer authentic credentials. Unfortunately for the Republicans, although they offered respected Judge Nathaniel Goldstein, outgoing Mayor LaGuardia bucked the party and forcefully endorsed the third party candidacy of blue blood Newbold Morris, a decision that virtually assured the Democrats of victory. Meanwhile the older party, desirous of avoiding a primary fight, chose highly regarded William O'Dwyer as the standard bearer for the post. Possessing more than a suggestion of a streak of independence, which evoked wariness among some city Democratic political bosses who would have preferred more tractability, O'Dwyer's eventual

victory demonstrated that he was indeed quite
popular. Altogether it appeared that even without
LaGuardia, the city would be in good hands.

Part of the LaGuardia heritage was that it
unmistakably altered the political landscape of
city politics. Commencing with his first try at the
mayoralty, for the next third of a century the two
major political parties invariably designated an
Italian American candidate for one of the three
principle citywide offices: mayor, city council
president, comptroller. Blatant ethnic balancing,
it was regarded as indispensable politics. Thus, in
June 1945 Republicans chose Judge Nicholas Pette of
Queens for city council president, while the
Democrats' first choice for the office of
comptroller was Bronx contractor and party stalwart
Lawrence Gerosa. Successful in forcing Democratic
party bosses to name him for mayor, O'Dwyer, who
wished to pick his own running mates, now chaffed
at their choice of Gerosa, who not only lacked
experience in municipal government but had also
offended O'Dwyer by neglecting to contact him prior
to the nomination. Among other names mentioned to
run for council president were those of George B.
DeLuca, Ferdinand Pecora and Robert F. Wagner, Jr.
Rejecting the Democratic county leaders choices not
only for comptroller, but also regarding the city
council president, O'Dwyer argued instead for the
nomination of public officials of proven experience
and ability, and preferably individuals known to
him personally with whom he could work: Lazarus
Joseph for comptroller and Vincent Impellitteri
for council president. Citing them as "splendid
colleagues . . . what pleases me most of all is
that they stand for things I stand for and for
which I have fought all my life."[16] But O'Dwyer
proved to be a most circumspect politician as he
instructed his brother Paul to conduct an
investigation into Impellitteri's background so as
not to be surprised by political skeletons in the
closet that might prove embarrassing.

In choosing Impellitteri, O'Dwyer cited his
performance as a lawyer, being especially impressed
with Impellitteri's work as counsel in a case that
was tried before the court over which O'Dwyer
presided. This evaluation suggests that
Impellitteri's legal career has not received the
attention it deserved. Thus, critics who have been

quick to infer that Impellitteri's background was
lackluster, tend to emphasize a mere party
functionary, that is a political machine man,
lacking remarkable talents or abilities, an
evaluation that should be revised in so far as his
legal experience is concerned. His work as a
lawyer, both while in government service and in the
private sector, commanded the respect of those who
were better informed by virtue of being close to
the scene and in a position to render suitable
evaluation. In the course of his career in the
highly visible and important New York County
District Attorney's Office Impellitteri headed the
rackets bureau that handled some of the most
notorious and difficult cases of the era. His
diligence and professional demeanor won the respect
of his colleagues and superiors, who duly promoted
him to successively higher positions in the
department. On occasion he joined the police in
conducting raids on racketeers while in one
instance he went to Europe in an unsuccessful
effort to extradite a fugitive who had fled to
Yugoslavia. It was not futile, however, because his
wife joined him, thereby affording an opportunity
for a short vacation.

One of the cases he prosecuted successfully was
that of William Rathbourne, an infamous forger who
was called America's Ace Swindler. The case evoked
such interest that the popular magazine, True
Detective, commissioned Impellitteri to write a
feature article in which the assistant district
attorney recounted an incredible story of a
scheming "con" man who attempted to continue his
criminal activities even after being sentenced to
Sing Sing prison.[17] Impellitteri's successful
prosecution of another noted criminal elicited
effusive compliments from the presiding judge.

If all of the assistants [district attorneys] would emulate
Impellitteri, I think that the District Attorney's office
would be a formidable engine of attack against the members of
the criminal society in this country.[18]

It is significant to note that while a young
assistant district attorney, Impellitteri won the
highest praise from his superior, Manhattan
District Attorney Thomas C. T. Crain, for his work
in criminal cases. In 1933, during his fourth year

in office, the thirty-two-year-old Impellitteri was
the recipient of extraordinary recognition. "Among
the younger men on the professional staff of the
New York District Attorney's Office no one stands
higher in my estimation both for fidelity, zeal and
ability   than   yourself,"   wrote   Crain   who
specifically cited a number of commendations that
had come across his desk complimenting the young
civil servant on "his excellent work."[19] Crain
undoubtedly was expressing his gratitude for the
support rendered by Impellitteri while Crain was
the   subject   of   judicial   inquiry   by   the   noted
reformer Judge Samuel Seabury. The "Bishop," as the
impeccable aristocratic descendent of the first
Episcopal bishop in the United States was called,
had   earned   public   esteem   by   handling   the
investigation of the James Walker administration
that forced the dandy "Beau James" to retire and
paved the way for LaGuardia's succession, was now
asked to launch an inquiry into Crain's conduct in
office. Although officially exonerated, Crain was
assuredly put on the defensive.[20] Nevertheless,
the letters complimenting Impellitteri's courtroom
activity were genuine expressions of respect for
rectitude,   sturdiness   and   professionalism.   The
writer of one of these letters was Sidney Hillman,
president of the Amalgamated Clothing Workers of
America, who expressed his "deep gratitude for your
magnificent handling of the trial of the four men
who   were   convicted   yesterday   of   attacking   and
assaulting our members and officers." (This was a
reference   to   a   case   of   antiunion   labor
racketeers.)[21]   In   a   personal   letter   to
Impellitteri in 1936, the newly elected Manhattan
District Attorney William C.Dodge, who had narrowly
defeated Ferdinand Pecora in the race for the
office, referred to an instance of Impellitteri
bringing a perpetrator to justice, declaring that,
"The conviction, no doubt, was due to your careful
preparation of the case." Complimenting him on
still another case, Dodge concluded, "Naturally, I
am proud to have you on the staff for I feel
assured that when you undertake the presentation of
a case, everything that is humanely possible for a
careful prosecutor to do, will be accomplished by
you."[22]   So   impressive   was   Impellitteri's
performance as an assistant district attorney that
there was open speculation in 1937 that he might

succeed to the post of Manhattan district attorney upon the end of Dodge's term.[23]   In   private practice Impellitteri was considered an extremely capable defense lawyer, whose expertise attracted the interest of colorful New York City criminal lawyer Samuel Leibowitz, then operating one of the most outstanding firms of its type in the city and one that was called in to handle some of the most widely publicized criminal cases of the day. While an associate of this firm, Impellitteri was entrusted with major responsibilities including the defense of a series of cases ranging from simple assault to matricide. One example was his role in 1939, in assisting Leibowitz prepare for the defense of Patrolman Alvin Dooley, president of the Long Beach Patrolman's Benevolent Association, who was charged with the assassination of Louis F. Edwards, mayor of that Long Island community. Dooley was simultaneously charged with critically wounding Edwards' bodyguard, Patrolman James Walsh. The sensational case attracted widespread attention as Impellitteri replaced as defense attorney Lorenzo Carlino, himself an emerging force in the Italian American community and father of future New York State Assembly Speaker Joseph Carlino. Among the more curious circumstances surrounding the case was the fact that Lorenzo Carlino, a Long Beach Republican leader, had been beaten by Edwards in a race for mayor a few years earlier, thereby rendering it awkward for him to act as defense attorney. The Impellitteri/Liebowitz team did its utmost to defend the client, with the dynamic Liebowitz consuming five hours of rhetoric in summation before the jury as they based their defense on temporary insanity. In the end Dooley was convicted of manslaughter.

These cases were tried before some of the most noted jurists of the day including William F. O'Dwyer, then a Kings County judge whose courtroom was the scene for the 1939 Rubel Ice Corporation robbery trial. A sensational case involving a 1934 armored car hold-up that gained notoriety as the largest cash hold-up in American history to that date, it caused authorities to take extra precautions. Reporters noticed that numerous armed guards were positioned in the courtroom as jurors were being selected for the ensuing trial of three men accused of being parties to the act.

Impellitteri was the defense counsel for one of the
defendants. Although the jury concurred in its
conviction, it is interesting to note that one of
the accused subsequently confessed his guilt, while
declaring the innocence of the other two, including
Impellitteri's client, thus enabling Impellitteri
to win a new trial for his client. Impellitteri's
professionalism and courtroom demeanor had so
registered with O'Dwyer that it came to mind when
the Democratic mayoral candidate considered his
slate in 1945.

The subject of Impellitteri's designation for the
city council presidency has elicited varying
interpretations ranging from the preposterous to
the convoluted. One Tammany Hall official amused
listeners with a tale that the choice was
determined by party bosses who consulted the
"Little Green Book", (a reference manual of city
officials) and who sought a Manhattan Italian to
balance the ticket. New York _Times_ reporter Warren
Moscow offers another interpretation by asserting
that it "had been engineered by O'Dwyer as a favor
to Marcantonio. Marc, for his part had used his
influence as a favor to his friend, Lucchese."[24]
The reference was to Thomas (Three Finger Brown)
Lucchese, an underworld figure from East Harlem,
who supposedly supported Impellitteri. Still
another version was attributed to Bronx Democratic
leader Charles Buckley, who purportedly told Moscow
that his predecessor Edward Flynn, prevailed on
O'Dwyer to rearrange the ticket in order to include
Impellitteri for ethnic considerations.

What is one to make of these intriguing but
contradictory versions? The one attributed to the
Marcantonio-Lucchese connection, while it may seem
plausible, has to be read against a background of a
prevailing anti-Marcantonio atmosphere that by
1950, found all the major New York City dailies
inveighing heavily against him for ideological
reasons. In addition, the reporter Moscow, was to
take a personal and active role in defeating the
mayor in 1953. O'Dwyer admitted that he and his
brother Paul had been in contact with Marcantonio
and the American Labor party, however, there was no
mention of accommodating Impellitteri, compelling
the conclusion that the account had not been
corroborated. The "Green Book" dictated choice can
be relegated to the hardly plausible, unless one is

prepared to believe that otherwise shrewd party bosses could chose a candidate for so important a position in so light-hearted a manner. The plausibility of the Buckley account has to be tempered by the awareness that it too lacks corroboration and by the fact that the original choice of Tammany Hall leaders included Italian American Gerosa for comptroller, presumably satisfying the desire for an ethnically balanced ticket. Against this background the O'Dwyer account that he rejected the choices of the county Democratic leaders because these leaders had ignored O'Dwyer in the process and that he had never met their nominees nor saw, at least in Gerosa, an individual possessing desirable municipal experience, appears most plausible. The fact that O'Dwyer knew and was favorably impressed with Impellitteri, as previously described, certainly helped. Nor was O'Dwyer unaware of the political dividends that inhered in linking himself on the ticket with so distinctively an Italian name. Having been a city political player for a number of years, O'Dwyer was fully conscious that the aroused city Italian Americans required special cultivation. O'Dywer lost no time in reminding the ethnic group of his genuinely close ties with them and their homeland.

Accordingly O'Dwyer expressed his sympathy with Italian Americans because of the criticism and vilification that they had endured in the early part of the war, as well the persistent stereotyping to which they were subject. Furthermore, during the early part of 1945, when it was still generally perceived that LaGuardia would run for a fourth term, O'Dwyer counted his wartime service as the head of the Allied Commission in Italy in 1944 and 1945 as being in his favor. He was especially pleased to note that his work in Italy as President Harry S Truman's special representative to supervise relief activities, received fulsome coverage in the New York _Times_ and _Il Progresso Italo-Americano_. In 1944, President Truman designated O'Dwyer to direct the recovery of the unfortunate country from the ravages of war by supplying desperately needed food, rebuilding devastated houses and taking steps to restore the agricultural and industrial bases of the country. Upon his return to New York O'Dwyer conspicuously

cooperated with Italian American leaders such as
Judge Juvenal Marchisio and Generoso Pope, who
spearheaded American relief efforts on behalf of
Italy. O'Dwyer was especially indebted to Pope who
had published a full account of his Italian
experiences in Il Progresso Italo-Americano.

Demonstrating an uncanny appreciation for ethnic
politics, which escaped the ken of other political
chieftains, O'Dwyer saw in Impellitteri, a
compatible running mate, one who, in a singular
way, could successfully draw the support of the
city's largest nationality bloc, accounting for
perhaps one of every six New Yorkers. Italian
American Democrats could now have little hesitation
to support a ticket that featured one of their own,
one who in many respects was more typical in his
ethnic background, than the more famous LaGuardia.
Impellitteri was born in Italy, was a member of the
regular Democratic organization and a practicing
Roman Catholic--all characteristics that would not
strain the credibility of their ethnic sensitivity.
Although receiving little scholarly attention, some
insightful researchers have noted that midcentury
marked a kind of transition in the religious
practices of Italian Americans. Whereas previously
they had been identified with a form of religiosity
that was less scrupulous regarding Mass attendance
and more attached to traditional Old World ethics
and feasts, they were now becoming assimilated into
the mores of American Catholicism, which is to say
a Hibernicized Catholicism. As Robert A. Orsi, who
produced an excellent study of the Italian parish
in East Harlem has written, "In the years after the
war, Mount Carmel became an Italian American
Catholic parish eager to conform to the styles and
values of American Catholicism."[25] Thus, this
leading "Little Italy," which had produced two of
the most progressive Italian American political
figures in LaGuardia and Marcantonio, was moving
perceptibly into the mainstream of American
Catholic religious life, a movement that was to
have a bearing on political directions.

Impellitteri enjoyed, furthermore, an untainted
reputation that evoked no real connection with the
underworld, the supposed Lucchese connection
notwithstanding. Although little known in the wider
community, Impellitteri possessed excellent
credentials within the ethnic enclave, having

accumulated a record of years of toiling within the vineyards of ethnic activity. In 1928, only four years out of law school, he was already being hailed by Italian Americans in his Connecticut home community where he impressed an audience of 500 with a "forceful and convincing" speech on the immigration question, religious bigotry and the evils of prohibition. New York's Italian-language newspapers promoted him as an up and coming political figure and a model for other young Italian Americans. "He is today another of those men of whom we feel proud and to whom we look up in our colony. His achievement and his brilliant success should be an inspiration to our youth who aim to make good."[26] Throughout the 1930's both as a representative of the district attorney's office and from the vantage point of a respected lawyer, he continued to make speeches both for the regular Democratic party and for the ethnic community. These activities kept his name alive within the leadership of Tammany Hall who were anxious to accommodate the growing Italian American element. Accordingly, his election to the presidency of the Rapallo Lawyers Association in July, 1940 enabled him to represent the most influential organization of Italian American lawyers in New York City and the state. The result was that at the age of forty, the mustachioed young attorney, then possessing no official public position but described simply as a "former assistant district attorney and a rather well-known city lawyer," was chosen to preside over an organization whose active membership included numerous city and state judges, congressmen, a borough president, the mayor of the city and the lieutenant governor of the state. Furthermore, it catapulted him to a position of considerable consequence by providing an opportunity for interaction with city political power brokers thereby rendering him a viable spokesman for a meaningful segment of the city's Italians. His name and his photograph now received steady exposure in the city's Italian media, especially _Il Progresso Italo-Americano_. Immediately upon his election to the presidency of the Rapallo Lawyers Association, he became a leader in Democratic politics. In the fall 1940 election, for instance, he served as chairman of the Italian American Lawyers Committee then vigorously campaigning for Franklin D.

Roosevelt's reelection and stressed the Democratic
administration's dedication to democratic goals of
benefit to the common man as the reason for
support. Impellitteri also cited the president's
appointment of numerous Italian Americans to
important positions in national government as
additional rationale to favor Roosevelt. During the
war Impellitteri had emerged as a major figure in
organizations like the American Committee For
Italian Democracy, an association of prominent New
York Italian American leaders dedicated to the
promotion of democracy in the land of their
ancestors. By comparison, Lawrence Gerosa of the
Bronx was not so conspicuous in Italian American
affairs, despite his fund-raising efforts on behalf
of his borough's Democratic party.

The Sicilian-born Impellitteri also enjoyed a
reputation of willingness to cooperate with his
party. In September 1943, for example, he agreed to
be listed as a temporary, "stand in" Democratic
candidate for justice of the state supreme court,
after the Tammany Hall leadership repudiated
Magistrate Thomas Aurelio, the original nominee,
over charges of consorting with underworld figure
Frank Costello. Embarrassed over the Aurelio-
Costello relationship, and desirous of proffering
an image of public integrity, the Tammany
leadership temporarily substituted Impellitteri for
the court position until it could convene, review
the situation and make a final nomination.
Understanding the tenuous nature of the
appointment, Impellitteri nevertheless allowed the
use of his name on the ballot, even if only
temporarily, very likely in the hope that he might
in fact emerge as the final choice, it was,
however, a hope that was destined to remain
unfulfilled because within a few days his name came
off the ticket. In sum, Impellitteri's residency in
Manhattan, the power center of city politics, his
association with numerous city Italian American
organizations, his leadership in veteran's
organizations, his ties with regular Democratic
party functionaries and his general amiability and
affability rendered him a valuable asset to the
O'Dwyer ticket. O'Dwyer took full advantage of the
city council president nominee by frequently
relying on Impellitteri to represent him before
important groups of the electorate. It is

interesting to note that some of these, especially labor unions, when failing to obtain O'Dwyer as their featured speaker during the hectic campaign period, importuned Democratic campaign headquarters to send Impellitteri in his stead.[27] Labor's favorable stance toward Impellitteri ought not be too surprising in view of the fact that for several years he had served as counsel for Local 282 of the Teamsters and Chauffeurs Union. In retrospect, O'Dwyer's selection of Impellitteri and its support by Democratic political leaders should be regarded as a wise display of knowledge about ethnic politics.

Political pundits were destined to be proven correct in their prognostication of a Democratic sweep in the fall 1945 election. Ironically a May 1945 New York _Daily News_, preferential poll saw former Mayor Jimmy Walker leading by a comfortable margin, followed by O'Dwyer. But the favorable response to the Walker name was merely one of sentiment because he was seriously ill and nearing the end of his life. The outcome of the election was in reality a foregone conclusion, the only question being the size of the Democratic plurality and inferences of the same for the upcoming Presidential election of 1948, namely a large O'Dwyer vote would hurt Republican Thomas E. Dewey, governor of New York. The O'Dwyer team won the election handily with O'Dwyer beating his nearest opponent, Goldstein, by over 685,000 votes. Lazarus Joseph defeated his nearest opponent McGoldrick by a 417,637 plurality. More impressive than Joseph's edge and almost as persuasive as O'Dwyer's margin was Impellitteri's plurality of 572,424 over Nicholas Pette--statistics that indicated abundant support for a relative unknown who had never before run for public office.

NOTES

1. Mary Louise DeNinno, "Ethnic and Political Consciousness in the New York Italian Community, 1940-1944" (Thesis, Master of Arts, San Diego State University, 1980), 189-90.

2. Dorothy Gallagher, _All The Right Enemies. The Life And Murder of Carlo Tresca_ (New York: Penguin Books, 1988).

3. "Proudly We Serve," Movie.

4. Louis Adamic, Two Way Passage (New York: Harper Brothers, 1941), 149.

5. New York Times, December 22, 1941.

6. Janet E. Worral, "Italian Prisoners of War in the United States: 1943-45," in Italian Americans in Transition, ed. Salvatore J. LaGumina, Joseph Scelsa, and Lydio Tomasi, (Staten Island: American Italian Historical Association, 1990), 253-61.

7. Edward Corsi Speech, "New York City Italian Americans, 1941," ECP.

8. Robert K. Lane, "The Way of the Ethnic in Politics," in Ethnic Group Politics, ed. Harry A. Bailey, Jr. and Ellis Katz (Columbus, Ohio: Charles E. Merrill Publishing Co., 1968), 89.

9. DeNinno, "Ethnic and Political Consciousness," 221.

10. Thomas Kessner, Fiorello H. LaGuardia and the Making of Modern New York (New York: McGraw-Hill, 1989), 487.

11. William O'Dwyer, Beyond the Golden Door, (New York: St. John's University Press, 1987), 210.

12. Jan Morris, Manhattan '45 (New York: Oxford University Press, 1987), 78.

13. David Halberstam, Summer of '49 (New York: W. Morrow, 1989), 19, 21.

14. Michael A. Musmanno, The Story of the Italians in America (Garden City: Doubleday, 1965), 216.

15. Noel F. Busch, "Joe DiMaggio," Life 6, no. 18, (May 1, 1939): 62-69.

16. O'Dwyer, Beyond the Golden Door, 218.

17. George Courson and Vincent Impellitteri, "Rathbourne's Chain of Crime," True Detective 30, no. 2 (May 1938): 30-32.

18. New York World Telegram, December 1, 1930.

19. Letter Thomas C.T. Crain to Vincent Impellitteri, December, Scrapbook, Series #1 VRI, NYMA.

20. Herbert Mitgang, The Man Who Rode the Tiger: The Life and Times of Judge Samuel Seabury (Philadelphia: J.B. Lippincott, 1963), 203-15.

21.. Letter Sidney Hillman to Vincent Impellitteri, July 2, 1931, Scrapbook, Series #1 VRI, NYMA.

22. Letter William C. Dodge to Vincent Impellitteri, January 31, 1936, Vincent Impellitteri Family Papers, (VIFP) in possession of Rose Comcowich.

23. New York Enquirer, May 30, 1937.

24. Warren Moscow, The Last of the Big Times Bosses, the Life and Times of Carmine DeSapio and the Fall of Tammany Hall (New York: Stein and Day, 1971), 63.

25. Robert A. Orsi, The Madonna of 115th Street (New Haven, Conn.: Yale University Press, 1985), 69.

26. Il Progresso Italo-Americano June 29, 1930.

27. New Yorker 21, no. 36 (October 20, 1945), 22-23.

4

Shouldering Responsibilities in a New Era

For the first time in several years New Yorkers celebrated January 1, 1946, as a holiday in the absence of war. Over a million frenzied horn-blowers, cowbell swingers and other din-creating revelers jammed Times Square where they frustrated police plans to contain them within a few midtown blocks, and thereby furnished the city with its noisiest New Year's Eve since the advent of 1941. While it devastated much of the globe, the Second World War transformed the United States into a boomingly prosperous nation with New York standing as a unique symbol of the metamorphosis. Never before had the ordinary American been so affluent. As if to accent the heady sensation the 1947 New Year's celebration was on an even higher scale as New Yorkers enjoyed themselves with perhaps only an inner feeling that this might be the last big splurge on the easy money of the war. Surely this was a reflection of a city happy to throw off the spirit of sacrifice and danger that had characterized the previous few years. Termination of bellicosity brought with it happy prospects of a return to mundane peacetime pursuits, as for example: an end to marriage postponements, procurement of adequate living quarters, the landing of meaningful jobs with futures, the resumption of education, the elimination of ration books as prerequisites for the purchase of necessary products like sugar, coffee and meat, and obtaining long-desired consumer items. One indication of the change in attitude was the tendency to engage in a national shopping spree. Having foregone purchases of desirable products for years because of the economic constraints of the lean 1930's or the scarcities due to war-time exigencies, Americans were now prepared to make up for lost time. With deprivation no longer the prevailing mood, Americans lined up to purchase the

latest labor-saving devices such as washing
machines and refrigerators as soon as they were
manufactured. News that nylon stockings were
available in mid-town Manhattan stores brought out
customers by the hundreds who literally stampeded
the retail outlets for the rare merchandise. People
likewise were willing to put in orders for the even
scarcer supply of automobiles and engage in black
market trading by paying exorbitant sums "under the
table" to expedite such orders. Another
manifestation of the buoyant mood was in the
penchant to buy expansive clothing that had not
been produced during the war. In such an atmosphere
the ordinary city shopper endured arrogance on the
part of clerks in many shops who took advantage of
their positions of possessing limited quantities of
coveted items. Conditions were always better for
the well-heeled customer who could afford to pore
over comprehensive collections of late afternoon
and informal dinner dresses in smart emporiums like
Saks Fifth Avenue or Bergdorf Goodman's department
store.

For certain the serious minded could point to
some disturbances on the otherwise pacific horizon,
such as the awful destructive power of the atom
bomb, the dire distress of societies severely
damaged by the war, and the elusiveness of full-
fledged harmony between nations. There were, in
addition, numerous domestic problems that cried out
for attention and equitable resolution. But in the
period prior to unraveling of international
relations that would soon gain acknowledgment as
the onset of an unrelenting Cold War, most people
took solace in a definite cessation of hostilities
and in an unmistakable veering towards a peacetime
economy and society.

As far as the status of their own municipality
was concerned, city residents exuded confidence
that the newly elected administration of William
O'Dwyer possessed the capabilities to commence a
more than competent control of city management.
Indeed O'Dwyer's 1945 election day record plurality
of 685,175, in an otherwise uninspiring election
that saw the fewest number of New Yorkers register
to vote since the days of Jimmy Walker, must be
construed as a ringing confirmation of the new
Democratic administration. The animated mood rested
on the conviction that O'Dwyer brought to the

headship of municipal government a "commanding
presence, the halo of a gang-busting District
Attorney," as Sayre and Kaufman aver.[1] O'Dwyer's
background projected the image of a newcomer
American who made out spectacularly well in this
land of opportunity. His was the heart-warming
story of the immigrant lad who worked as a
patrolman, became a Fordham University Law School
Graduate, lawyer, District attorney, county judge,
and brigadier general in the United States Air
Force during the Second World War. In short, when
O'Dwyer first came on the scene, "he had more class
than any other guy that ever came down the pike,"
in the words of one professional journalist.[2] New
York City in 1946 faced in microcosm the spate of
problems confronting the nation as a whole in the
immediate postwar years: labor unrest, housing
shortages, corruption in government, crime, fiscal
constraints, tense intergroup relations, inadequate
transportation and educational facilities, and
abuse of the environment. Some examples, as in the
fields of labor, housing and transportation are in
order. Labor organizations, which had grown in size
and strength in recent years but that had seen
their power circumscribed due to wartime exigencies
and restrictions, were now prepared to obtain a
greater share of the country's economic largesse.
Cities like New York, which were home to municipal
unions for its uniformed employees, were in the
forefront of the labor agitation of the period.
Almost immediately on O'Dwyer's ascension to
office, Michael Quill, whose ability to spout the
union line with a mellifluous Irish brogue that was
carefully crafted for selective public consumption
and who was president of the powerful Transport
Workers Union (TWU), became the first to test the
city administration's mettle by threatening to
strike unless demands for wage increases were met.
Simultaneously New Yorkers were subjected to a fuel
oil deliverers strike and a tugboat workers strike.
These labor problems were resolved in due course
with O'Dwyer even eliciting praise for refusing to
succumb to the TWU threat and not caving into
Quill. At the same time the transport workers did
receive wage increases. Indeed in preparing the
city budget in 1946, O'Dwyer, after consultation
with City Council President Impellitteri and other
city officials, agreed to a modest increase in the

salaries of many municipal employees. As a strong
advocate for housing, O'Dwyer eagerly testified
before federal legislative committee hearings on
behalf of a new national government housing measure
and demonstrated his administration's commitment to
the cause of adequate housing by leading New York
City to open its first postwar, low-rent housing
project even before the national government acted.
Finally, the O'Dwyer administration completed a
project launched by aviation enthusiast LaGuardia,
establishing a major international airport for the
city, albeit following a different plan than that
of the former administration. Whereas LaGuardia had
argued for a wholly city-owned and city-financed
facility, O'Dwyer, convinced that this was beyond
the municipality's fiscal ability, approved a plan
to allow the New York Port Authority to construct
the airport and operate it under lease for fifty
years.

Critics of Impellitteri, who, as city council
president, was second in the hierarchy of municipal
power, have charged him with passivity, implying
that his performance was that of noninvolvement and
functioning in a purely ceremonial role. Whatever
the grounds for some of the criticism, it should be
kept in mind, however, that to be a somewhat
compliant supporter of the administration was
inherent in the very nature of the office and that
in that sense it was comparable to the office of
vice-president of the United States who normally
does not publicly dispute the president. The truth
of the matter is that Impellitteri presided over
the city council, which, because it was then not
vested with extensive powers, was a body that
concerned itself with many trivial items and that
despite imposing titles and descriptions, there was
more shadow than substance to its functioning.
Ordinarily the council had been content to follow
the administration's lead and ratify its wishes.[3]
Accordingly, in the absence of incompatibility
between mayor and city council president would it
be realistic to expect outspokenness and
contrariness approaching divisiveness? Unlike later
examples of individuals elected city council
presidents as a result of winning primary
designations on their own, that is, Rudolph Halley
and Carol Bellamy, and therefore in competition
with the mayor, Impellitteri was handpicked by

O'Dwyer and was expected to be an administration player and supporter. This anticipation was to be more than fully realized as O'Dwyer frequently placed the responsibility for carrying out major city programs into Impellitteri's hands. It should also be remembered that O'Dwyer determined to take a more direct and vigorous role than his predecessor LaGuardia, in the deliberations of certain aspects of city government. Thus, although the city council president ordinarily presided over meetings of the powerful Board of Estimate, O'Dwyer let it be known at the outset of his administration that he would attend future meetings of the Board as presiding officer. When unable to attend he would send a representative; only then would Council President Impellitteri preside. This was a radically different management style than LaGuardia's who rarely attended meetings of the board.

Early during the O'Dwyer term, the Sicilian-born city official demonstrated his ability and perseverance in dealing with sensitive city issues that came before the puissant Board of Estimate and which other city officials avoided by their deliberate absence or by assigning subordinates to represent them. The delicate negotiations between the city and its municipal unions in the spring of 1946 are a case in point. By mid-April, O'Dwyer and his colleagues on the Board of Estimate were confronted with unmistakable signs of keen disaffection from city employees who remained dissatisfied with city plans to increase the budget to allow for a mere modest wage increase. Over 100 union representatives addressed the board in a record-breaking session that saw over 5,000 city employees in attendance in the hearing room which was constantly filled and emptied. The session lasted from 11:00 a.m. to 3:30 a.m. Evincing a strong distaste for this type of encounter, Mayor O'Dwyer and other members of the board deliberately and gratefully absented themselves, choosing to send representatives in their stead. Conspicuous by his presence was Impellitteri, "who presided throughout the entire fifteen hours of the hearing, was the only elected member of the Board of Estimate to exercise the 'patience and fortitude' required for the task."[4] It was a thankful mayor who complimented Impellitteri for taking the onus

of a major burden off his shoulders while
demonstrating "a full and detailed understanding of
the material presented by more than 100 spokesmen
for city employees." Impellitteri's efficient and
workman-like performance in this instance, as on so
many other occasions when he substituted for the
city chief executive as acting mayor over the
years, elicited well-deserved praise as a
"friendly, scholarly man," who endured an extremely
busy daily schedule.[5]

Impressed by the city council president's
conscientious conduct, O'Dwyer came to rely on
Impellitteri on matters that had international
repercussions, such as the selection of New York as
the headquarters for the United Nations. Although
the municipality had long enjoyed prestige as the
premier city, it was to be challenged in the
postwar period by the likes of Boston,
Philadelphia, and San Francisco, all of which
sought the world organization for their own
municipalities. In other words, these cities were
in competition with New York and all importuned
United Nations officials to locate in their
municipalities. Not prepared to relinquish the
prestige that would attach to the city that housed
the organization, New York officials were energized
to undertake aggressive actions to settle the
matter in New York's favor. For some months city
officials acquired increments of private and city-
owned land along the East River in order to turn
the acreage over to the United Nations in a move
considered by O'Dwyer to be the most important act
in city history. It was, therefore, somewhat
surprising and revealing to note that O'Dwyer, who
was away on vacation, entrusted Impellitteri with
the task of completing the formalities of
negotiations by officially making the presentation
of the city property to the peacekeeping
organization. Thus, October 18, 1947, was an
extraordinary day for the immigrant council
president who represented the city and in a sense
the nation, when he met with and welcomed Secretary
General Trygve Lie and other United Nations
officials from around the world, and earnestly
urged them to accept the city's land for their
official world headquarters. With massed bands of
the army, the navy and the New York City Police
Department offering a program of marches and with

city, state and world figures in attendance, Vincent Impellitteri tendered the official offer on behalf of the city. In making the presentation Impellitteri heralded the step as another chapter in the great universal effort toward global understanding. He cited the numerous advantages that accrued to the organization by remaining in the city and stated that New York's commitment to the United Nations headquarters was reflected in the realization of the financial and material assistance provided.

We believe that the advantages of remaining in this city, in this particular area, with all its conveniences, with its great accessibility, with the absence of any need of condemnation of land, plus the willingness and the eagerness of the city to make further contributions in improvements, should turn the scales in favor of this location as against any other.[6]

The successful conclusion of this episode ranked as a highlight of O'Dwyer's mayoralty and it also demonstrated the consequential role Impellitteri played. Long after his tenure as mayor was over, Impellitteri harkened back to this event as a matchless climax of his career.

That O'Dwyer entrusted Impellitteri with the most important aspects of city administration is further borne out by reference to the responsibilities given him with respect to the preparation and presentation of the city budget as well as by his designation as city spokesman before the New York State government. On April 1, 1948, acting as agent for O'Dwyer, Impellitteri publicly presented before the Board of Estimate, the largest budget yet in city history at $1,137,000,000. In presenting the budget, Impellitteri reproved the overly parsimonious state government, stressing once again the impossibility of expanding city services without the city receiving its share of city-paid revenues from the state. The city, he soundly asserted, was at an enormous disadvantage because, although it was at the limits of its legal power to tax, demands for services and inflationary pressures constrained its enterprise. Impellitteri also explained that the limited increase in city real estate revenues were deceptive because they were more than offset by the ongoing inflationary spiral. The New York <u>Times</u>, although not overly

enthused about the budget, nevertheless conceded it
could not argue with the proposal to keep spending
within legal limits.

Two weeks after submitting the plan it was once
again Impellitteri who held the limelight during
discussions over budget proposals. Public hearings
on the budget were regarded as New York City's
equivalent to New England town meetings. It was the
one chance for the ordinary New Yorker to come to
City Hall and have a say in city affairs and indeed
a couple of hundred city residents seized the
opportunity over the four days of a marathon
session that was more akin to an endurance test for
city officials, especially the presiding officer.
These annual hearings attracted advocates of many
opinions ranging from good government groups to
those who made little sense yet still had to be
heard. The hearings tended to be so crowded that
they required the assignment of extra police to
prevent demonstrations and disorders including
boisterous applause, a feat in which they were not
very successful. Such sessions were recognized as
extraordinary strains to the presiders who
understandably could easily lose forbearance and
patience. It was likewise understandable that few
political leaders, especially O'Dwyer, relished the
wearying task and gladly passed it on to the city
council president, whose patience and demeanor was
up to the ordeal. For his part, Impellitteri came
through the difficult affliction admirably by
allowing the citizens to express themselves while
making a judicious use of the gavel to force
participants to stay with the subject under
discussion. Even Republican bastions applauded
Impellitteri because he "was equal to the trying
job. His experience in the often tumultuous City
Council seemed to help."[7] Later on in the month it
was once again Impellitteri who presented the
city's case to the New York State government when
he beseeched Governor Thomas E. Dewey to veto a
Republican sponsored higher fare bill.

The widening breach between Russia and America in
the months following the end of the Second World
War confronted Americans with the disturbing task
of trying to deal with an ideologically committed
antagonist bent on world domination under the
Communist label. By early 1946, there were
unmistakable signs that the United States was tired

of "babying" the Russians, in the words of
President Truman, and that the time had come to
take a hard line. Russian Premier Josef Stalin's
chilling assertion that there could never be
lasting peace with capitalist nations was answered
by Western powers' denunciation of an "Iron
Curtain." In this distrustful atmosphere, Western
nations struggling to recover from the
extraordinary devastation of the war, looked to the
United States for help. Regarding itself as the
main bulwark against the threat of international
communism, the United States responded with the
Truman Doctrine, the Marshall Plan (European
Recovery Program), and the formation of the North
Atlantic Treaty Organization (NATO)--a combination
of economic and military steps designed to
strengthen the West and "contain" communism.

The years 1946-1949 were especially difficult for
Italy, which, like many European countries, was
beset by crisis after crisis as it desperately
tried to feed its people and stem the Communist
tide. As the critical April 1948 elections
approached it appeared that the Italian Communist
Party, the largest in the free world, could be on
the threshold of electoral success. Such an
unwelcome prospect was regarded with fear and
trepidation as forces within and without Italy
campaigned in favor of the Christian Democrats. For
the Catholic Church the campaign took on the
semblance of a crusade as it inveighed against
atheistic communism and exhorted its followers to
save the country from the godless scourge. Against
this background numerous figures in the United
States, including former secretaries of state and
other high officials, were actively involved in a
propaganda effort to convince Italian voters to
defeat the Communists at the polls. The anti-
Communist crusade elicited the interest of an
assortment of individuals, including implausible
opportunists like Italian American publicist Guido
Orlando who succeeded in promoting himself as "pope
of publicity" and who wildly claimed personal
credit for causing Italians to vote for the de
Gasperi Christian Democrats.[8] No participants,
however, were as active and genuinely concerned as
Italian American leaders who joined together in an
extraordinary effort to influence the outcome via
extensive letter-writing campaigns and shortwave

radio messages. Throughout the country one could
find individuals such as Mayor Thomas D'Alessandro
of Baltimore, for example, who chaired the
Committee for Italian Democracy and who coordinated
a letter-writing campaign that produced 140,000 to
150,000 letters per day as American Italians urged
their relatives and friends in Italy not to vote
Communist. In New York leading Italian Americans
like labor leader Luigi Antonini used his popular
radio program to urge Italians to vote against the
Communist Party. Publisher Generoso Pope of Il
Progresso Italo-Americano, promoted the campaign in
his media outlet by printing convenient form
letters that could easily be cut out and that bore
the message, "Vote for freedom for Italy and for
Italians, or you may never vote again."

It has been observed that religious observance
among Catholic Italians was weak until the 1940's,
when after the conclusion of the war, a discernible
strengthening of Catholic ties in Italian American
communities was manifest. Therefore, it was not
surprising to find religious entreaties against
Italy's Communists. This development dovetailed
perfectly with United States policy concluding that
religion was a bankable commodity as a moral weapon
in the Cold War.[9] Monsignor Alphonse Arcese, well-
known pastor of a Brooklyn Italian parish,
broadcast appeals over short wave radio to Italians
imparting the message, "Italians vote for the
parties that are with God."

For Vincent Impellitteri, a native born son of
Italy, the anti-Communist crusade was a cause of
supreme importance in which he was determined to
play a major part. Appropriately he played a
conspicuous role in the New York letter-writing
campaign and also ventured to the airwaves to
broadcast direct messages in Italian to voters in
the land of his birth. Eleven days before the
crucial April 18 election, for example, he
broadcast a stirring plea to Italians not to cast
their votes that would permit, "your beautiful land
to become enslaved under the crushing heel of
communism." He further noted the inevitable
consequences of becoming a Communist satellite
nation that perforce would then effectively
preclude access to western friends. Impellitteri's
efforts in this activity were so effective that
they elicited the personal acknowledgment of

President Truman not only at the time but also in subsequent years as the president sought every opportunity to bolster his anti-Communist campaign. Thus it can be seen by this representative cross-section of leaders that Italian Americans were mobilized and indeed inspired to participate in the anti-Communist campaign. The solidarity effort was very effective as Italian voters resoundingly defeated the Communist party and conversely gave major support to the Christian Democratic party. The victory of Italy's Christian Democrats over the Communists struck a positive responsive chord within New York City's Italian American community as evidenced in a warm outpouring of the ethnic group to hear Fr. Riccardo Lombardo, S.J.,one of Italy's leading anti-Communist voices during his 1949 visit to the city.[10] Sensing this as an activity that elicited popular support, Impellitteri was to refer to his role in this campaign frequently in subsequent years. Nor was this the only occasion in which he enlisted in the campaign to aid postwar Italy. Significantly, even earlier in 1947, he responded with alacrity to a request that he become a member of a national committee formed to work on behalf of a bill to legalize an increase in Italian immigration.[11]

Impellitteri's anti-Communist activity was evident within the New York City political system. In 1937 the city had initiated a proportional representation experiment as a means providing opportunities for minor political ideologies to obtain a forum and degree of representation in proportion to their percentage of the population. By 1947 the political innovation had become a critical center of controversy with Democrats in the city council particularly because of the presence of left-wing councilmen. Accordingly, Impellitteri joined in the chorus of condemnation of the system as officials called on voters to approve a referendum abolishing the it. Denouncing proportional representation as an "ignoble experiment which should be discarded and relegated to the ash-heap," he cited his own sad, personal experience as evidence.

One mortifying example of this, which I can never forget, was the impertinent affront to Cardinal Spellman and the Catholic Church when Communist councilmen cast the only votes

against a resolution congratulating Cardinal Spellman on his
elevation; a resolution which had the full support of all the
other members of the council regardless of their political or
religious faiths.[12]

Political life during O'Dwyer's first
administration comported with the image of a
typical, partisan controlled atmosphere in which
the Democratic party was preponderant, and in which
the party's strongest club, Tammany Hall, sought a
return to its traditional role as patronage
dispenser. It was also a time that saw relations
between the Tammany leadership and O'Dwyer
alternate between feuds and cooperation. Tammany
Hall, which regarded itself as the traditional
determiner of politics, recognized that it was
compelled to deal with a mayor who, as the highest
Democratic elected city official, had exhibited
disturbing streaks of independence, but who
nevertheless held the reigns of power at City Hall.
Whether this independence, which was sprinkled with
appropriate words of reform, was genuine or merely
rhetoric for public consumption, was a matter of
conjecture. The reform approach revolved around the
denunciation of underworld influence in the
political arena--a charge that was readily
acknowledged by political insiders who explained
that the association of criminal elements and
Tammany Hall leaders had been a fact of political
life for years and that it had intensified because
these leaders had been frozen out of city political
influence during the LaGuardia mayoral years.
Conspicuously the underworld figure most frequently
mentioned in this connection was Francesco
Castaglia, an Italian American popularly known as
Frank Costello, the "prime minister" of the
Syndicate in New York. Long involved in gambling
enterprises, Costello, it was averred, hungered for
respectability by associating with respected judges
and political leaders. In donning the mantle of
reformer, the mayor, who had himself been charged
with having a close acquaintance with Costello, was
apparently attempting to control power brokers
within the hall, while seeming to cleanse it.
    In addition to the intraparty jockeying for
influence, the political climate in the city was
characterized by an interethnic struggle for power
that further blurred the horizon. The latent desire

for control of Tammany Hall by Democratic Italian American elements who had become fed up with what they considered discrimination in patronage matters, had been under way for years. The Italian bloc, which included a fascinating alliance with Jewish district leaders, now began a determined effort to oust the Irish leadership and replace it with its own people. Louis Eisenstein, a veteran Tammany stalwart provided an insider's view of the development.

Back in the early 1930's, when the Hall was dominated by Irish names, factions developed along geographic lines and clashes whirled around personalities . . . . Now, allegiances based on "national origins" dominated Tammany's internal affairs. Italian leaders banded together, first in self defense, later to advance their interests.[13]

However, when in the late 1940's the contest for power had reached the point where the sons of Italy were finally to emerge triumphant, it would take a careful effort to control the delicate balance between the two groups without weakening the Democratic party. As a New York <u>Herald Tribune</u>, editorial narrated, "Scarcely a week passes but that the 'Irish group' or the 'Italian group' is stirring a new plot, and deep significances are read into O'Dwyer's latest appointments."[14] Given his own ethnic roots O'Dwyer was deeply aware of the meaning of control of Tammany Hall by the Irish who for decades used this power as a vehicle to obtain desirable civil service jobs for ethnic group members. Simultaneously he was sensitive to the Italian American determination that they no longer be shunted to peripheral political positions. Indeed with one of every seven New Yorkers of Italian background this ethnic group could lay claim to being the largest single nationality element in the city and thus could no longer be ignored in its quest for power. The Italian element furthermore, now included significant numbers of the second and third generations whose increased literacy and familiarity with city affairs evinced a growing political consciousness. Moreover, members of the ethnic group now possessed that other necessary ingredient for successful politicking, namely money, albeit some of it traceable to crime

syndicates that were interested in utilizing their
bounties to exercise influence in Tammany Hall
because of the obvious reciprocal benefits that
could accrue from a powerful political organization
in their debt. While the extent of this connection
is debatable, what should not be overlooked is the
seemingly unusual phenomena of the promotion of
both their own economic interest and their ethnic
group's interest on the part of a number syndicate
figures such as Costello. It is not necessarily an
incongruity to couple principle and self-interest,
as one Costello biographer explained,

> What did Costello get out of politics? Was he simply being
> the fixer for the Mafia and the other elements of organized
> crime? Of course, he was an agent for the Mafia, but there
> were other reasons for his heavy involvement in political
> affairs. He enjoyed the delicious feel of power. He also
> sincerely believed that Italians were entitled to a greater
> share of the political spoils, and many of the men he put on
> the bench were Italian Americans.[15]

Against this background O'Dwyer determined to use
Impellitteri in order to direct events so as to
maximize the political benefits to himself.
Impellitteri was to serve as a kind of liaison
between O'Dwyer's administration and segments of
the Italian American ethnic group. Nor was O'Dwyer
plunging into untested waters for he well
understood how valuable his Italian-born colleague
had been in the 1945 mayoral campaign, (ostensibly
unknown, Impellitteri had run only slightly behind
O'Dwyer in the popular vote). Indeed, in view of
the rather slim plurality of O'Dwyer over Goldstein
on the Democratic line alone, exclusive of American
Labor party backing, O'Dwyer needed all the help he
could muster. O'Dwyer frequently relied on
Impellitteri to be his political spear thrower when
the occasion called for an attack on another
popular Italian American political leader. In this
atmosphere it was politically expedient for O'Dwyer
to have Impellitteri, rather than an Irish
American, publicly rebuke former Mayor LaGuardia,
for example. Thus, in May 1946, when Impellitteri
chided LaGuardia for opposing the City Planning
Commission's decision to turn down a $15,000,000
bus terminal in Manhattan, he marshalled an
effective argument that LaGuardia himself had
appointed the members of the commission. "The City

Planning Commission should be happy that its appointing officer is no longer Mayor," observed Impellitteri.[16] Impellitteri likewise criticized LaGuardia for leaving the financial affairs of the city in worse condition than had been indicated earlier. The latter assertion was not mere political posturing as Kessner concluded in assessing LaGuardia's lack of coherence in the development of city programs. "LaGuardia laid no plans to set New York on a solid fiscal footing."[17]

An adept politician, O'Dwyer sought to transform Tammany Hall by ousting the incumbent leadership, which consisted of hapless Edward V. Loughlin, titular head of the organization, and Clarence Neal and Bert Stand, the acknowledged powers behind the scene. City Hall's denial of patronage positions to Tammany Hall during the first year of O'Dwyer's administration so weakened the ruling clique of Loughlin, Neal and Stand, that it was merely a matter of time before the triumvirate would be ousted thereby enabling O'Dwyer to name his own people to head the organization. Ethnic considerations were thus intertwined with political machinations as Democratic Italian Americans sought to promote Carmine DeSapio to a major position in the Tammany Hall leadership. Impellitteri was deeply involved in the meetings and negotiations that finally led to a pact between the Irish and the Italian insurgents. Consequently, in December 1946 Impellitteri, accompanied by Third District leader Frank Sampson and DeSapio, informed O'Dwyer that they had entered into an agreement to support DeSapio for a high Tammany post, thereby further weakening Loughlin and setting the stage for O'Dwyer to name Sampson to succeed him.

Carmine DeSapio, who for years had waged primary fights with the Irish, provided the leadership as the Italian element sought to gain control of Tammany Hall. Ambitious for the command of Tammany Hall, DeSapio nevertheless sensed that he was not yet strong enough to take over for himself and would thus have to wait for a more propitious time. In the meantime DeSapio and other Italian leaders such as Samuel DeFalco, were content to oust the ineffective incumbent Loughlin and settle for a Tammany leader of their choosing, providing that DeSapio be given a prominent post. Replacing

Loughlin, who was merely Tammany's titular head, was only part of the problem because Neal, as chairman of its Committee on Elections and Stand, as secretary of Tammany Hall, were the real forces behind the scenes and eventually would have to be dealt with. Mayor O'Dwyer could hardly avoid political stratagems because, as the highest ranking Democrat in the city, he was, ostensibly, the leader of the party. Impellitteri, because he held the second highest city post as well as by virtue of his Manhattan residency and his Italian visibility, was bound to be a major player in the political maneuvering. As an illustration, it was an accord reached by the O'Dwyer-Impellitteri leadership with the Italian insurgent group led by DeSapio that provided DeSapio with the necessary votes to become elections commissioner on the Board of Elections, at $10,000 a year, and to support Frank Sampson as the next Tammany boss. In actuality membership on the Board of Elections was the most important and most prestigious reward within the organization apart from the leadership of Tammany Hall itself.

Meanwhile on January 6, 1947 it was reported that O'Dwyer, who had starved the incumbent Tammany leadership for six months by depriving them of patronage jobs, had devised a plan to establish a new, civic minded Tammany organization to be divorced from underworld influence. This was a reference to the open association between Frank Costello and Neal and Stand. It was also maintained that the maneuver would further weaken the latter duo and provide the O'Dwyer-Impellitteri team with a greater opportunity to refashion the New York County Democratic organization. For their part Neal and Stand sought to retain their power by throwing their support to DeSapio for Tammany leadership and thereby frustrate efforts to promote Sampson, O'Dwyer's choice. However, in the end the O'Dwyer-Impellitteri side was able to prevail as Sampson succeeded Loughlin while DeSapio was forced to remain content with the position of election commissioner. The events could allow O'Dwyer to project a reform image, but in the minds of observers it was misleading. "Both camps benefitted from the charade. O'Dwyer could legitimately claim that he was cleaning up Tammany, even while Costello's influence remained strong."[18] The events also constituted a snub of DeSapio and undoubtedly served to sour relations between the Tammany leader and the council president, thereby providing a background for a future destructive feud between him and Impellitteri.

Temporarily devoid of the top Tammany post, DeSapio nevertheless reigned as the most influential Board of Elections member and a major power wielder. As a New York Times, political reporter explained, the position placed DeSapio above the common herd. "It made him the man to whom all other leaders had to turn for help with their problems in the primaries and general elections. He was the clearing house through which all election-machinery patronage had to pass."[19]

The elevation of Sampson to Tammany chieftain meant the ouster of Neal and Stand from their positions of influence and an occasion to test the newfound power, an opportunity that came quickly in the spring of 1948 when a seat on the coveted surrogate court opened up. In view of the fact that Sampson was O'Dwyer's man and that he had been district leader of Impellitteri's assembly district prior to becoming county leader, his decision that the court post go to Impellitteri was not totally surprising. It soon became evident that Sampson was in fact serving as the organization's titular leader, because the real power now gravitated to a quartet of men that including Francis X. Mancuso, Sidney Moses, Harry Brickman and Carmine DeSapio, with the latter poised to exercise the major role. Thus, in a direct rebuke to Sampson, DeSapio rejected Impellitteri in favor of Francis A. Valente for Surrogate Court of New York County, one of the prize plums of the judiciary establishment. Clearly this would become another basis for future antagonism between DeSapio and Impellitteri. To be sure the move also constituted a slighting of O'Dwyer's protegé, Sampson, however, it was more likely interpreted as a source of concern to O'Dwyer because it would take the guardianship of estates of infants out of Irish hands and turn it over to Italians who were supposedly less scrupulous regarding Catholic dogma. Observers of the city's political power brokers always included "Fiftieth Street" or the "Power House," as Cardinal Spellman's residence was called, as a major player especially at a time when a large portion of

Tammany organization people were Catholics.[20]

Politically, the city witnessed the emergence of
a classic juxtaposition of sparring ethnic groups:
the Irish and the Italian blocs. While this
explanation is in reality an oversimplification of
political machinations, O'Dwyer, nevertheless, was
compelled to move carefully so as not to openly
alienate the "Italian bloc." The crafty Irish mayor
performed this deftly by denouncing the DeSapio
move as an example of Tammany corruption, and then
proceeding to tantalize the political establishment
by maintaining that he intended to promote the
candidacy of an Italian, one with whom he had
influence, for the surrogate court in the upcoming
primaries--Impellitteri. The DeSapio faction
retaliated by voting Sampson out and replacing him
with Hugo Rogers, Manhattan borough president and a
leader of the Black voting bloc. Within a year
DeSapio felt strong enough to take over as the
undisputed Tammany leader. In the meantime the
O'Dwyer-DeSapio feud furnished New Yorkers with an
image of an administration fighting against corrupt
bossism. Critics charged that the whole incident
was pure camouflage, because in the end O'Dwyer
accepted Rogers and withdrew Impellitteri's name
from consideration. It was not clear whether
Impellitteri genuinely sought the judicial post or
whether as a team player he allowed the mayor to
use his name as a necessary part of the infighting.
According to the account of J. Raymond Jones, then
Harlem Democratic leader, the vote within the
Manhattan Democratic organization was virtually
evenly split between Impellitteri and Valente and
that only Jones's rejection of the city council
president prevented his elevation to the court.
Jones admitted that he did this in order to advance
the candidacy of an African-American for the court
of general sessions.[21] In any event the DeSapio
forces withdrew Valente's name and thereby accepted
a compromise choice, who promptly lost to a
Republican-Liberal candidate.

The national elections of 1948 aroused unusual
local attention as it pitted President Harry S
Truman against New York Governor Thomas E. Dewey.
Although incumbency is normally an advantage, the
prevailing political wisdom perceived Truman
campaigning under a disadvantage because of his
civil rights position and a seemingly devastating

split within the Democratic party. It was felt that
the normally complacent Democratic South had been
alienated by Truman's procivil rights stands and
stood ready to back Dixiecrat Strom Thurmond, who
was running on a separate ticket. In the North,
Truman was expected to be adversely affected by the
candidacy of Democrat Henry Wallace, who ran as the
Progressive party candidate. Thus, although a large
part of the country had developed a certain
affection for the perky Missourian, the consensus
was that he did not possess sufficient presidential
stature to win on his own. Virtually all the
nation's political pundits predicted that the
urbane, sophisticated Republican New York governor,
who had run a respectable campaign against Franklin
D. Roosevelt in 1944, was the odds-on favorite. The
capable governor of the nation's premier state, who
enjoyed a distinguished national reputation and who
had solid Republican backing, could not fail to win
against the feisty but hapless man from
Independence, Missouri. The results were startling
as the expected strength of the Dixiecrats and the
Progressive parties failed to materialize and
Truman achieved a majority from much of the farm
areas and the big cities. In the latter instance
keeping New York City Democratic was the important
function entrusted to the O'Dwyer-Impellitteri
leadership that campaigned faithfully on behalf of
the regular ticket. Impellitteri's activity in
endorsing Truman saw the city council president
venture far beyond city borders as, for example, a
campaign trip to Utica, New York demonstrates. On
October 27, 1948 a Democratic organization rally
turned out 1,200 people who paid tribute to
Impellitteri who enthusiastically promoted Truman's
candidacy as immensely preferable in the face of an
inactive Republican controlled Congress. He
asserted that for Italian Americans Truman's
election had a special meaning because they were
"grateful that Italy has been a beneficiary of
American friendship and generosity as expressed
through the Marshall Plan." He also maintained that
the Democratic party, in contradistinction to the
Republican party rewarded Italian Americans with
more opportunities for careers in public
service.[22]

In so far as local races were concerned, there
was the usual bickering within Democratic ranks as

Tammany leaders vied with insurgents. One of the
more interesting cases involved Franklin D.
Roosevelt, Jr., who, because of DeSapio's
opposition, was initially denied Tammany support
for a Congressional seat, and was apparently
offered the city council presidency in its stead.
According to Impellitteri, the DeSapio strategy
called for Roosevelt to replace him as council
president in 1949 whereupon the late president's
son would become mayor upon O'Dwyer's resignation.
Rejecting that intriguing orchestration, Roosevelt
ran and won the Democratic primary nomination for
Congress. In two years Impellitteri would compare
his own battle to run as an independent against an
unsavory machine to what the more famous Roosevelt
had done.[23]

As O'Dwyer's first term was reaching its
conclusion, political observers were only mildly
surprised in June 1949, to learn that the mayor had
chosen not to run for reelection. The announcement
elicited praise for the mayor's ability to grow in
office, that is, although he had inherited a crop
of governmental problems because of a stringent
wartime operating basis, O'Dwyer's administration
had tackled many headaches successfully despite a
huge inflationary spiral that escalated city
management costs. Speculation and rumors abounded
that the purported decision not to run could be
attributed to his advancing age--he was approaching
fifty-nine, his weakened physical condition,
attractive offers from the private sector and
matrimonial plans.[24] O'Dwyer's explanation was
that he had come "to the conclusion that I had
about enough of the office of Mayor."
Notwithstanding all of these considerations, it was
also speculated that whatever credence lay in them
was offset by the belief that because fellow
Democrats regarded him as the strongest possible
Democratic candidate for the office, they would
overcome his reluctance and importune him to
acquiesce. In the event that he remained
intransigent in his decision, other prominent
Democrats were identified as possible party
candidates: District Attorney Frank S. Hogan of New
York County, former Comptroller Joseph D.
McGoldrick, Brooklyn Borough President John
Cashmore and Supreme Court Justices James J.
Bennett and Ferdinand Pecora. Although his name was

not originally included among the potential
successors, Vincent Impellitteri soon emerged as
another one worthy of receiving consideration. That
Impellitteri was interested in succeeding O'Dwyer
was manifest in a statement issued after Democratic
leaders supposedly designated Pecora as their
choice. The selection of Pecora was also a
reflection of the wishes of Carmine DeSapio and the
behind-the scenes underworld leader Frank Costello,
whose influence in Democratic politics was said to
be so enormous that he compelled the other leaders
to sign undated letters of resignation for future
use. Designation of Pecora did not meet unanimous
agreement within the Italian bloc of Tammany Hall
leaders as the example of Judge Francis X. Mancuso
demonstrated. Mancuso's decision to support
Impellitteri against Pecora so angered the
influential Costello that he resorted to the
drastic action of filling in a date on the
previously signed resignation letters and summarily
forced Mancuso out of his Tammany leadership
position. As George Wolf, Costello's lawyer has
written, "Frank [Costello] simply filled in the
date of Mancuso's resignation, turned it in, and
the next thing New York--and Mancuso--knew the
Tammany leader had resigned."[25] Impellitteri
regarded the Pecora designation a mere formality
whereby Democratic leaders discharged a debt of
gratitude to Generoso Pope, and now announced that
he himself was available should the leaders want
him. These manipulations drew comments from some
popular observers of city affairs such as popular
columnist Ed Sullivan who advised Generoso Pope
that if he wanted to plump for an Italian American
who could not be attacked at any point,
Impellitteri, whose vote total in 1945 startled
leaders, "is made to order."[26]

From the outset the press and political reporters
were dubious about O'Dwyer's decision against
running for reelection, and indeed, O'Dwyer
himself, after repeated meetings with Democratic
party leaders, confessed a weakness in his resolve.
Any uncertainty about O'Dwyer's running terminated
completely by the end of the summer of 1949, when
he once again agreed to be the official standard-
bearer for the Democratic party, with Impellitteri
and Joseph similarly receiving nomination for
council president and comptroller respectively.

Newbold Morris was once again O'Dwyer's opponent in
what was expected to be a somewhat rigorous
campaign but with the end never in doubt because
Morris could not excite the body politic. Indeed to
some Republican leaders like Edward Corsi, who,
perhaps because he himself was under consideration
for the Republican-Fusion mayoralty nomination,
regarded Morris' candidacy "a mistake" with
predictable results. What made 1949 different from
1945 was the action of the American Labor party.

   In the 1949 campaign, unlike the previous one,
O'Dwyer was not to have the American Labor party
line, then considered a critical asset. Instead
that third party nominated fiery Congressman Vito
Marcantonio, who could be counted on to wage an
energetic campaign, which while not expected to win
the mayoralty, could very well cut deeply into the
Italian American pool of voters that the Democratic
party sorely needed. This might give Newbold
Morris, the Republican and Fusion parties candidate
an important boost. Rumors were rampant that
notwithstanding the party's nomination, Democratic
district leaders were selling out O'Dwyer. "I think
what undoubtedly has happened is that these Italian
leaders up in Harlem and in the areas generally
dominated by Marcantonio must rely for their
following on Italians and Puerto Ricans . . . "
explained an O'Dwyer supporter as he expressed
concern on the eve of the election.[27] Under the
circumstances, it was all the more imperative for
O'Dwyer to harness the support of significant
Italian American leaders, such as newspaper
publisher Pope. It was also obviously vital that
Vincent Impellitteri play an major role in the
campaign. O'Dwyer's Democratic Italian American
allies fulfilled their mission handily as
Impellitteri and Pope led the attack on
Marcantonio. For weeks prior to the election
Marcantonio's name scarcely received mention in Il
Progresso Italo-Americano, except when he was the
subject of criticism. Called on to siphon off the
Marcantonio appeal in the Italian community,
Impellitteri devoted at least two radio broadcasts
to the task as he disparaged the Congressman for
being a false friend of Italy. Specifically aiming
his address at Americans of Italian origin he
chided Marcantonio "for begging for votes on the
ground that he is a friend of Italy and the Italian

people. I say flatly of this statement that it is a lie." A denial that he was engaging in red-baiting notwithstanding, Impellitteri nevertheless, cited Marcantonio's opposition to the Marshall Plan and his failure to become involved in the anti-Communist letter-writing campaign, as startlingly similar "to the regular Moscow line." Fulminating against Marcantonio for not participating in the 1948 letter-writing campaign, Impellitteri reminded his audience that he himself had written hundreds of letters asking Italians not to vote for Communists and contrasted that with Marcantonio by asking rhetorically, "How many letters did Vito Marcantonio write in that campaign to save Italy?" Impellitteri charged that Marcantonio's purpose in the mayoral race that he did not have a chance to win was merely an attempt to be a spoiler by taking votes from O'Dwyer and thereby aid Morris. "I can assure that Vito Marcantonio will fail--just as he failed to prevent this country from giving aid to a stricken and hungry Italy." Using blunt language Impellitteri appealed to New York Italian Americans to reject Marcantonio. "In short, I am asking you to take the word of Vince Impellitteri, a New Yorker of Italian origin, over Vito Marcantonio, who is also a New Yorker of Italian origin."[28]

Ethnic considerations were evident also in the selection of candidates for the position of president of the city council. Hence, within the Fusion and Republican parties, the names of Edward Corsi and Justice Matthew Deserio circulated, with the latter receiving the nomination of the Republican, Fusion and Liberal parties in an obvious attempt to attract the city's large Italian American vote. That this lead was followed by influential organs like the New York _Times_, which also endorsed Deserio, rendered Impellitteri's designation as the Democratic party's nominee for the post critical. Indeed, the election demonstrated Impellitteri's immense popularity as he effortlessly defeated Deserio by nearly half a million votes, while O'Dwyer received 1,266,000 votes to 956,000 for Morris and 356,000 for Marcantonio-- a plurality, although not a majority. Impressively Impellitteri's 1,321,232 votes led the Democratic ticket in a conspicuous demonstration of his attraction to rank and file New Yorkers.

NOTES

1. Wallace S. Sayre and Herbert Kaufman, Governing New York City: Politics in the Metropolis (New York: W.W. Norton Inc., 1965), 696.

2. Folder: "Campaign," VIFP.

3. Sayre and Kaufman, Governing New York, 607-22.

4. New York Times, April 15, 1946.

5. New Yorker (April 3, 1948): 22-23.

6. New York Times, October 19, 1946.

7. New York Herald Tribune, April 18, 1948.

8. New York Journal American, April 10, 1949.

9. Goeffrey Moorhouse, Imperial City: New York (New York: Holt, 1988), 73.

10. The Catholic News, September 17, 1949.

11.. Letter from Vincent Impellitteri to Victor Anfuso, March 15, 1948, Victor Anfuso Papers (Staten Island: Center for Migration Studies).

12. "Press Release," October 29, 1947, VIFP.

13. Louis Eisenstein and Elliot Rosenberg, A Stripe of Tammany's Tiger (New York: Robert Speller and Sons, 1966), 181.

14. New York Herald Tribune, January 1, 1947.

15. Leonard Katz, Uncle Frank, The Biography of Frank Costello (New York: Farrar, Straus and Cudahy, 1973), 123.

16. New York Times, May 7, 1946.

17. Kessner, Fiorello H. LaGuardia and the Making of Modern New York, 561.

18. George Walsh, Public Enemies: The Mayor, the Mob, and the Crime That Was (New York: W.W. Norton, 1980), 143.

19. Moscow, Last of the Big-Time Bosses, 67.

20. Luther Gulick Memoirs, Oral History Project, Butler Library, Columbia University.

21. John C. Walter, The Harlem Fox, J. Raymond Jones and Tammany, 1920-1970 (Albany: State University of New York Press, 1989), 102-3.

22. Utica Observer, October 28, 1948.

23. Folder: "Speech Material," VIFP.

24. Murray Snyder, New Republic (June 14, 1949): 11-13.

25. George Wolf, Frank Costello, Prime Minister of the Underworld (New York: Morrow and Co. 1974), 163.

26. New York Daily News, June 20, 1949.

27. Interview, George S. Combs, The 1949 Election in New York State, Oral History Project, Columbia University.

28. Radio Speech, October 1949, VIFP. Il Progresso Italo-Americano, November 1,3,6, 1948.

5

The "Unbossed and Unbought" Candidate

Visions of relief from the debilitating effects of languorous heat, oppressive humidity and stifling stillness, not politics, preoccupy the mind during the dog days of summer. These are periods when those who can manage it spend as little time as possible in the city, trying instead to get away from it all at the end of work week, thereby giving New York the appearance of a deserted metropolis. This was the setting in the summer of 1950 as New Yorkers grappled with such momentous issues as the quickest way to cool off at nearby beaches and pools and the enjoyment of cold, refreshing drinks at backyard barbecues, rather than the ponderous concerns of international crises or municipal politics. Even as New Yorkers raced to the sunlit seashore or to cheer on their favorite baseball team in noisy but historic stadiums, ominous events were beginning to intrude on the indolent atmosphere. Like Americans throughout the land, New Yorkers awoke to a bright, gloriously sunny June 25, prepared to partake of a round of their normal Sunday summer activities: swimming, visiting friends and relatives, taking leisurely strolls, tending to their gardens, listening to radio baseball games or in some instances viewing the national pastime on primitive black and white television monitors amidst a sense of complacency-- an attitude of casualness that was to be rudely interrupted before the day was out. On that same day tens of thousands of tenacious North Korean troops burst across the 38th parallel in a sneak attack that almost overran United States ally South Korea. Surely the North Korean invasion was a matter of the gravest import compelling the United States to undertake major decisive military decisions. The president responded to the crisis promptly by ordering the armed forces into action to help the United Nations stem the tide of the

North Korean Communist onslaught. United States
involvement in the war affected the entire nation,
however, the extent of the seriousness of the
situation was not fully appreciated in the first
few weeks of combat as was reflected in heady talk
of a war of short duration. Originally labeled a
"police action," it was in fact a ferocious war
which, by the time an armistice was signed in 1953,
took the lives of an estimated 5 million people
including 54,248 Americans.

New Yorkers, while not unaware of the gravity of
the event, paid only limited attention; the
prevailing attitude was that the fighting in that
far off country was an unusual aberration in an
otherwise tranquil milieu. As for concern over
significant political developments closer home,
such as in their own city, summertime New Yorkers
were similarly comparatively indifferent.
Furthermore, the big city elections had taken place
only eight short months before and the upcoming
fall elections for statewide offices could be dealt
with after the summer's end. However, on August 15,
1950 Mayor O'Dwyer's announcement that he was
resigning his position in order to serve as
ambassador to Mexico was certain to disturb the
lazy, somnolent atmosphere. Ordinarily a startling
development, the statement was met with only mild
surprise since for months there had been ongoing
speculation over how long O'Dwyer would remain in
office. Surely anyone familiar with the mayor's
gyrations regarding his race for reelection in
1949, first ruling himself out, then reversing the
decision; his numerous absences from City Hall
because of a combination of personal and health
reasons thought his midsummer pronouncement less
than astonishing. O'Dwyer's decision was attributed
to several causes including the continuing strain
of the burdens of the office on his deteriorating
health, his advanced age, his recent marriage to
attractive, brunette apolitical model Sloan Simpson
and the imminence of scandal that was to rock the
city in subsequent months. Veteran political
reporters aver, however, that the determination to
have O'Dwyer resign had been made by nationally
prominent Democrats long before, even prior to his
running for a second term.

Interestingly news of the resignation did not
result in a surfacing of a sense of impending doom

and abandonment or that it presaged municipal collapse. Indeed there was every indication that the city was to be in good hands, as even the Republican New York <u>Herald Tribune</u> observed, "Because of Mayor O'Dwyer's numerous and extended absences from the city Vincent R. Impellitteri, who will move into the mayor's chair, is not entirely inexperienced in that post." The paper simultaneously advised that there had not been sufficient opportunity to judge Impellitteri as an executive or administrator in large affairs, albeit crediting him with being a likeable, friendly and engaging person. Invoking the city charter now elevated the city council president to acting mayor, where he would serve until the next general election, that is, until November 1950. The question of why O'Dwyer chose September 1, as the official resignation date led to the widely held speculation that it was orchestrated by Bronx Democratic leader and National Committeeman Edward Flynn, to provide the backdrop for a blatantly favorable partisan political climate. Evidently the move was not designed to give Impellitteri any particular edge in the upcoming contest. As one City Hall reporter explained, O'Dwyer had no intention of building Impellitteri up as a logical successor. "He never lets the acting Mayor make an official appearance by himself. Impellitteri always finds himself overshadowed by a personal envoy of the Mayor."[1] Indeed there is no evidence to support the thesis that any major Democratic leader envisioned the city council president as O'Dwyer's permanent heir. A strong argument to support this interpretation resides in the designation of the date of resignation. Had O'Dwyer delayed his official resignation until after September 20, the special mayoral election would have taken place in November 1951, thereby providing Impellitteri with more than a year of experience as acting mayor, thus placing him in a commandingly favorable lead against potential rivals. A September 1, resignation, however, left Impellitteri with a limited opportunity to govern the city on his own. That Impellitteri was eager to take the helm of city government was manifest in the celerity with which he abbreviated his planned three week vacation at Fire Island, Long Island, to five days, in order to assume the post of acting mayor.

Politically the momentous turn of events began rampant conjecture regarding the list of eligibles to succeed O'Dywer and complete the remaining three years of his term. Among the first Democratic names to emerge were those of Manhattan District Attorney Frank Hogan and Comptroller Lazarus Joseph, soon to be joined by Justice Ferdinand Pecora's name. Conspicuous by its absence was the name of Vincent Impellitteri, who was thought to be purely a fill-in until the end of the year. But the acting mayor did not choose to be merely a substitute figure. With intensive coaching under the tutelage of the outgoing mayor, Impellitteri was determined to demonstrate that he possessed the ability and knowledge to deserve consideration for the post in his own right. "I have been working with Mayor O'Dwyer for the last four years as a member of the Board of Estimate and I am fully aware, I think, of most of the problems that have come up during his administration."[2]

In addition to the impact on city politics, the change in city government, which necessitated a special election for mayor in 1950, was also expected to have major ramifications for the state and the nation. Thus, it was surmised that the special city election would strengthen chances to elect a Democratic New York governor against popular two-term Republican Governor Thomas Dewey, and possibly position Democrats to capture the nation's largest bloc of electoral votes for the upcoming presidential election of 1952--votes that had gone to Republican Dewey in 1948. Likewise, an expected outpouring of city Democratic votes in 1950 would enhance Democrat Herbert Lehman's chances for election to the United States Senate. All in all the political intrigues of 1950 were sure to cockle the hearts of Democratic party leaders who delighted in masterminding electoral developments for the benefit of their party.

By August 1950, DeSapio, who had been chosen the sole leader of Tammany Hall, had been persuaded to establish good relations with Flynn, whose influence with the White House was considered a desirable asset. Consequently, it would behoove Tammany Hall to link itself with and cooperate with Flynn, who was credited with organizing the political contortions that led to O'Dwyer's resignation scenario in favor of the ambassadorship to Mexico. The strategy envisioned a special election for mayor in 1950 that would strengthen Democratic chances for the previously mentioned statewide offices and the 1952 presidential election. That ethnic considerations were of paramount importance in the political equation was clearly evident in the selection of candidates and the alignment of political parties. The prevailing view was that the Liberal party, which had broken with the Democrats when it opposed O'Dwyer in 1949, had in effect been compromised in 1950 as a result of deals with the Democratic party to support certain legislative and judicial local candidates. Because the Liberal party likewise had endorsed Democratic candidates for statewide office, it was presumed that this position would frustrate any possibility for advancing a Jewish figure for mayor, the conventional wisdom being that Democrats would nominate a Catholic for mayor, a Protestant for governor and a Jew for Senator. However, with the elevation of Impellitteri as acting mayor on September 1, Democrats risked alienating Italian voters unless they named an Italian, thereby propelling Ferdinand Pecora as the choice of preference over Hogan and Joseph. Because Pecora was a Protestant, this necessitated juggling the Democratic lineup with a scenario that foresaw an ideal Democratic ticket headed by Pecora, a liberal Protestant Italian running for mayor with Herbert Lehman, a liberal Jew for United States Senate and Walter A. Lynch, an Irish Catholic for governor. It was said that DeSapio concurred with the Flynn plan, even though he had his own list of several names for mayoral candidates, including Impellitteri at the bottom of his list. Unsubstantiated rumor also had it that the politically influential underworld figure Frank Costello also promoted the choice of an Italian American as the city's chief executive.

As fall 1950 unfolded political fever ran high in the city as it did in the rest of the nation. This was the time of year when telephone poles and billboards were plastered with politicians' faces and names, when mail boxes bulged with partisan propaganda extolling the virtues of the contestants and when sonorous loudspeakers blaring the praises of candidates rent the air. To run for any public office took plenty of stamina and a storehouse of

nervous energy, traits even more in demand for
those running for New York City mayor. Expected to
be one of the most exciting elections of the year,
it was also evident that it would be one of the
most exhausting physical exercises so that whoever
the victor, he was going to have to work arduously
for it.

The special election occasioned by O'Dwyer's
resignation resulted in an extraordinary disruption
of city politics. Having only recently expended
considerable energies and money for the mayoral
election only several months previously, political
parties would now have to provide for a strenuous
replay. The circumstances did, nevertheless, hold
out unique opportunities for the parties concerned.
For a unified Democratic party, it presented the
likelihood of potent political advantage on local
and national levels. For the minority Republican
party, the late summer development held a
potentially different and somewhat ambivalent
meaning. To face a Democratic party with such a
preponderant advantage in registration was not a
happy prospect. If, however, the unity of the
Democratic opposition could somehow unravel, it
would render less ominous the normally dispiriting
minority Republican disadvantage. It soon became
evident that this scenario was indeed unfolding
thereby energizing Republicans to designate a
quality candidate with potentially wide appeal
among the city electorate. Early speculation that
Walter S. Mack, chairman of the Pepsi Cola
Corporation and stalwart supporter of Republicans
LaGuardia and Wendell Wilkie, was destined to be
the Republican front-runner, soon succumbed to the
reality of ethnic politics. Manhattan Republican
leader Thomas Curran, who had been Impellitteri's
Fordham University Law School classmate, recognized
that the city's Italian American electorate had
been energized and would not take kindly to
bypassing a qualified Republican Italian American
candidate. This attitude was clearly apparent as
Italian American Republican leaders applied strong
pressure in an unsuccessful effort to have Edward
Corsi become the lieutenant governor nominee on the
Dewey ticket. Astute assessment of recent political
developments was translated to mean that Corsi
would receive a prominent place on the Republican
ticket in order to counter even the appearance of

alienating the Italian vote. "Republicans are not going to miss the boat in the race for this vast reservoir of votes," was the evaluation.[3] Accordingly, Republicans chose as their mayoral aspirant Corsi, who indeed possessed excellent credentials: an esteemed Italian name with a formidable reputation within Italian political circles, a distinguished career as a noteworthy journalist in the Italian and English language press, a dedicated social worker, an enviable record in administrative experience as the United States commissioner of immigration, the head of the City Department of Welfare and the state industrial relations commissioner and prior experience in running for public office, in sum, the background of a very well-qualified candidate. In addition, he possessed the most desirable ethnic background supplemented by genuine connections to Italy and the Italian American community.

Initially the regular Democratic and Republican candidates saw this as a contest primarily between themselves, and hence a contest in which they did not have to pay much attention to minor party candidates. Not surprisingly they paid little heed to Paul Ross, nominee of the American Labor party, correctly concluding that since Vito Marcantonio, that party's most famous leader had come in a distant third in the 1949 mayoral election, the lesser-known Ross posed no genuine threat. Impellitteri's assertion that if denied the Democratic party designation he would run as an independent was dismissed as an annoying deviation for the Democrats, while for Republicans this represented an interesting opportunity, a wedge that rendered the Democratic party somewhat vulnerable, yet hardly an area that warranted inordinate expectations. Thus, virtually ignoring Impellitteri, at the outset of the 1950 campaign Pecora and Corsi concentrated their political fire on each other, a decision they soon regretted because it was in fact a decision to engage in substantial wishful thinking.

In accepting the Republican nomination for mayor, Corsi emphasized a thirty year record of public service in spite of a background of deprivation and poverty. In fact, he sought to convert his poor immigrant beginnings to advantage, that is, in the absence of family monetary means, he worked his way

through high school and college and that, on
graduation, he eschewed a money-making career in
favor of social service. He referred to his first
job as director of Harlem House, as an opportunity
to help society's less fortunate even as he, as an
impoverished young immigrant lad, had been assisted
by the same settlement house. He reminded New
Yorkers that in that position he made loyal
citizens of many immigrants and taught them
English. (Ironically simultaneous with the 1950
election, shrinking contributions were forcing the
same Harlem House to curb its social service
programs.) He described his tenure as the nation's
commissioner of immigration under both Republican
and Democratic administrations as a welcome chance
to overhaul government handling of new arrivals in
order to provide a more decent, warm-hearted and
humane treatment. Corsi also sought to carve out
for himself major ground as labor's best friend
among all the candidates. In a display of an
inflated sense of identification with union
organizations, Corsi belittled Pecora's prolabor
claim in Republican campaign literature that said
that "Corsi dominated the labor scene like no other
candidate for Mayor in the history of the City of
New York."[4] Administrative experience was another
strong feature of the Corsi campaign as he stressed
his leadership position in the Bureau of Welfare,
which had dispensed relief programs and welfare
benefits during the depth of the Great Depression,
as a major example of his role in bringing succor
to hundreds of thousands of New Yorkers in
distress. Accordingly he was able to exult that he
had managed successfully the biggest enterprises on
national, city and state level governments.

In addition to boasting of his record in the
realm of social work, labor and government
administration, Corsi also endeavored to link his
Democratic opponent with the public's growing
awareness of corruption that was the sorry legacy
of the O'Dwyer administration. Pointing to the
dubiousness of the Tammany sponsored O'Dwyer
mayoralty, Corsi contrasted this with the image of
integrity that was the hallmark of LaGuardia's
tenure. Time and again Corsi attempted to establish
the LaGuardia link as one of his strongest suits,
reminding New Yorkers that he had served the city's
greatest mayor in a conspicuous role. "We threw out

politicians. We sent some of them to jail. We gave
the city food, shelter and clothing--without
tribute or graft to any gang."[5] Honesty and
efficiency in city government became typical
staples of Corsi campaign oratory as he inveighed
mightily against Democrats asserting that he would
clean up the corruption that hampered the city.
Corsi was relentless in his attacks on Pecora, whom
he described as the hypocritical "elder-respectable
front" whose pompous declarations for cleaning up
New York City were betrayed by the reality of the
knowledge that as Tammany Hall's nominee, Pecora
was "too beholden" to the organization. Corsi
likewise criticized Impellitteri as the Junior
Tammany candidate, the "reluctant dragon" whose
proclamation of independence was palpably false
because Impellitteri had himself previously sought
Tammany Hall endorsement. As for Impellitteri's
clamor against corruption, Corsi wondered aloud how
this could be because as city council president he
had ample opportunity to investigate corruption
charges but in fact never did so. "Impy the
Innocent" is not so innocent, intoned Corsi who
accused the acting mayor of being in league with
Tammany leaders Robert Blaikie, Frank Sampson and
Harry Brickman. Conveniently forgetting his own
earlier association with the controversial Vito
Marcantonio, now fighting for his political life as
all except the most extreme left-wingers opposed
his reelection to Congress, Corsi cynically charged
Impellitteri with being in the debt of the East
Harlemite congressman. When the earlier
relationship between Corsi and Marcantonio was
pointed out, Corsi's defenders sought to play it
down contending it was mere politeness rather than
"a love feast." The Republicans stressed instead,
Corsi's opposition to Marcantonio in recent years.
In sum, Corsi attempted to depict both major
opponents as unworthy candidates.

In dismissing Impellitteri's interim mayor record
as negative Corsi revealed his own desperateness by
maintaining that the mayor condoned bookmaking by a
convicted gambler (Harry Gross) in Rikers Island
prison-- basically an unverified charge. And in the
same accusatory but uncorroborated vein Corsi
charged that the Experience party candidate

begged Generoso Pope Jr. to get the nomination for him. And

this is important. It was only after this same Tammany machine
rejected the junior candidate that he proclaimed himself an
independent, although he was quite willing to enter into its
servitude.[6]

On a broader level Corsi's seventeen plank platform
for New York City stressed, among other things, the
need to develop civil defense, a new Parking
Authority to facilitate traffic, improvements in
transportation, educational and health facilities,
and a number of traditionally familiar good
government programs.
   In keeping with his virile physical image, a
deceptively pugnacious-looking, prematurely bald
Corsi whose receding hairline and searching eyes
were supported by bulging flesh in the upper
cheeks, sought to convey an image of an upright but
hard-hitting, no-nonsense campaigner as in the
LaGuardia tradition. Unfortunately for him he was
no LaGuardia when it came to politicking, lacking
the theatrics of the Little Flower, he proffered
instead the visage of a soft-spoken, serious,
rarely ruffled humorless figure. Thus, his
estimable calls for caring welfare and social
benefit programs were betrayed by ineptitude and
opportunism on the campaign trail. Accordingly,
although LaGuardia might personally have
experienced exasperation at Vito Marcantonio's
public position, he never broke with him, whereas
after a period of hesitation, Corsi capitulated to
political expediency, (their earlier friendship
notwithstanding) when he publicly disassociated
himself with Marcantonio in a vain effort to stir
support on anti-Communist grounds. Lacking that
intangible chemistry of rapport with the public,
that absolute requirement of populist politics, the
uncharismatic Corsi failed to fire the imagination,
advancing instead an image of a competent but
essentially colorless Republican nominee who
elicited only lukewarm response from his own party
leaders. This was especially true of Governor
Thomas Dewey who was running for reelection and was
considered a likely Republican presidential
candidate in 1952. Formally supporting Corsi for
mayor, Dewey only sparingly used the political
pulpit to promote his cause. It was an open secret
that an informal agreement between Dewey and
Impellitteri was in effect whereby Dewey would do

little to help Corsi while denouncing the city's regular Democratic party, thereby aiding Impellitteri's candidacy. For his part Impellitteri reciprocated by giving lip service support for Walter Lynch, the Democratic gubernatorial candidate, which would work in Dewey's favor. Under these circumstances Corsi was destined to fight an uphill battle.

It was the hapless fate of Ferdinand Pecora to bring mixed signals into the mayoralty race. He was the bearer, on the one hand, of an aura of impeccability because of his acknowledged years of state and national government service highlighted by his performance as chief counsel for the United States Senate Banking and Currency Committee, which exposed evil practices in bank and stock businesses and which led to the establishment of the Security and Exchange Commission. His performance for probity and uprightness in office won merited universal acclaim and served to invest Pecora with a strong image of integrity enjoyed by few figures in the public arena. His subsequent years of distinction as a New York State Supreme Court Justice further enhanced a mien of respectability. On the other hand Pecora's unseemly politically partisan steps left an image of ambiguity. Long an advocate of "good government" (he was active in Theodore Roosevelt's Bull Moose campaign of 1912), he now seemed to betray a public trust by accepting the nomination for mayor from the tainted Democratic Tammany leadership with the result that he quickly used up the reservoir of goodwill that had been extended to him by virtue of his earlier career. Try as they might, Democratic efforts to capitalize on Pecora's prestige as a way of deflecting attention against charges of bossism and criminal influence in Tammany Hall were unavailing. New Yorkers saw the dichotomy.

If the art of politics is the art of the possible, even the Tammany association might not have been such an insuperable handicap. That is, had Pecora been designated Democratic candidate for mayor years earlier when his name was first proposed, he might well have been elected. However, proper timing is essential in politics so that the ripeness of one year does not necessarily hold for another year, especially when the sponsoring political organization has in the interim become

besmirched with scandal. Furthermore, at sixty-
eight years of age Pecora was encumbered by an
additional generational handicap. Short of stature,
wiry, sporting a full head of hair generously
sprinkled with grey and white streaks, and
bespectacled with thick lenses, Pecora was
evidently the senior citizen of the campaign. Not
without some ingenuity pro-Pecora organs attempted
to convert chronological liability into electoral
asset by acknowledging that Pecora's election to
City Hall would be a climax to his career rather
than the stepping stone to higher office which
would naturally tempt younger office-holders.
Understandably this raised questions of physical
fitness for so demanding a job that had only
recently had proven too strenuous for the much
younger William O'Dwyer. Conscious of the
persistency of the age issue, Pecora labored to
convey of picture of a vigorous, sprightly, hard-
working nominee who indubitably possessed the
stamina required as he progressed through a round
of activities such as reviewing his mail, greeting
various groups of supporters, recording radio
speeches, conducting live television appearances,
delivering speeches throughout the city and meeting
with top strategists such as DeSapio and Generoso
Pope, Jr., who attempted to assume some of his late
father's political broker role. To convey a
positive image about Pecora, his public relations
people featured a story about a reporter who
accompanied the Democratic candidate through a
"typical" sixteen hour campaign day that began at
8:15 a.m. and continued in a nonstop, yet
"unhurried" manner until 1:30 a.m., stopping only
occasionally to sip from a flask of honey,
glycerine and lemon juice to keep his vocal chords
pliable. In an ongoing effort to dispel the "old
man" image, especially in contradistinction to the
young, slim, immaculate and energetic-looking fifty
year old Impellitteri, it was said that the sixty
eight year old jurist had a constitutional
inability to sleep more than six hours and that he
was "invigorated" by campaigning. Plainly the
worried Democratic nominee was increasingly aiming
his attack on Impellitteri, whom he labeled the
"Expediency party candidate."

Pecora was also vulnerable in the area of
politicking, that is, the art or technique of

elective politics. Could a well-deserved reputation
to an appointive public position as counsel be
easily translated into the realm of public
campaigning? Was the jurist's background sufficient
to ingratiate himself to a cynical public? Did it
not require a talent and ability possessed by few
to mingle freely with ordinary folk, to enthuse and
excite the body politic, prior achievements
notwithstanding? More than a few political
aspirants have met their match in the field of
elective politics in a city like New York whose
citizenry seeks a candidate with whom it truly
relates--an individual who has been tested by
elective contests. It is of course true that Pecora
had twice run for and handily won the state
judgeship, however, contesting for such an office
is generally on a different level, requiring a
minimum of partisan campaigning when compared to
the mayoralty. Clearly Pecora was facing a major
hurdle; even within his own party he was confronted
with defections of important district leaders. When
polls and astute observation rendered it clear to
party chieftains that Pecora's campaign was
flagging, they sought the help of national
Democratic leaders such as President Truman who,
while studiously avoiding a meeting with
Impellitteri while on a city visit, took time from
his busy schedule to arrange a lengthy photographic
engagement with Pecora. It was of dubious benefit.
Even more questionable, if not disastrous, was the
decision to bring into the campaign, former
Secretary of the Interior Harold Ickes, the
forceful but crusty New Dealer polemicist, who went
about the city speaking on behalf of Pecora.
Controversial and out of office since 1946, the
involvement of the abrasive Ickes was regarded as
more of a liability and provided critics with a
field day as they ridiculed the move. "Why in
heavens, Judge, did you let them take the crumpled
curmudgeon off the political dump heap and prop him
up to speak your praises? You can't be that hard
up."[7]

As for his platform, suffice it to say that
Pecora stressed New Deal social welfare and
prolabor issues. However, linking such
progressivism with a continuation of O'Dwyer's
programs was a serious misstep since,
notwithstanding the acknowledged progressivism of

many O'Dwyer programs, the public was increasingly
reminded that the O'Dwyer years saw the spread of
the seamier side of political life. Once again bad
timing would hurt Pecora. Accordingly, although
Impellitteri, as did Pecora, favored many of his
predecessor's plans, the acting mayor was able to
avoid undue identification with the O'Dwyer
association by emphasizing his "independence."

In August 1950, few professional politicians had
regarded Impellitteri's assertion that should he be
denied the Democratic nomination for mayor he would
run as an independent as anything more than a ploy
for a plum judicial post. The fact that he later on
did become a judge only served to encourage the
impression that the judicial post was all he ever
wanted to cap his political career. Nevertheless,
Impellitteri was serious about running for mayor,
convinced that he deserved to be nominated not only
because he possessed hands-on experience in the
post but also because the 1949 election showed him
to be the most popular Democrat running for
citywide office. Hardly had he been sworn in as
acting mayor on September 1, 1950 than he declared
his candidacy for city chief executive in the
upcoming special election. His assertion that he
was the choice of the five Democratic borough
leaders was essentially for public consumption
since he simultaneously proceeded to organize his
own independent political organization: the
Experience party. This could be read as a sure sign
that he did not expect to become the official
nominee of the Democratic party. Illustrating his
resourcefulness, Impellitteri proceeded to
accumulate an impressive petition of 44,000
signatures, far more than the 7,500 necessary to be
placed on the ballot. The effort was facilitated by
the free use of space in the medium-sized Abbey
Hotel, owned by Louis Zuch, who first hired the
future mayor as room clerk at the Ansonia Hotel
many years earlier. Now designated Impellitteri's
campaign headquarters, the Abbey provided limited
space of a ballroom, two large adjoining rooms and
six bedrooms for a small staff under the brilliant
red-headed Irishman William Donoghue, to conduct
mailings, arrange speaking schedules, distribute
campaign buttons and literature and raise small
funds in a shoestring operation that was dwarfed by
the competition, especially the Democrats. Housed

in sixty rooms in the Hotel Commodore, the traditional Democratic campaign headquarters, that also housed the Liberal party, the Democrats paid fifty-five workers to conduct a costly campaign estimated to exceed $2,000,000. Republican campaign expenses also must have been high to cover the cost of almost an entire floor of the Hotel Vanderbilt, which had never been used for such purposes previously and which required 150 man hours of labor to convert bedrooms to electioneering offices replete with mimeograph machines, typewriters and switchboards. By contrast Impellitteri's campaign costs, which depended on people sending in single dollar bills and which had only one large contribution ($10,000 sent in by John Raskob, a wealthy old friend of Al Smith), struggled with a total budget of $125,000, only one sixteenth of the Democrats costs.

In announcing his independent candidacy Impellitteri emulated the 1933 scenario where Democrat Joseph V. McKee attempted and failed to obtain official endorsement as the mayoralty candidate of his party. Like Impellitteri he ran as an independent, however, in a losing contest. For his part in 1950 the Sicilian-born acting mayor was determined that this scenario would have a happier ending. It was understandable that Impellitteri's announcement of insurgency met with polite and even patronizing acknowledgment. The odds against him were, after all, daunting, what with the absence of substantial funding and a scant two months to assemble a viable political organization capable of slugging it out with much better financed and experienced political machines. That he was able to do so is a testimony to his uncommon, indomitable personal resolve, to his surprising organizational talents and to his perspicacious exploitation of a serious split within the Democratic party. His conviction notwithstanding, to popular reporter Inez Robb Impellitteri was engaged in a nearly impossible task, reminiscent of a David and Goliath struggle that could not fail to elicit "a sneaking admiration for any nervy little guy with a slingshot." Impellitteri's audacious challenge "induced the shakes in both the regular Republican and Democratic organizations."[8]

Impellitteri possessed several major assets as he geared himself for an uphill campaign. His first

advantage was the assemblage of a very effective
campaign team that included William Shirley, a
Scotch Irishman with a theater and business
background whose affinity with Italian Americans
was reflected in his ability to attract many of
them to purchase land in his Shirley, Long Island
real estate development. Indeed Shirley, Long
Island would boast of one of the largest
concentrations of Americans of Italian descent for
decades to come. He was a close social friend,
assumed the post of chairman of the Independent
Citizens Committee for Impellitteri and was also
instrumental in raising funds. Herman Hoffman,
campaign manager and a useful liaison to the Jewish
community whose financial and political support
proved to be a most desirable asset (as was the
aforementioned Donoghue), was highly valued as
personal secretary to O'Dwyer and now proved
indispensable to Impellitteri as his executive
secretary. A political professional with priceless
experience, the knowledgeable Donoghue was an
expert strategist who time and again made
suggestions that Impellitteri followed to
successful conclusions. Donoghue's frequent
memoranda are examples of perceptive wisdom.
Appropriately anticipating a potentially major
issue, he advised Impellitteri to introduce a
resolution to the Board of Estimate calling for a
10 percent increase in the salaries of underpaid
city employees in an effort to go beyond mere
campaign promises, as in the cases of Pecora and
Corsi, and thereby stand ready to assume the
responsibilities for seeking justice before the
election. Donoghue also emphasized the preparation
of radio speeches on principal themes, the
necessity of harnessing a speech writing unit, the
preparation of a budget for radio and television
spot announcements highlighting Impellitteri's
achievements to be specially aimed at foreign
language stations and planned itineraries for sound
truck use with care to be exercised to tailor the
message to the ethnic backgrounds in different
neighborhoods. "For instance, if you have a sound
truck in Brownsville [Jewish] we should emphasize
the support of Lehman; if you have a sound truck in
Harlem [black] we must emphasize the fact that Mrs.
A. Philip Randolph, wife of the President of the
Sleeping Car Porters, is active in the mayor's

campaign."[9]

A second important asset Impellitteri brought into the campaign was a highly commendable record of appointments during his short tenure as acting mayor. Heading the appointment list was his designation of Thomas Murphy as police commissioner, a move that proved to be a master stroke during a time of increased concern over revelations of scandals traceable to the former administration. Having gained national fame as the vigorous federal prosecutor of Alger Hiss, the tall, mustachioed Murphy, who was the brother of the popular Johnny "Fireman" Murphy, ace relief pitcher of the New York Yankees, had his own score to settle with Democratic leaders and took the opportunity to serve in this visible post. Much to the annoyance of Tammany Hall stalwarts, Impellitteri now possessed the temerity to go after common hoodlums who were implicated in efforts to intimidate the Democrats who supported him. Impellitteri also directed Murphy to move against politics in the department by revoking Generoso Pope, Jr.'s honorary deputy commissionership, hence unseating one of arch enemy DeSapio's biggest allies. Murphy's administration of the Police Department, which promoted officers on merit basis, won commendation even from Republican outlets. "Clearly the Police Department is getting a large amount of new and young blood where it counts . . . . The philosophy is to be tough and real . . . . Keep it up Mr. Commissioner."[10] Impellitteri's appointment of Murphy was considered such a positive move that even the Republican candidate Corsi stated he would retain the commissioner if elected. Hardly less important was Impellitteri's retention of Robert Moses in his multiple administrative roles. A virtual legend and institution in his own time, the aggressive and brilliant Moses was regarded as the foremost city planner, the peerless builder of highways, tunnels and bridges and the stern guardian of the city's parks and beaches. In a word he was a veritable institution who had served the city and the state in so many capacities through Democratic and Republican administrations, that it was unthinkable not to retain him. This appointment also elicited favorable comment. The designation of individuals to lesser positions as in the case of the city park commission also won praise.

The ability to take advantage of the dissonance within Democratic ranks proved to be a major Impellitteri advantage. This was especially so in the case of a triumvirate of Manhattan leaders who were able to sway a significant number of votes in that critical borough. Harry Brickman, veteran head of the second assembly district, perennial insurgent Robert Blaikie, maverick leader of the seventh assembly district, and Frank Sampson, leader of the third assembly district and former boss of the county provided valuable experience for the embryonic Impellitteri organization. Nor were they alone as other lesser-known but locally important leaders of Democratic clubs throughout the city also broke with Tammany Hall. By throwing their lot with Impellitteri, these leaders were taking a calculated risk, but such was the state of affairs in the party that the unity desired by DeSapio was decisively unraveling. This development, furthermore, rendered all the more credible Impellitteri's claim of being "unbossed" and obligated to no machine.

Arguably the single most potent political weapon in the Impellitteri campaign arsenal was his assertion of blatant efforts to buy him off with a judgeship. Repeatedly Impellitteri subjected the public to an unremitting bombardment of charges, echoed elsewhere, that the Tammany Hall leadership sought to bribe him with guarantees of a New York State Supreme Court judgeship with a fourteen year tenure and handsome salary of $28,000 per year, which rounded out to nearly $400,000 for the entire tenure, if he withdrew from the race in favor of Pecora. Attributing the offer to the Tammany Hall boss served to further discredit DeSapio. Impellitteri's spurning of the offer struck responsive chords with cynical New Yorkers who were already inclined to believe the worst of political bosses and now had fresh evidence of their arrogance and crass underhandedness. Denial of the charge proved futile for the Tammany leadership which at first hesitated, then belatedly tried to deny making the offer by countercharging that Impellitteri himself had requested the judgeship. This led to a ringing denunciation of DeSapio and underscored Impellitteri's self-description of being "unbossed, and unbought."

Carmine DeSapio, if any sense of personal decency remains, must feel deep shame today . . . .

As a matter of fact, this offer was made directly to me by Carmine Desapio in his home. I made his judgeship offer public on September 5th. That was six weeks ago. It has never been denied. Now they have developed this lying defense.[11]

Impellitteri charged the Flynn-Costello-DeSapio leadership with an outright subornative effort in order to get him out of the race, an offer he resolutely declined. "I could have taken that bribe and retired to the comparative security and sanctuary of the judicial chambers." Impellitteri's rejection of the offer elicited more favorable response than any other issue during the campaign. As one editorial concluded, "It makes a simple and effective narrative, thick with skulduggery, of how a candidate refused to be shoved into munificent obscurity and insisted on bucking the political powers."[12]

A fifth Impellitteri asset was his success in garnering an array of endorsements from within and without the Democratic party. Former United States Postmaster and National Chairman of the Democratic party James Farley, now feuding with National Committeeman Edward Flynn, for example, was lavish in his support of the independent candidate. The endorsement of Daniel Finn, scion of an old established political family with deep roots in the Democratic party, was as helpful to Impellitteri as it was damaging to the regular Democratic ticket. Having been humiliated and defeated by DeSapio for district leadership in Greenwich Village a number of years earlier, one can imagine how avidly Finn savored the opportunity to gain revenge by opposing DeSapio's choice. Even though Finn no longer headed a Democratic stronghold, he still commanded a following among Irish Americans. The endorsement of respected Columbia University Professor Raymond Moley, contributing editor of _Time_ magazine and former advisor to Franklin D. Roosevelt, was another major asset. Moley actively campaigned in Impellitteri's behalf by making a major radio address a few days before the election in which he injected a personal note, namely that as Roosevelt's advisor he personally heard Pecora agree with the president that at age seventy men are often unable to perceive their own infirmities;

yet the jurist now sought an extremely difficult
job at the same age. Accordingly, Moley opined that
he could not support Pecora because of his age and
his lack of relevant administrative experience.
"The best preparation for a job is acting for the
man holding it. That, Impellitteri has done . . . .
Let us keep Impellitteri where he is and let him
finish the job."[13]

The support of powerful Robert Moses was
important as was the backing of more than a few
leaders within New York's black community like Mrs.
A. Philip Randolph, wife of the important labor
leader. Other political endorsements of importance
included those of Sydney P. Baron, former secretary
of the InterCounty Republican Committee. The
inaction of certain politicians also aided
Impellitteri, as in the case of Representative
Franklin D. Roosevelt Jr.'s silence (tantamount to
acquiescence) when he failed to oppose his home
district Democratic Club's rejection of Pecora.

In addition to blessings from professional
politicians, Impellitteri had the backing of a
number of sports celebrities, such as boxers Barney
Ross and Joe Louis, with whom he had developed a
personal relationship. In endorsing Impellitteri,
Louis's message conveyed a simple but effective
thought.

As a man who has engaged in many stiff fights I admire another
fighter. Particularly when he fights for clean, decent, honest
government and is a sincere fighter for equal rights for all
men. Good luck to you and after November 7 when I come to town
I'd like to drop in at City Hall and congratulate you
personally. Lots of luck.[14]

It is no wonder that many years later the
autographed photograph of the world heavyweight
champion graced a wall in Impellitteri's bedroom
alongside world famous figures like British Prime
Minister Winston Churchill and General Douglas
MacArthur.

In the immediate postwar years, with memories of
indebtedness to the armed services so fresh and
because of heightened tension traceable to the
developing Cold War, the cultivation of veterans
support in the community was considered a definite
advantage. By a large margin Impellitteri was the
beneficiary of a vigorous veterans organizational

sponsorship throughout the city, which was merited by virtue of years of personal involvement. A proud veteran of the navy, he had served as past state and county commander of the Catholic War Vets and past commander of a few veterans organizations; moreover, he continued to be active in veteran affairs long after holding public office. How important was the rapport between veterans and Impellitteri is revealed in the defection of an election district captain in Pecora's home assembly district. "I cannot in good conscience support Ferdinand Pecora . . . in view of the fact that in my capacity as Commander of Veteran organizations I have never had any help from him but many practical helps from Mayor Impellitteri." In an effort to undermine this potentially crucial support of former servicemen the opposition resorted to a vile level of politics as it insinuated that the pro-Impellitteri veterans organizations included bigots and hatemongers. To impugn his reputation as a fair and unbigoted person was personally repugnant to Impellitteri, who was in truth a decent minded, tolerant man who deliberately spurned offers of help from hatemongers. Offended, he charged his opponents with conducting "the filthiest campaign" as they desperately attempted "with lying statements and libelous literature to turn the people of every racial and religious group in the city against me, and against each other." The smear tactics proved to be highly unsuccessful as veteran organization leaders immediately joined in denouncing the vicious rumors as totally unfounded.

Statements that Mayor Impellitteri solicits or accepts the support of bigots and mongrel peddlers of hatred are deliberate lies . . . .
    I have known Mayor Impellitteri for years and I know of his sincere, unremitting and vigorous work for tolerance and brotherhood . . . .
    In saying these things on behalf of my friend, Mayor Impellitteri, I speak as an Orthodox Jew and a life-long member of the Zionist Organization of America.[15]

Labor support is always a crucial factor in New York City mayoralty elections and thus it would be of interest to iterate this aspect of the campaign. A major portion of official labor backing, as for example Michael Quill's Transport Worker's Union, (TWU) went to the regular Democratic candidate,

Ferdinand Pecora. However, there were significant
exceptions and numerous defections within organized
labor's rank and file that benefitted Impellitteri.
For example, several locals of the TWU repudiated
Quill and endorsed the acting mayor instead. Major
backing for Impellitteri came from American
Federation of Labor (AFL) unions through the Non-
Partisan Committee of the Central Trades and Labor
Council, divisions of the Brotherhood of Locomotive
Engineers, locals of the Moving Pictures Operators
Union and the Utilities Workers of America, among
others. Most impressive was the support rendered by
key municipal workers unions such as the United
Firemen's Association that insurgent elements
rejected their own leadership's endorsement of
Pecora by circulating pro-Impellitteri messages for
fire department bulletin boards. "We must show
Mayor Impellitteri that the rank and file . . .
were not consulted as to our wishes . . . because
our sympathy was with the Acting Mayor, a tried and
proven friend."[16] The insurgents were well-
justified in their estimation of Impellitteri
because, in contradistinction with O'Dwyer, and
even at the risk of incurring the mayor's
displeasure, he displayed friendship and
cooperation with professional firefighters from the
beginning of his tenure as council president. In
1946, Impellitteri alone within the administration
was willing to chair a committee that sought to
rehabilitate the firemen's Death Benefit Fund
campaign. It was also Impellitteri who, unlike some
unsympathetic members of the Board of Estimate,
took a strong stand in support of a cost of living
bonus and upward adjustments in base pay. "He was
in your corner, then, and he is in your corner,
now," wrote one insurgent leader as he criticized
the United Fireman's Association president.

Finally there was the personality of the
candidate himself. At five foot eight and a half
inches (some sources say nine and a half), and 172
pounds, with brown eyes and flat black hair that
was beginning to gray and thin and that was parted
slightly left of center, he presented the visage of
a neat, pleasant looking man. The olive-skinned
shoemaker's son, with somewhat irregular but
carefully crafted facial features, whose ready and
winning smile put people at ease, was a most
likeable political figures. He possessed, moreover,

a welcome sense of humor during an otherwise feisty
campaign. Thus, as bulbs flashed during a picture
taking session, one of them went off with a loud
bang causing everyone in the room to jump. "Hey I'm
only the Acting Mayor," he cracked, thereby
eliciting general laughter. Even his nickname
"Impy," a friendly abbreviation of his full name,
which most people continuously misspelled, served
to endear him to the public. His attractive,
slender, blonde wife was referred to as "Mrs.
Impy." Compared to the overly austere rectitude of
Judge Pecora or the seemingly aloof Corsi,
Impellitteri exuded an atmosphere of genuine
friendliness that won the attention even of his
critics. The Sicilian challenger, furthermore,
needed all the goodwill of his personality to
overcome some negatives such as a failure to
receive as high a rating as his competitors from
the Citizens Union who assessed Corsi and Pecora as
qualified for mayor. Basically a shy person,
Impellitteri's effrontery in taking on the power
bosses established him in the public mind as the
personification of the average unorganized citizen
fighting against clubhouse politics. In a word he
was a likeable, dependable person, one with whom
rank and file New Yorkers felt comfortable. This is
not to say that he avoided invective. Indeed during
the campaign he demonstrated a willingness to utter
strong statements as he slugged it out with his
competition in rounds of frequently bitter and
caustic charges and countercharges.

That this was one of the city's dirtiest
political campaigns was conceded by virtually all
observers--a phenomenon all the more ironic
considering the generally positive reputations
enjoyed by the three major candidates. So
adversarial and antagonistic was the campaign that
upon learning that vandals had attempted to
intimidate Impellitteri's campaign headquarters
workers, one newspaper, citing the election day
murder of Joseph Scottoriggio in East Harlem in
1946, called for special alertness against possible
violence on election day. The campaign was marred
by charges of underworld associations, insinuations
of anti-semitism and fascism, blatant appeals based
on ethnicity and destruction of Experience party
campaign headquarters. The campaign "set new
records for hogwash, character assassination and

general smearing," stated the New York <u>Daily News</u>.
All of the candidates concurred in the assessment
that this was "the filthiest political campaign the
city has ever seen," yet each contributed to the
low-level tone even if reluctantly. As one
researcher concluded, "The general approach of the
candidates was negative rather than positive,
destructive rather than constructive, personal
rather than ideological or programmatic."[17]

In an election featuring three candidates born in
Italy, it would be singularly enlightening to trace
attempts by each to garner their countrymen's votes
and the ethnic group response. For Corsi the
phenomenon presented several problems because he
had hoped to capture the Italian ethnic vote by
donning the mantle of LaGuardia, who had succeeded
in moving the Italian element away from its
traditional partisan fealty. Indeed, more than any
of his competitors, Corsi could best lay claim to
the LaGuardia vote given the important role he
played in LaGuardia's administration. Corsi's
undeniable association with the first Italian
American mayor notwithstanding, the emulation of
LaGuardia's extraordinary political feat was simply
not possible in 1950. The situation was so
different that no single candidate could
convincingly present himself as the spokesman for
an ignored ethnic minority as in 1933. Indeed all
three major candidates presented excellent
credentials when it came to identification with the
Italian community thereby seeming to give the
advantage to Pecora and the Democrats as the
preponderant party in the city. Firmly ensconced as
a Democratic party bastion, the influential Italian
daily <u>Il Progresso Italo-Americano</u>, in a betrayal
of its journalistic responsibility, totally ignored
Corsi, while it provided Impellitteri with only
token coverage, thereby projecting the impression
that Italian American organizations unanimously
supported the eminent jurist. Thus, once the
campaign began in earnest and in response to
Impellitteri's ouster of Generoso Pope, Jr. from
his honorary post in the police department, the
Italian newspaper tried to avoid any coverage of
the mayor with the exception of minor mention
during Columbus Day celebrations. Otherwise the
paper was bereft of Republican and Experience party
mayoral activities as it concentrated on Pecora

with a fulsome biographical account augmented over several days replete with photographs, activities and positions, in addition to a generous display of organization support for Pecora within the Italian community. Generoso Pope's largess to Pecora, who had been a close personal friend of his father's extended not only to newspaper coverage but also to Pope-owned Italian radio stations like WHOM, which carried anti-Impellitteri propaganda. On November 3, for example, a pro Pecora Italian broadcast featured a fictional discussion between "Tony and Joe" that denounced the acting mayor for ignoring Italians when it came to positions in city government. "With so many important nominations he didn't even dream of appointing an Italian," Joe complained to Tony. Predicting that this action could only arouse resentment among the city's Italians, Joe further whined. "That's why we need a competent, scrupulous, sensible man like Ferdinand Pecora." The radio script ended with a jingle:

> For Mayor and our guide,
> The people trust Pecora, the Italian
> A vote for Pecora, a vote for Pecora
> It's a boon to the Italians,
> I can tell you that.[18]

Despite the Il Progresso Italo-Americano's propaganda barrage for Pecora and its policy of ignoring the opposition, numerous Italian ethnic city organizations did support the Experience party candidate as attested to by correspondence sent to Impellitteri on organization stationary. The election results would show that Impellitteri was the emphatic winner among his ethnic group garnering 48.6 percent of its support to 23.5 percent for Pecora and 17.8 percent for Corsi. By contrast the support for Impellitteri among Jews was 21.2 percent versus over 44 percent for Pecora and only 5.8 percent for Corsi. Blacks endorsed Impellitteri with 37.0 percent of their votes compared to 37.4 percent for Pecora and 13.7 percent for Corsi.[19]

An interesting aspect affecting the Italian American candidates was posed by the Tresca Memorial Committee headed by Socialist Norman Thomas, his party's perennial presidential candidate. The Tresca Committee was dedicated to

the memory of the slain radical leader and used its
prestige to demand ongoing investigation of the
unsolved 1943 murder of Carlo Tresca. When the
committee's communications to the three Italian-
born candidates went unanswered, Thomas decided to
go to the press to expose their inaction in the
face of a crime against one of their own
nationality. Belatedly Corsi, who had been a friend
of Tresca and whose own father was a political
exile from the same town in Italy as Tresca,
responded with assurance that as mayor he would
command a probe of the crime. There was no response
from either Impellitteri or Pecora.

To obtain the blessings of major municipal
newspapers, always a sought after priority among
politicians striving for political office, takes on
particular relevance in New York City because of
the extraordinary role the media has in shaping
public opinion locally and beyond city limits. The
major English language dailies tended to align
themselves along expected paths as the principal
Republican organs endorsed Corsi, the left-wing
organs supported Ross, the liberal Democratic
newspapers backed Pecora and some independents
subscribed to the Impellitteri candidacy.
Accordingly the New York Herald Tribune, and the
New York Times, articulated their preference for
the GOP candidate as the best qualified.
Interestingly the New York World-Telegram and Sun,
hedged its bet by maintaining that while Corsi was
its first choice, it would only be a little less
happy to see Impellitteri win. The Scripps-Howard
newspaper saw the baneful influence of Tammany Hall
as the most important issue and if a victory by the
Experience party nominee Impellitteri was the only
way to avoid it, as the polls indicated, so be it.
Crediting Impellitteri with "guts," this newspaper
opined that although it did not expect the removal
of Tammany Hall, an Impellitteri victory would
break the Flynn-Costello-DeSapio element.

The very liberal New York Post, practically a
home organ for the Democratic party, shrilly
trumpeted charges of political connivance at
Impellitteri while it championed Pecora as the
truest advocate of liberal principles. In what
could only be considered cleverness or naivete, in
view of the fact that he was designated by party
bosses, the Post, also maintained that Pecora had

the intelligence and ability to withstand the pressures of Tammany Hall. For Impellitteri the New York _Daily News_, emerged as his staunchest supporter. Not as widely esteemed as some other city newspapers, the _News_, as the most popular newspaper in the city and with the largest circulation, was of immense help in portraying Impellitteri as the unbossed, unbought, independent candidate. The paper summed up its views as follows on the eve of the election: "we think this independent, boss-free, courageous and experienced man is the best fitted of the four candidates for the job."[20]

The polls had indeed illustrated that Impellitteri "has stolen the show," as one newspaper put it. Originally considered a long shot with little chance of defeating the better financed and time-tested major parties, especially the Democratic organization, it soon became apparent that the underdog had caught the attention and admiration of the public. One of the more revealing polls was a Hunter College public opinion survey conducted in October 1950. Supposedly representing a cross section of New Yorkers as to residential location, age, sex and economic status, the survey showed that Impellitteri was preferred by 34 percent versus 28 percent for Pecora. Corsi was faring poorly with 10 percent, while Ross trailed badly with only 6 percent. The no opinion tally was 22 percent. Voter analysis indicated that although Impellitteri was a candidate without a basic vote, he was attracting support from all quarters except the American Labor party. A study of the poll demonstrated that there was a virtual split among Democrats in Manhattan, Brooklyn and Queens with the Bronx alone showing beneficial partisan loyalty for Pecora. The Republican vote was also split with half of its polled members indicating Impellitteri as the choice. It was also evident that among independents the acting mayor was the overwhelming recipient of large backing.[21] The impressive pro-Impellitteri trend was confirmed in the usually rather accurate New York _Daily News_, straw poll which canvassed 15,000 people in all 67 assembly districts. The first straw returns of October 24 showed surprising Impellitteri strength in all boroughs as he led with a commanding 52.5 percent, an absolute majority over the combined ballots of his opponents. With subsequent <u>Daily News</u> polls demonstrating continued Impellitteri strength, it was evident that many voters were disgusted with regular "business as usual" politics of the official parties, preferring the independence of the acting mayor. The swing to Impellitteri was widespread geographically and economically with support among all income groups, much to the surprise of poll takers as they concluded that he led his rivals across income bracket lines "on a scale unequaled here since . . . early in the New Deal . . . . "

New Yorkers awoke to a November 7 election day that sported fair skies and seasonably cool temperatures, such conditions seemed calculated to bring out record numbers of voters. The 1950 election saw a sequence of the largest registration in city history followed by the largest turnout on Election Day. In a reflection of voter disenchantment with traditional parties, the 1950 election showed more registered independents then ever before, confirming a national trend. "In the confused fall of 1950, the outcome was more than ever in the hands of the nemesis of prophets, the independent voter."[22] Independents joined huge segments of the Democratic, Republican and American Labor parties in fashioning innovation in city electoral history as 1,156,060 of them elected Impellitteri, the first independent candidate to win in modern city history. Pecora's tally was 937,060, while Corsi placed third with 382,795, and Ross last with 149,182.

NOTES

1. New York <u>Daily News</u>, February 29, 1948.

2. New York <u>Herald Tribune,</u> August 24, 1950.

3. New York <u>Herald Tribune</u>, August 20, 1950.

4. New York <u>Post,</u> October 26, 1950.

5. New York <u>Herald Tribune,</u> September 26, 1950.

6. Script, WNEW Radio, October 30, 1950, <u>VIFP</u>.

7. New York <u>Daily Mirror,</u> November 1, 1950.

8. Script, Inez Robb, October 4, 1950, Box 48, file: Mayoralty Campaign 1950, <u>VRI</u>.

9. Memorandum, October 17, 1950, file: Memorandum-Miscellaneous, <u>VIFP</u>.

10. New York <u>Herald Tribune,</u> October 22, 1950.

11. Statement by Mayor Vincent R. Impellitteri, October 22, 1950, file: Press Releases, VIFP.

12. New York World Telegram, October 28, 1950.

13. Speech by Raymond Moley, November 2, 1950, file: Press Releases, VIFP.

14. Telegram, Joe Louis to Impellitteri, November 6, 1950, file: Press Releases, VIFP.

15. Speech, file: Press Releases, VIFP.

16. Memorandum, Independent Fact Finding Committee-UFA, file: Correspondence A-M, VIFP.

17. Nicholas V. Montalto, "The Influence of Ethnicity on the Political Behavior of the New York City Italian American Community Since World War II" (Thesis, Master of Arts, Georgetown University, 1969), 84.

18. Italian language broadcast translation, Mayoralty Campaign, file: Mayoralty Campaign 1950, Box 48, VIP.

19. Chris McNickle, "To Be Mayor of New York. The Transfer of Political Power From the Irish to the Jews and the decline of the Political Machine in New York City, 1881-1977" (Dissertation, Ph.D., University of Chicago, 1989), 401-4.

20. New York Daily News, November 6, 1950.

21. Public Opinion Survey, Ellen E. Brennan, file: Correspondence A-M, VIFP.

22. Time 56, no. 19 (November 6, 1950): 23.

6

Tasting the Fruits of Victory

Celebration was in the air on the evening of
November 7, 1950 as it became clear that "David had
defeated Goliath." In defiance of the experts, the
odds, and history itself, the unpretentious
shoemaker's son, Vincent Impellitteri, had been
elected to the second most significant
administrative position in the world's most
powerful nation without the support of one of the
two major parties. What had eluded the much better
known newspaper tycoon William R. Hearst in his
quest for the city mayoralty on an independent line
in 1905 had now been accomplished in stunning
fashion by the immigrant from Sicily. As voting
tabulation proceeded on election night, 5,000
ordinary yet excited New Yorkers joined in the
festive occasion, crowding the block in front of
the Abbey Hotel to pay tribute to the man who had
defied the bosses and who contentedly accepted
concession speeches from his opponents. Appearing
with his pretty, overjoyed wife, attired
conservatively in a dark blue suit, white shirt and
dark tie and puffing away incessantly on a slim
cigar, the exuberant and confident mayor deftly
answered reporters questions. Reflecting on the
bitterness of the campaign, which at times caused
candidates to lose their tempers and indulge in
undignified displays bereft of civility, he
admitted he too was tempted to cater to unbefitting
behavior but seldom yielded thanks to the calm
temperament he had inherited from his mother. It
was important for rank and file New Yorkers to be
present for it was as if one of their deserving
own, an underdog with whom they could identify, who
had captured the coveted prize that they could
share by osmosis. It was an impressive and
unprecedented victory indeed as the acting mayor
not only outpolled the Democratic candidate by
219,527 votes, but failed of an absolute majority

over the combined total of his three rivals by only
156,225. For his part the elated Impellitteri
expressed sincere thanks to supporters for helping
him reach "the climax of everything I have worked
for all of my life." On November 14, the occasion
of the formal inauguration of the 101st mayor, once
again thousands of pleased city residents were on
hand despite the severity of the weather.

It was axiomatic that a festive atmosphere
suffused the city's huge Italian American community
understandably elated at Impellitteri's victory. In
actuality promoters of political activity within
the ethnic group were in the happy position of
supreme exultation because all of the major
candidates were of Italian descent and that what
had seemed so impossibly remote only a couple of
years ago now was reality. Never in their wildest
dreams would they have thought it possible for
three Italian-born men to run for the exalted
office of New York City mayor—yet that is
precisely what happened. Exhibiting a chauvinistic
flush of euphoria, <u>Columbus</u>, an ethnic magazine,
saw the 1950 election as a confirmation of its
prediction some years earlier, that in the election
of LaGuardia, the sons of Italian immigrants had
come of age. It was, moreover, an affirmation of
America as a land of opportunity.

> We deem it a great privilege to dedicate this issue of
> <u>Columbus</u> to the new Mayor of the City of New York, Vincent R.
> Impellitteri—the youthful, dashing, genial founder of the
> Experience Party, another example of the most alluring
> opportunities offered by the American Democracy to its loyal
> adopted citizens.[1]

Celebration was not confined to New York City as
two other smaller municipalities in nearby states
joined in. One was Bayonne, New Jersey, birthplace
of Elizabeth McLaughlin Impellitteri, the mayor's
wife, who had become deeply immersed in his winning
campaign. The blond, gray-eyed, attractive woman
who met Vincent on a blind date in 1924, married
him in 1926, and seemed to be completely at ease
with life in Gracie Mansion, was now prepared to
share the amenities as well as the responsibilities
of being the "First Lady" of the city. Like most
wives of prominent politicians of that era whose
loyalty was unquestioned, Elizabeth Impellitteri

terminated her secretarial job in a Manhattan
office and contentedly accepted the self-imposed
role of supportive helpmate who, despite some
active campaigning, preferred noninvolvement in
purely political issues. Most of her public
appearances were on behalf of numerous, worthy
charitable causes such as the Heart Fund drive or,
as befitted her earlier modeling career, being
photographed sporting some of the latest designs in
women's fashions; she was considered one of the
best-dressed women in public life. Without children
of their own, the Impellitteris did not seek
adoption as a desirable option as did the
LaGuardias. Despite a gregarious inclination on his
wife's part, Vincent preferred the sedateness of
evenings at home. Consequently although they
socialized occasionally with family and close
friends, much of the Impellitteris' social life
while Vincent was mayor consisted of going out to
dinner at a quiet Italian restaurant on Houston
Street, dancing, particularly the rhumba, and for
the mayor, swimming at the New York Athletic Club.
Their favorite retreat outside the city was Fire
Island.

An even bigger celebration took place in Ansonia,
Connecticut, home to much of the large Impellitteri
clan and the town where Vincent spent his childhood
and adolescence. On a cold December 16, 1950, in
what undoubtedly was Ansonia's most memorable bash,
the guest of honor who was appropriately attired in
protective winter clothing, was greeted by almost
the entire community along with citizens of nearby
towns, who showered "Jimmy" Impellitteri's
motorcade with good wishes from the moment he
crossed the Ansonia-Derby town line. After a brief
visit at his sister's home, he stopped at Ansonia's
City Hall where he spoke to a cheering crowd of
3,000 and then finally he was the guest of honor at
the local State Armory--the only place large enough
to hold the 700 banquet guests, including family,
relatives and former teachers and classmates.
Revealingly, in his address, Impellitteri expounded
on themes of national defense as a consequence of
having met with President Truman only the previous
day; he called for solidarity in the face of the
recently proclaimed national emergency caused by
the Korean War. The newly elected mayor likewise
urged his audience to remain strong supporters of

the United Nations, recalling his own role in
opening that organization's headquarters in New
York and his hope that people would back the
international organization in the face of brutal
aggression.

Impellitteri's election also elicited favorable
comment from newspapers in disparate regions of the
country. The Chester Reporter, in South Carolina
marveled that three candidates for the city
mayoralty were of Italian parentage and Catholic
(which was incorrect). It also found it fascinating
that in America an immigrant who, had he remained
in the provincial Sicilian mountain town of his
birth, might never have risen beyond the modest
post of policeman, here won the second highest paid
municipal office in the country.[2] Editorial writers
in Glens Falls, New York interpreted Impellitteri's
election as vindication that the era of the
individual was not over and that common people
would not have to put their trust in political
bosses after all. "Within this state Vincent
Impellitteri of New York proved conclusively that
people still admire individual initiative and
independence." It was stated further that New York
City's Democrats had erred in knuckling under to
the dictates of the Liberal party and the Congress
of Industrial Organizations (CIO), which provided
Impellitteri with high ground against the "boss"
issue.[3]

Like many a politician who had just completed an
exhausting political campaign, it was not
surprising to find Impellitteri take time out for a
respite with his wife. Accompanied by Walter
Shirley and his wife, probably their closest
friends, the Impellitteris went to Cuba where they
were greeted by local officials and where Vincent
could indulge in cigar smoking, one of his lifelong
favorite pastimes, and where he could temporarily
put aside administrative worries. Although some
politicians like President James K. Polk never
seemed to take vacations, it is more normal to find
political leaders interrupting their duties for
relaxation, aware of the need to remove themselves
temporarily from the stress of the job. The careers
of New York City mayors offer varying experiences.
Some workaholics like LaGuardia railed at his
vacationing administrators: "Does a military
commander take a vacation in battle?", while more

did in fact take ample time off. Thus, James Walker's vacationing habits became infamous, while O'Dwyer's mayoral absences were such that it provided his successor with numerous opportunities to substitute for him. From the outset Impellitteri showed a tendency to interrupt his strenuous public duties with more relaxed pleasurable activities. The city's first family enjoyed its full share of opportunities to journey to summer places on Long Island, the Shirley's Palm Beach estate or the warm embraces of the sun in Cuba where they could swim, go out to dinner and dance. These were the Impellitteris' principal leisure activities, both prior to and after the mayoralty tenure. Although most of it can be attributed to partisanship which labeled any time outside of the city as "vacation" (even when in fact Impellitteri was on a thirty-four day mission for the United States State Department), the frequency of his vacations sparked its share of criticism; how seriously it impaired city administration is arguable.

It was just as well that Impellitteri went to Cuba for vacation following the election because immediately upon his return he was thrust into the exacting issues of the day, some affecting the entire nation, while others were peculiar to the city. The Korean War was the overriding national concern. For several months, commencing with the inception of hostilities in June 1950, Americans had experienced alternations between joy and relief and worry and dismay. The nation seemed to be fully supporting of President Truman's decision to send American combat troops as part of a United Nations force under General Douglas MacArthur to help turn the tide of an apparent disaster to South Korea. By November it appeared that the United Nations action had fully stemmed the tide and that it merely remained to launch a "final offensive" before a successful conclusion to the conflict. This assessment was predicated, however, on the belief that the Chinese Communists would not intervene. This belief proved to be totally and disastrously erroneous when, on November 26, Chinese forces came in "with both feet" thus changing the context of the war. By the end of 1950 the situation could not have been grimmer militarily with Chinese Communist forces inflicting severe damage to United Nations personnel as they began a slow, methodical and

punishing advance to the 38th parallel. This
contrary development provided the backdrop for a
national debate over the future course of American
overseas involvement with some people being highly
critical of the Truman Administration: Former
President Herbert Hoover advised extrication from
Korea, while Senator William Howard Taft opposed
further mobilization and sending of troops overseas
and former Ambassador Joseph P. Kennedy recommended
retreat from virtually all overseas commitments. On
the other hand there were many voices calling for a
strong response on the part of the United States:
Secretary of State Dean Acheson and Republican
Governor Dewey of New York, for example, urged
further mobilization. Against this background the
president issued a declaration terming the
situation a "national emergency" and called on all
Americans to recognize that they were in a genuine
war condition. It was like a replay of the scenario
of nine years earlier as young men received their
"greetings" from the president of the United States
to report for induction into the army. News that
atomic energy research was being accelerated so
that the horrifying vehicles of destruction were
now being mass-produced, was somewhat mitigated by
the knowledge that simultaneous atomic research
also held enormous beneficial potential in health
and energy fields. With Congressional backing the
Truman administration developed a civil defense
plan to help municipalities prepare themselves
against atomic attack. For New York this presented
special problems because of the virtual
impossibility of providing effective shelter for
massive populations without the expenditure of huge
sums of money to construct tunnels in deep rock in
addition to a proposed new Second Avenue subway.
The nature of the problems clearly precluded an
immediate solution, however, some basic steps could
be taken.

As a responsible public official, Mayor
Impellitteri responded by calling for unity behind
the American effort and for the need to concentrate
on civilian defense preparations. On January 20,
1951 he proclaimed Civilian Defense Week stating
"We must prepare to protect our families and our
homes and our Community because of the crisis that
confronts the nation." Two days later he confessed
his fear of the consequences of inadequate defense

preparations, "if the bombs fall upon us, it will be too late." Coupling the warning with a request for federal funds, he endorsed the call for construction of civilian defense public shelters. Impellitteri appointed former Police Commissioner Arthur Wallander, now a Consolidated Edison Company official, to head the city's Civilian Defense Commission and energetically prodded the development of plans for bomb shelters, siren tests, air raid drills, traffic programs, and so on. A measure of the extensiveness of defense preparations can be gleaned from Impellitteri's March 1951 annual message to the city council, in which the mayor proudly boasted that in allocating almost $7,250,000 for civil defense purposes, New York City was expending a greater sum for such objectives than any other city or state. The energy exerted by the Impellitteri administration in this activity notwithstanding, on the whole New Yorkers, responded to the emergency, as did many Americans, with a degree of indifference. Accordingly, efforts to produce volunteer aircraft spotters always seemed to fall short of desirable goals; a lukewarm response perhaps best attributed to the ambiguity surrounding the Cold War, which unlike World War II, with beginning and end dates fixed in people's minds, as historian Ronald Polenberg suggests, seemed amorphous.[4] Aggravated anxieties over the decision to conduct war on a limited basis were further exacerbated in March 1951 when Truman fired MacArthur for open and public defiance of presidential policy in urging an escalated war. Under the circumstances Americans placed great emphasis on good-paying, steady jobs, eating more nutritious food and owning their own homes. One study of the time indicated that the average American of 1951 earned $1.96 an hour, paid $25.00 a week or $1,300 a year for food. Despite this picture of complacency, Impellitteri nevertheless remained true to the President's objectives and proved to be a strong backer of combat forces, at one point sending 100 city flags to Korea. In December 1951 Impellitteri, along with his Civil Defense Director Wallander, conducted one of the most successful and remarkable air raid drills of the period. Only occasionally interrupted by barking dogs, for seven strange minutes the streets of New York were stilled in response to 1,000

blasting sirens that initiated the preparation
practice. Bridges were cleared, busses came to a
halt and passengers led to previously designated
shelters where they were joined by patrons and
entrepreneurs who left their shops attired in their
traditional occupational garb. There were only a
few flaws, including the arrest of a man for
sassing a female air raid warden.

    The Truman-MacArthur controversy was the backdrop
for one of the most stirring events of the era. An
"American Caesar," as the legendary imperious
general came to be known, was near the end of an
extraordinary military career begun by his father
before him in the middle of the nineteenth century.
Like his father, Douglas MacArthur had extensive
experience in American wars and served as the army
chief of staff. As noble a hero as any World War II
American military leader, he symbolized the spirit
of heroism and commitment that won the undying
gratitude of Americans. Remaining in the Pacific
theater following the surrender of Japan, he was
named the commander of that nation and oversaw its
remarkable transformation from a militarist state
into a democracy. Given the assignment to stem the
Communist North Korean tide in 1950, he performed
his task brilliantly until the entry of Communist
China altered the situation and led to the policy
conflict with President Truman, who, despite the
tremendous damage to presidential popularity, had
no choice but to dismiss him. Now at last, after
many years of military service, the warrior was to
return to his homeland to receive the honors due
him from a grateful public. MacArthur's demeanor,
his ability to exploit Truman's low popularity
rating and his uncommon oratorical gifts that
became enshrined in a memorable address to both
houses of Congress in which he recalled an old West
Point melody, "Old Soldiers never die, they just
fade away," was the background to his description
of himself as "an old soldier who sought to do his
duty as God gave him the light to see that duty."
That stellar performance before a somber Congress
and an adoring public that jammed the galleries
elevated him to a stature of unparalleled esteem.
The announcement that he was coming to New York was
the setting for the greatest welcome conferred on
any recent hero. When Grover Whelan, who served as
host to important city visitors, learned that

MacArthur was coming to New York City, he interrupted Mayor Impellitteri, then attending an important Board of Estimate session, to goad the mayor into allowing the city to honor him. Although Impellitteri was on good terms with Truman, he discussed the matter with the Board of Estimate and decided that it was an appropriate gesture. The result was that in April the metropolis greeted the general with its heartiest reception ever as an admiring public estimated at 7.5 million people, who generated 2.8 million tons of trash for the Sanitation Department, came to see him riding in his familiarly characteristic army uniform, in an open two-tone Chrysler limousine with a beaming Sicilian-born mayor. For nearly seven hours the motorcade wound its way through 19.2 miles of city streets packed with deliriously joyful and cheering people crammed into all available sidewalk space and perched on trees, ledges and rooftops. That this was a peak in Impellitteri's mayoralty is evidenced by the fact that until the end of his life a photograph of the event had a prominent place on Impellitteri's bedroom wall.

Little enthused over the war in Korea, New Yorkers were more absorbed with an assortment of interests of a personal and parochial nature such as obtaining adequately compensated jobs and the changing nature, of city demographics. For entertainment there were always the movies including early 1950's Academy Award winners "All About Eve," "An American In Paris," "The Greatest Show On Earth" and "From Here To Eternity." At the New York Paramount, the foremost cinema mecca in the city, the sensational comedy team of Dean Martin and Jerry Lewis were gleefully amusing audiences with their humorous antics and slapstick. Hollywood productions, it seemed, were undergoing important transformations as out of the movie capitol came a new bevy of apprentice goddesses like Debra Paget, Debbie Reynolds and Marilyn Monroe. Contrary to the dismal prognostication of doomsayers, the Broadway legitimate theater, a New York leisuretime mainstay, continued to attract large audiences with a combination of diverting new plays like "I Am A Camera," which led to stardom for Julie Harris, and engrossing revivals such as the smash hit "Pal Joey." In the meantime "South Pacific" was winding up its second year on Broadway

with never an unsold seat. Broadway also provided
such prize-winning offerings as Tennessee
Williams's "The Rose Tattoo." There were, in
addition, television shows that then were produced
extensively in New York City at that time, and vied
with the movies as one of the favorite means of
entertainment as viewers were glued to their sets
watching the antics of Milton Berle and Jimmy
Durante or the glamour of Faye Emerson. Sports-
minded New Yorkers found the baseball world much to
their liking considering that the New York Yankees
had won three straight pennants, the only remaining
question was could they repeat in 1952, for the
great DiMaggio had played his last game in the
World Series of the previous year. In 1951 New York
boxing enthusiasts were shocked to learn that
"Sugar" Ray Robinson, arguably the best fighter
pound for pound of the era and the pride of the
city, had lost his middleweight title to English
fighter Randy Turpin. However, 61,370 excited New
Yorkers crowded together at the Polo Grounds in
September of that year to see Robinson recover his
crown. This was a source of great joy to New
Yorkers as a whole and especially pleasing to the
mayor, who had developed such a friendship with
Robinson that the boxer campaigned for him in
African American neighborhoods and also played a
prominent role in Mrs. Impellitteri's Heart Fund
drive.

Patronage, which has always been a concomitant of
American municipal governance, is inevitable for
New York City mayors and political life under
Impellitteri proved to be no exception. Acquiescing
in the axiom that the spoils system is the
lifeblood of politics, Impellitteri was, in effect,
agreeing with the opinions of professional
politicians like Edward J. Flynn. "As long as men
are elected to public office who are politically
ambitious (and who enters a political race who is
not?) the practice of the spoils system will
continue."[5] By appointing Frank Sampson, leader of
a minority Tammany faction, to oversee patronage,
Impellitteri contributed to a brewing controversy
even as he left for the Cuban vacation. Critics
denounced the appointment as a vivid betrayal of
the notion of independence and a brazen replay of
political machination in emulation of the most
notorious Tammany Hall chieftains of the past like

Boss Tweed.[6] The Impellitteri-Sampson technique was
to get rid of officeholders who had supported
Pecora and replace them with Impellitteri men. In
an effort to prove to his supporters that they were
being favored, on December 27, 1950 Impellitteri
conducted a mass swearing in of eight new
appointees who had steadfastly campaigned for him.
Having thus paid his obsequious compliances to
Experience party loyalists, Impellitteri
nevertheless, had no intention of cutting himself
off from the regular Democratic organization
especially from Flynn, with whom he soon attempted
a rapprochement.

Reintegration within the Democratic party was not
incongruous after all, since even prior to the
election and continuously after the victory
Impellitteri identified himself as a faithful party
member. Even as late as July 1950, only two months
before he began to denounce the Tammany leadership,
Impellitteri dutifully sang the praises of the
Tammany Society. "It was a strong force for good
government in 1790 . . . . It is an equally strong
force for good government today."[7] Soon after the
election he would be approving regular Democrats
for office, as for example, his endorsement of
Joseph T. Sharkey for president of the city
council, "even though he did not support me."
Within days of the election there were fresh
reminders of pending reconciliation as powerful
elements within regular Democratic ranks, prompted
by the fuel of patronage now under Impellitteri's
control, took the initiative to arrange an accord
with the insurgent mayor. One of the most notable
examples at propitiation saw Generoso Pope, Jr.,
previously vociferous in his denunciation of
Impellitteri, now incredibly attempt to excuse his
earlier ferocity as behavior attributable to his
emotional Latin background that became even more
pronounced in the heat of the campaign. "The period
of combat is nevertheless over, and there ought now
begin collaboration and cooperation." He maintained
that what distinguished a democracy from a
dictatorship was that after the electoral war was
over victors and vanquished could move ahead
without recrimination. In an attempt at nonpartisan
statesmanship, Pope reminded readers of the
significance of the fact that the three major
candidates for mayor were Americans born in Italy.

Rome was not built in a day. In the victory of Mayor
Impellitteri everyone can find a sense of satisfaction because
one of our own has been chosen the head of our city and we
take the auspiciousness of this victory to mean that the day
will not be long in which other Americans of Italian origin,
Italians will be called, because of their own merits, . . . In
this state of mind, to Mayor Impellitteri, our sincere
congratulations and our liveliest best wishes.[8]

Despite the rapprochement with many Democrats in
various boroughs, there was to be no detente with
Carmine DeSapio, head of Tammany Hall. On this
point the mayor was adamant. While in most other
respects pragmatic about the need for quid pro quo
in politics, when it came to relations with
DeSapio, Impellitteri succumbed to that rarely used
but nevertheless stubborn streak within his
character in remaining obstinate and unrelenting in
his opposition to the Tammany chieftain. The irony
of the situation was evident when two years after
his mayoralty was ended, Impellitteri reflected on
DeSapio without animosity. Early in the
administration, however, and contrary to reports
that his nomination of a pro-DeSapio woman to a
city magistrate post represented a bid for peace by
the Mayor, Impellitteri rejected repeated
opportunities at reconciliation and consistently
depicted DeSapio as the Manhattan Democratic
organization's source of infamy that had to be
eradicated. So intent was he in his anti-DeSapio
vendetta that the mayor would spend years of
needless and ultimately futile effort in trying to
oust the Tammany leader--a course of action that
perhaps seemed feasible in the brief interlude
following the special election of 1950 when in fact
the pro-Impellitteri forces of committeemen within
Tammany Hall failed by one vote to defeat DeSapio.
DeSapio's position seemed so vulnerable that many a
political observer was readying his political
obituary. "It's only a matter of time before
DeSapio will have to yield his leadership . . . .
DeSapio has no chance of effecting a
reconciliation."[9] So weak did DeSapio's position
appear in early 1951, that many Manhattan
Democratic officeholders held their distance rather
than publicly embracing his actions and thus
antagonizing Impellitteri. One of the best examples
is furnished by Manhattan Borough President Robert
F. Wagner, Jr., who, because he surmised that

DeSapio might well be displaced as leader of Tammany, upset a DeSapio strategy to strengthen his position in the Tammany executive committee, by declaring his willingness to work with the mayor and resist taking sides in the intraparty political fight. But DeSapio was as intelligent and as wily a political leader as any Tammany Hall head in many a decade and accordingly knew how to direct a Phoenix-like resurrection from the politically dead by changing his approach and his image in the postelection period. "I felt something drastic had to be done to disprove the public impression of me and my organization," he confessed to Time, and indeed over the next few years he confounded skeptics by systematically setting about to change Tammany's public image. He was successful in seeking out able and competent candidates for public office and soon became lionized as a mature, modern-age, new-style political statesman who won national acclaim and prestige as few Tammany Hall leaders had ever done. DeSapio thereupon outmaneuvered his rivals, frequently Impellitteri supporters within the party structure, and thus strengthened his position within the New York County Democratic organization. Accordingly, although Impellitteri appointed Harry Brickman deputy treasurer in the Department of Finance and Hugo E. Rogers as special counsel to the Traffic Department, where they served faithfully without compromising their integrity, DeSapio was able to wrest from them control of their home districts by enlisting the support of his own allies Louis DeSalvio and Prosper Viggiano, thereby enabling the Tammany leader to realign local political district geography and in the process isolate Impellitteri. DeSapio became just as obstinate in denouncing Impellitteri thereby precluding any real chance at a truce between the two. The rupture would prove to be especially damaging to Impellitteri in 1953.

Political infighting was a constant as was the persistency of the difficulties surrounding the governance of big cities. Chief among these problems was the budget, that is how to come up with the money necessary to carry out responsible city programs. "His first job is money," wrote one reporter, "money to implement the hard-hitting civilian defense organization he has created. Money to lick the housing shortage . . . and money to

continue the necessary school building program, and
correct some screaming inequities in civil service
salaries."[10] Thus, financing the city's needs
became a complex of funding for already existing
municipal programs, their expansion, the
inauguration of new programs and the need to
increase salaries of city employees. This required
a delicate balance of city-generated income
augmented by cooperation from the New York state
legislature, specifically, approval to increase the
city sales tax from 2 percent to 3 percent A city
sales tax of 1 percent had originally been adopted
in 1934 in order to assist the city finance relief
costs on a pay-as-you-go basis. In the face of
extraordinary postwar expenses, the O'Dwyer
Administration had doubled the city sales tax to 2
percent thereby rendering it the biggest income for
the city next to the real estate tax. What
originally was advanced as a temporary measure had,
in effect, become a permanent city fixture. Unlike
previous city administrations that had frequently
engaged in partisan sparring with a Republican-
controlled state government in Albany, the
innovative Impellitteri sought to cultivate State
legislative approval on a bipartisan basis. In a
refreshing departure from the past he courted
backing from Republicans as well as Democrats as he
outlined a five point program for state aid. He
also adroitly illustrated his political skill by
successfully securing the backing of major
Democratic leaders such as Bronx Chairman Edward J.
Flynn, Brooklyn Chairman Francis J. Sinnott, and
Democratic State Chairman Paul F. Fitzpatrick. In
addition, Impellitteri enlisted the approval of
James Roe, the Queens Democratic leader, who
brought the unanimous support of that borough's
Democratic state legislators. The marshalling of
intraparty support gave the mayor the upper hand
against DeSapio who, although reluctant to bolster
the mayor, nevertheless, could not appear to be
insensitive to the city's needs, and accordingly
directed Manhattan Democratic state legislators to
favor the Impellitteri sales tax increase plan. In
sum, it was abundantly clear to most that a sales
tax boost was essential to balance the books and on
March 5, 1951, Impellitteri formally asked the
state legislature to approve his request for a tax
escalation, fully realizing it invited outcries and

resistance. Walter Hoving, vociferous chairman of
the anti-Sales Tax Commission, assailed it as a
"shortsighted" means of providing cost of living
bonuses for city employees. Since it was estimated
that much of the increased sales tax burden would
be borne by corporations and business, the mayor
dismissed such criticism as self-serving. "There
has been a great deal of shedding of crocodile
tears by certain special groups who, in a desire to
benefit from their own interests, exerted much time
and money to depict the proposed addition of one
percent sales tax as a 'heavy burden.'"[11] On the
other hand, while the New York _Times_ labelled the
sales tax a bad idea, it realized that under the
circumstances there was no reasonable alternative
to pay for the huge outlays of city expenses in the
postwar period. It nevertheless called for
economies in city government and applauded
Impellitteri for supporting the mayor's management
survey, which was designed to study ways of
streamlining municipal government. After some
feuding with Albany, including a successful protest
against a bill that would have exempted gasoline
from the sales tax, thereby preventing the city
from imposing an auto use tax, the city was allowed
its request as Impellitteri signed the sales tax
increase measure into law on April 20, 1951.

Financing municipal activities would continue to
be a major preoccupation as officials struggled
with a desire to fund an increased array of
services and an accelerated capital building
program designed to compensate for many years of
little or no construction due to war-related
circumstances. Moreover, fiscal problems were
further exacerbated by relentless inflation.
Because much of the funding came from merchandising
tax exempt municipal bonds, it was the source of
serious concern when early in 1951 the United
States Treasury Department proposed the end of that
exemption partially on the grounds of the need for
the federal government to generate revenue during
the national emergency. Impellitteri lost no time
in journeying to Washington to testify and argue
against the premise, depicting it as a dubious
proposal to "rob Peter to pay Paul, and Peter is
already up to his ears in financial difficulties."
He reminded Congress that the proposed tax would
result in only a relatively small boost in federal

revenue, while placing a heavy burden on local
governmental bodies. His astute analysis
demonstrated that given the nature of municipal
bonds, payout is extended over many years thus
placing limits on possibilities to tax interest.
Furthermore, he pointed out that a very substantial
portion of ownership of tax-exempt bonds was by
institutional investors who were not subject to the
progressive rates of the individual income taxes.
In a successful effort to defeat the proposal he
pleaded with lawmakers not to further saddle
municipalities with handicaps as they tried to
finance local government.

When the mayor of an American city recognizes that the cost of
living has far outstripped the salary scale of faithful
municipal employees, he has a titanic and frequently
impossible burden to rectify the inequity because of his
inability to raise the money needed to meet pay raises. Our
power to tax is strictly controlled by the State and by
existing taxes imposed by the Federal government . . . . We in
municipal finance and our citizens who must pay the bill are
at our wit's end and simply cannot stand the additional burden
you propose to ask us to assume.[12]

During Impellitteri's first year as mayor, a
great deal of attention was directed at the Mayor's
Committee on Management Survey, which was created
under O'Dwyer and headed by Director Luther Gulick
of the Institute of Public Administration, to study
ways of economizing city government. Since
Comptroller Lazarus Joseph, an Impellitteri rival,
was chairman of the committee, it was not
surprising that some discord existed between the
Impellitteri administration and the management
survey committee. This was especially true when the
committee suggestions clashed with the views of the
imperious Robert Moses, city construction
coordinator and a member of the committee. The
opinionated but talented Moses could be counted on
to defend vigorously his turf of municipal power
and few could cross him without being bloodied in
the process. He was a match for even the strongest
mayors like LaGuardia, who frequently had to accept
Moses on his own terms. To a considerable extent
Moses articulated the Impellitteri administration's
relationship to management survey committee
proposals. Consequently, he rebuked Joseph for
inferring that large-scale economies in city

operations could easily be effected. Moses denounced such inferences as misleading. Not one to proffer a modest image, Moses referred to his own "considerable personal experience" with matters of economies in government on state and federal levels by virtue of his work with former governors, mayors and presidents. He admonished Joseph to consider the increased demands on a city that was growing in population and was expected to house over eight and a half million people in ten years. Since so much growth had taken place in nearby suburbs, it necessitated the development of an extensive infrastructure embracing transportation, roads, public housing, schools, parks, health facilities-- all of which required additional capital, debt and interest amortization. He argued further that the Impellitteri administration recognized that people no longer were satisfied to live in slums and that they properly sought a greater share of the good things of life. While he acknowledged the desirability of economy, he assailed as "so much moonshine," the deliberate cultivation of the notion that enforced efficiency would actually result in tremendous cuts in city operating budgets. Fancying himself the wielder of a clever, if scathing pen, Moses lashed out at those like Senators Estes Kefauver and Charles Tobey of the Senate Crime Investigating Committee, who called on the city to engage executives with professional expertise to run city departments, while simultaneously fostering disincentives via a besmirching of all municipal personnel with unproven charges of corruption.

> To paraphrase the sapient words of the Immortal Bard, there will be cakes and ale, wagering and other sports after Senators Kefauver and Tobey have returned to the hills of Kentucky and New Hampshire from whence, as the Bible says, cometh our help. Wise reformers don't give too many cathartics. A few more doses of Senator Tobey, and the town will be thirsty for another Jimmy Walker![13]

For his part Impellitteri, while refusing to join in with Moses's negative characterization of the Kefauver Committee, nevertheless, agreed with his "keen analysis" of the city's fiscal problems. The mayor asserted that the city's financial problems were caused by skyrocketing costs of materials and labor, and consequently went far beyond the few

economies suggested by the committee. He further
reiterated his desire to provide needed pay raises
for city employees thereby reaffirming his
steadfast commitment that the city should be at the
forefront of providing public employees with
suitable salaries and satisfactory working
conditions. But Impellitteri also expected much
from city employees, especially administrators. One
of his first acts after being elected mayor in his
own right was to address a memorandum to heads of
all City departments and agencies directing them to
avoid even a hint of corruption. Lashing out at the
dubious practice of soliciting gratuities on
holiday evenings, he warned them "under no
circumstances, to solicit or encourage in any
manner or form gratuities or honorariums from our
taxpayers."[14]

Because the press frequently cited suggestions of
the Mayor's Committee on Management Survey as the
unquestioned guide regarding economies of
operation, it tended to evaluate Impellitteri on
how closely his administration adhered to its
recommendations. While the results were mixed, and,
therefore, the administration avoided extremes of
unstinting praise or total condemnation, the first
nine to twelve months of Impellitteri's tenure
could be said to have elicited mildly positive
ratings. Indeed, one survey of city newspaper
editorials for 1951 found that he received
favorable comment forty-five times and unfavorable
comments forty-seven times. Considering the fact
that only one newspaper (the New York Daily News)
was originally in his favor and that the rest of
the city dailies were either opposed or neutral
during the 1950 election, this could be construed
as rather remarkable. Also to be considered is the
fact that a number of the unfavorable editorials
were repetitious and were in some instances
reversed following mayoral actions, it could well
be said that in reality that the number of
unfavorable reactions was considerably lower.

The major criticism was in degree rather than
philosophy, that is, although he was moving in the
right direction in beginning to implement the
mayor's committee's suggestions for economies, he
could have moved more swiftly to effect further
reform of city management. At the same time,
however, Impellitteri received favorable reviews

for certain economic steps he undertook as, for example, in September 1950 when he ordered 108 city-owned automobiles withdrawn, saving the city $492,000 a year. "Frankly, we never thought we would live long enough to see anything like it," commented the New York _Times_, as it congratulated the mayor. The newspaper likewise commended Impellitteri for following up the mayor's committee recommendation by setting up a Bureau of Management Improvement and more than once recognized economies instituted by Impellitteri. In an innovation that held out promise for the city to use the valued counsel of talented individuals from the city's private sector, Impellitteri received deserved credit for bringing into his administration an experienced business administrator who agreed to work gratis. The move was deemed "unique in our times."

Housing was one of postwar America's most crucial problems. Years of nonconstruction because of the national depression and extended neglect during the Second World War when military matters were understandably of more urgent concern, had left the nation with an acute housing shortage as well as a surfeit of substandard dwellings. Although a nationwide problem, it had particular impact on the nation's oldest and largest cities like New York. Private enterprise could and did help fill the housing needs of those who could afford it, but the housing needs of the city poor could not be met without major government involvement and assistance. Although resisted by conservative elements, in 1949 Congress enacted a law to provide government funds for thousands of low-cost housing starts. Led by the imaginative Moses, New York City took the national lead in using the law's provisions to carry out a massive slum clearance program to tear down deteriorating Victorian-age tenements and replace them with new housing units for the poor. The result was that beginning with O'Dwyer's term and even more under Impellitteri, the greatest housing construction program in city history took place.

Like Mayors LaGuardia and O'Dwyer before him and Wagner and Lindsay following him, Impellitteri called on the talented Moses to function as the main architect of the city's housing development: mapping out sites for slum clearance and planning strategies for interaction among city, state and federal authorities and private financial segments to implement the construction of major city housing projects. Indeed Robert Caro, whose massive tome on Moses's power brokering is otherwise scathingly critical, nevertheless asserts that Moses deserves credit for masterminding virtually all major publicly financed city construction in his time, maintaining that the master builder jealously orchestrated every step of the process. A review of the Impellitteri Papers undeniably corroborates Moses's powerful role, however, these same sources also indicate that Moses was not the exclusive important factor in this regard. Other vital performers on behalf of public housing included Philip Cruise, chairman of the New York Housing Authority and the mayor himself, both of whom warrant recognition for their influential roles in facilitating the construction of public housing. Although Impellitteri generally gave Moses free rein, he was not, as Caro infers, a mere puppet pulled along by strings manipulated by Moses.

In 1951, when Congress leaned toward a disastrously reduced housing program that would sharply curtail federally financed city housing, the nation's mayors became alarmed and pleaded with Impellitteri to play a prominent role in countering the move. Nor did Impellitteri disappoint them as he demonstrated genuine leadership by personally sending telegrams to the entire city Congressional delegation (the largest in the nation) and to other national legislators urging their opposition to antipublic housing legislation. The mayor could depend on sympathetic national legislators, in some instances former Fordham University Law School classmates now serving in Congress, to inform the entire Congress of the detrimental impact that would result in a cutback of the housing program. Taking the initiative, the mayor then announced he was sponsoring a meeting in City Council Chambers to which renowned political leaders and housing advocates were invited to launch a public rally against the Congressional action. As an attention getter the June 1 meeting was preeminently successful and accordingly elicited the gratitude even of President Truman who telegraphed an encouraging message to him while sailing on the USS Williamsburg.

I hope the public meeting you have called will arouse the citizens of the largest city in the country and the entire nation to a realization of the danger which threatens us all if the real estate lobby succeeds in killing public housing. Keep up the good fight.

The well-publicized and well-attended meeting heard the mayor bluntly decry the Congressional bill that would savage twenty city housing projects already approved and under way and would indefinitely postpone thousands of other desperately needed dwellings. "No substantial progress can continue to be made without adequate Federal assistance . . . Is this really the best we can hope for? I refuse to accept that." When Congress reversed its position on August 15, and approved public housing expenditures increases, a good deal of the credit was attributed to the pressure so ably managed by Impellitteri on this occasion.

Impellitteri's advocacy of publicly assisted housing construction remained constant throughout the rest of his term even in the face of vigorous protest. It was inevitable when old buildings were razed, poor tenants dislocated and neighborhoods permanently transformed, that the city housing program produced its share of critics. On a number of occasions when local citizen groups and chambers of commerce made known their opposition to particular projects, they received extensive media coverage. A proposal to renovate a midtown West Side neighborhood in 1952 is a case in point as the press provided fulsome coverage, replete with photographs and interviews with quotable laments from affected residents. This neighborhood contained a mix of nationalities--Germans and Irish, Italians and Jews--gripped with a ferment of anger and revolt, who signed petitions by the thousands to save their neighborhood from demolition. Unfortunately for them the area was judged to be a slum so that even though the mayor was not without sympathy, he undoubtedly saw its demise as a sad but inevitable price for the creation of new and desirable living quarters. Consequently, notwithstanding hearings and protests, the mayor allowed Moses to proceed in furthering public housing in the city. The determined Construction Coordinator had long since been convinced that tenement slums were "cancers"

that must be eliminated before proper housing could
be erected. He was impatient, moreover, with any
interruption to his vision of massive housing
construction with the result that the Impellitteri
years saw one of the most extensive construction
programs of housing projects in the United States.

An analysis of Impellitteri's first annual
message as mayor reveals his self-perceived tasks
including, in part the continuing implementation of
some of the capital improvement programs begun by
the previous administration and including, in part,
the establishment of his own stamp on city policies
in the areas of expansion of debt limit exemption,
an accelerated rate of school construction and
greater attention to traffic relief. The message
was received in the affirmative as was his call for
enhanced revenue and more state aid. Reappointment
of Police Commissioner Murphy, and noninterference
with his operation won due attention. Murphy had
earned warranted national renown for handling the
tough job in such a manner as to eliminate "pay-
offs" and thereby enhance police morale (a most
desirable commodity against a background of
emerging scandal traceable to the O'Dwyer years).
Indeed an augmentation in departmental personnel
for the police department represented the one
substantial increase in Impellitteri's
$1,366,000,000 1951 budget, the largest in city
history. To be certain there were critics of
Impellitteri, mostly from left of center, however,
he also enjoyed a substantial degree of favorable
evaluation. By and large Impellitteri's
appointments to numerous judicial positions,
including Irving Cooper as chief judge of special
sessions, elicited deserved approval even from
Republican sources such as the New York Herald
Tribune, and the New York Times, for his refreshing
willingness "to take seriously the recommendations
of the bar associations . . . . But on the whole
the Mayor's record in the matter of judicial
appointments has been good."[15]

His appointments to other important positions in
municipal government, including Henry McCarthy as
welfare commissioner, Jacob Grumet as fire
commissioner and George Monaghan as police
commissioner following Murphy's resignation,
likewise won contemporary commendation as positive
moves.

As for evaluations based on longer term analysis,
reference will be made to the careful study of the
New York City mayoral office undertaken by Theodore
Lowi. As Lowi correctly stated, in the modern era
every mayor strives to achieve efficiency of
specialization while making policy implementation.
Specifically, whereas New York City mayors of an
earlier era were more likely to appoint
"generalists" (frequently lawyers) to important
municipal offices, from the time of the city
charter change during the LaGuardia years, the
tendency has been to place less reliance on
generalists and simultaneously provide a greater
role for specialists who possessed job oriented
skills. In effect this meant augmented influence
for various specialists, such as doctors and
engineers, lawyers also benefitted, however, but
only those with specialized training. This was a
response to the realization that with the growth of
municipal government operations and simultaneous
development of career bureaucracies operating
within virtually autonomous departments, it was
increasingly necessary to name political executives
who had made careers of departmental specialties in
order to exercise a modicum of control.[16] It is of
significance to note that Impellitteri appointed
more people with job oriented skills to his cabinet
than any prior mayor with the exception of
LaGuardia. Mayor Robert F. Wagner's record in this
connection was only slightly higher.

Despite a rather positive early administrative
record, it was the unlucky fate of Impellitteri to
be compared with LaGuardia--a comparison from which
he was bound to suffer. Accordingly, in April 1951
a New York _Times_-sponsored teachers' seminar found
city political affairs observers drawing a parallel
between LaGuardia and Impellitteri both of whom had
run and won as independents. However, unlike
LaGuardia, who exercised extensive reform by
ridding his administration of old party hacks,
Impellitteri did not sweep clean many agency heads
and administrators and replace them with
independents devoted to the science and art of
government. The conclusion was that the
Impellitteri had misled the public with his
independent stance and that his administration
would not result in municipal management with the
same high LaGuardia standards. While this

observation has some merit, it was not altogether
fair in that Impellitteri, unlike LaGuardia, had
always considered himself a Democrat and part of a
Democratic administration before he became mayor,
he therefore knew, worked with and was on the same
wavelength with many colleagues. He had not run on
a platform of throwing out all the rascals.
LaGuardia, by contrast, was replacing a Democratic
regime that had been ensconced in power for many
years and he had won his office in considerable
part on the issue of cleaning house of the rascals
of the Walker administration. In other words, the
circumstances were not exactly alike, and one could
not expect the same developments. LaGuardia and
Impellitteri were, furthermore, different in their
temperament and philosophy. Not to be overlooked
was the benefit of Impellitteri's independence that
helped obtain needed approval for the city budget
with its tax increase from a Republican controlled
state government.

While conducting the city administration brought
its share of headaches, the job also had its
enviable array of perquisites among which was that
of receiving the honor of a virtual head of state
when traveling abroad. No example illustrates this
better than Impellitteri's extraordinary visit to
Italy in 1951. In early July 1951 reports emanating
from Italian newspapers told of an impending good
will trip to be made by Impellitteri to Italy "on a
special mission of friendship for President
Truman." Feigning surprise at the report,
Impellitteri quickly let it be known that he
welcomed such an opportunity, which soon became
reality with confirmation of plans that he was to
make the trip on behalf of the president and the
State Department. In actuality even before the
proposed trip the United States Department of State
had seized every opportunity to enlist
Impellitteri's support to firm up ties between
America and Italy. Accordingly, a State Department
official communicated that department's desire that
Impellitteri issue a favorable statement extolling
the virtues of democracy for Italy in anticipation
of May Day 1952, a day normally preempted by
Communist advocates to celebrate the superiority of
their ideology. Without hesitation Impellitteri
cooperated even to the point of issuing, with only
minor mutation, the written statement prepared by

the State Department. "You have proven the value of liberty. You have demonstrated the power of faith. You have again revealed the vitality of Italy." Likewise in July 1952, using the occasion of America's July Fourth celebration and the coincidence of the birthday anniversary of Italian unification hero Giuseppe Garibaldi, the State Department importuned Impellitteri, replete with a supplied written statement, to issue a message linking the two events as a means of developing Italian-American friendship. Once again Impellitteri demonstrated his loyalty in collaborating by affixing his signature to the prepared missive with only slight modification.

Garibaldi was a great and good European, and no doubt were he alive today, he would have been foremost among statesmen in supporting those measures designed to assure the defense and security of Western Europe. The man who, a century ago, raised the flag of the Italian Risorgimento, would certainly have rejoiced to see Italy cooperating today with the other free nations of the world, in behalf of peace and freedom.[17]

The proposed trip to Italy was, therefore, very much in conformity with the United States government policy of "containment," which was designed to prevent the further spread of communism; thus the determined Truman was prepared to move with alacrity in support of governments threatened by ruthless Communist advancement in Europe in the postwar years. "In Italy, a determined and aggressive effort is being made by a Communist minority to take control of that country."[18] Impellitteri soon met with President Truman to discuss the journey, which included, both Italy and a side junket to Israel. The announcement met with expected derision as some critics wondered aloud about the need for such a sojourn and the deleterious effects of a lengthy absence from City Hall. The hostile New York <u>Post</u> could not resist the temptation to comment that while the city floundered the mayor was "fiddling" away in Rome. Unmentioned and accorded little more than speculation, undoubtedly in the minds of some, was the parallel between the present scenario and Truman's appointment of O'Dwyer as Ambassador to Mexico, a move that was regarded with dubiousness. However valid were the detractors' arguments, they

overlooked the important fact that a critical
aspect of the developing Cold War strategy was the
maintenance of warm ties with Italy and Israel.
Thus, an extended process of cultivating Italy, and
preventing its Communist party--the largest in the
Free World--from sharing governmental power, was
consequential to the Truman administration and the
United States. Prominent anti-Communist Americans
with Italian connections were enlisted in the cause
as, for example, Republican Connecticut Governor
John Lodge, who with his Italian-born wife also
made a goodwill visit to Italy in 1951. As for the
mayor of New York City, there was no denying that
in 1948 Impellitteri had played a highly meaningful
role in urging Italy to vote against the
Communists. The fact that New York City housed more
inhabitants of Italian and Jewish background
outside of Italy and Israel was not lost on the
president. To enlist an Italian-born American
politician then holding a position of public esteem
as prominent as any American of Italian descent in
the important task of promoting friendly relations
between the two nations was a major stepping stone
in the construction of American foreign policy.
That Impellitteri figured so significantly in this
endeavor may have escaped the ken of many observers
and critics, however, it did not escape the
tenacious mind of President Truman. For his part
Impellitteri saw this as an opportunity to cement
relations with Italy by offering himself as an
example to the Italian people of how a poor
immigrant could rise through the democratic
processes, to become mayor of the largest city in
the world. Hence it was that on September 18, Mayor
Impellitteri, his wife and a few aides flew to Rome
to begin a whirligig of hearty ceremonies, joyous
greetings and generous receptions replete with
medals, honors and plaques. The outpouring of
public dignitaries, the honors and scrolls bestowed
on him by municipal and regional governments as
well as the national Italian government, the huge,
friendly crowds of ordinary Italian citizens who
came out to greet him, were visible testimonies to
the depth of affection between the two countries.
Because this occurred against a background of
difficulty and shame for a proud nation that was
suffering from the devastating physical and
psychological effects of a lost war, the reception

accorded Impellitteri also possessed a special
meaning because in recognizing him Italians were
really honoring themselves. They were acknowledging
that prestige and honor could indeed originate from
humble but sturdy Italian roots. Few Americans of
that era, LaGuardia not excepted, were embraced by
Italians as enthusiastically as Impellitteri as
cities and towns vied with each other to provide
the most memorable occasions of pomp and
festivities. He was, after all, one of their own
who had made good in America, one who had been born
in Italy--a fact even LaGuardia could not claim.

And thus it happened that Vincent Impellitteri
stood at the center of the lustiest reception Italy
accorded any celebrity since the end of the Second
World War. That Italians were elated and
appreciative of this visit in which the mayor acted
as an informal ambassador was manifest in the
importance they attached to it. A large Italian
police force had to struggle to restrain tens of
thousands who had waited for hours and lined the
streets from Ciampino Airport to the city of Rome
to catch a glimpse of the man. Rome's Mayor
Salvatore Rebecchini spoke for Italians in general
when he greeted Impellitteri with the observation
that the Italian populace "followed with great
interest and who received with extreme joy the news
of your meritorious election to the maximum
civilian capacity to which you have honorably
risen." Italian newspapers welcomed him as a self-
made man, who by force of his own strength and
tenacity rose to a brilliant position. They
likewise commented on his typical Sicilian physical
features, the warm disposition of Southern Italians
and an abiding affection for the land of his
ancestors. Interestingly one newspaper welcomed the
contrast between his poised, pensive and composed
manner with that of the frenetic, hand-waving,
emotional LaGuardia.[19] In the course of his
Italian sojourn Impellitteri met with Pope Pius
XII, the president of the Italian Republic Luigi
Einaudi, members of the nobility, chambers of
commerce and mayors of the most important Italian
cities, however, the most poignant stop on his tour
unquestionably was in Isnello, his birthplace.
Still remote with its narrow, curvy roads not
designed for easy access for the long, sleek, gray,
borrowed Pontiac carrying its famous guest, Isnello

remained a sleepy village of 4,200 souls perched at the foot of a grey precipice hundreds of feet high. Bereft of television and movies, the town still employed a town crier who proclaimed the impending visit by blowing his trumpet and instructing residents that "all animals--donkeys, goats, sheep and pigs--are to be shut in the houses and are not to walk on the public road."[20] Although impoverished, Isnello approved the relatively considerable sum of $600 to finance a reception for its most famous son, the son of a poor village cobbler. Upon arrival in the town Mayor Impellitteri was greeted with banners proclaiming "Welcome Impy" in English, high flying fireworks, cries of "bravo Vincenzo" and the pealing of church bells from San Michele, where he had been baptized as an infant and where he joyfully heard mass and publicly shed tears for the first time in memory of his associates. Out of respect for his mother, and in the inimitable Sicilian dialect, Isnello women greeted him with a traditional Sicilian proverb "Bedduzzo De Mamma." He was also immediately swamped by dozens of relatives, many of whom expressed hopes that he could aid them to come to America. Some were so affected that they ascribed magical, if not miraculous powers to Impellitteri and even the vehicle that brought him. To touch the car, it was felt, would bring them closer to their dream of going to America. The accomplished Italian writer, Carlo Levi, who was present during the visit, provided a literate and vivid account of its meaning to Isnello's inhabitants.

There was something mysterious about this man Impellitteri whom they were awaiting, and whom no one knew, because he had been taken away as a baby of one year old, fifty years ago; and who was now returning, surrounded with glory like a saint from paradise, from America; and who, though unknown to everybody, was nevertheless one of them. There was something mysterious about his birth, as about that of Homer, and of Christopher Columbus (or, to be more precise, of Jesus Christ); and there was something miraculous about his return and his approaching epiphany.[21]

In addition to those Italians who came to see him in person were many from all walks of life who, unable to make personal visits, extended their heartfelt thanks in other ways. The most famous of these was ninety-one-year-old former Italian premier, Vittorio Emmanuele Orlando, perhaps the world's oldest statesman and a fellow Sicilian, who wrote an apology to the mayor that infirmities kept him from personally greeting the Sicilian-born American official. Orlando interpreted Impellitteri's visit as an opportunity to create an indissoluble link between the United States and Italy as "they again join in the fond hope of further advancing civilization and greater power for both countries.[22] While Impellitteri could do little about bringing back to America all those who entreated him, he did bring some tangible gifts in the form of $800 to rebuild a convent and, after consultation with Isnello's mayor, $2,400 for a necessary public work for all the townspeople-- public baths. Deemed most desirable in 1951 when no more than a dozen villagers had fixed, modern bathtubs, with time and growing affluence, these public facilities fell into disuse. An occasion of unparalleled personal joy to Impellitteri, the Italian visit deserves to be recognized as an immensely successful step toward the implementation of American foreign policy. Accordingly, as the Sicilian-born mayor was completing his first year in office, he could not help but be pleased that, domestic administrative problems notwithstanding, he was making a positive mark in advancing American foreign policy. It would merely take a return to New York, however, to realize that city problems not only persisted but actually intensified.

NOTES

1. Columbus 36 no. 1 February 1951): 1.
2. Chester Reporter, November 13, 1950.
3. Box 49, file: Mayoralty Campaign 1950, VRI.
4. Richard Polenberg, One Nation Divisible (New York: Penguin Books, 1980), 86.
5. New York Times, December 31, 1950.
6. Glen Cove Record, November 23, 1950.
7. Chelsea-Clinton News, July 13, 1950.
8. Il Progresso Italo-Americano, November 9, 1950.
9. New York Daily News, December 24, 2950.
10. Sunday Mirror, March 18, 1951.
11. Message from the Mayor to the Board of Estimate and Council, April 2, 1951, Box 1, file: Art Communication, VRI.

12. <u>Congressional Record</u> 82nd Cong., 1st sess. (March 7, 1951), A2670.

13.Letter from Robert Moses to Lazarus Joseph, August 9, 1951, Box 1, file: Comptroller, <u>VRI.</u>

14. Memorandum No. 1, November 16, 1950, Box 65, file: Memos to Departments, <u>VRI</u>.

15. New York <u>Times</u>, July 12, 1951.

16. Theodore Lowi, <u>At the Pleasure of the Mayor</u> (Glencoe, Ill.: Free Press, 1964), 59-64.

17. Telegram from Bill McMenamin to Ed Carr, July 2, 1952. Letter from Ed Carr to Jack Tierney, April 25, 1952, Box 59, file: Mayor's Messages, <u>VRI</u>.

18. Harry S Truman, <u>Memoirs by Harry S Truman, Years of Trial and Hope</u> (New York: Signet, 1965), 279.

19. <u>Il Momento</u>, September 20, 1951.

20. Carlo Levi, <u>Words Are Stones</u> (New York: Farrar, Straus and Cudahy, 1958), 35-36.

21. Levi, <u>Words Are Stones,</u> 37-38.

22. Letter from V. E. Orlando to Impellitteri, October 4, 1951, Box 59, file: Mayor's Messages, <u>VRI</u>.

7

A City of Headaches, A City of Hope

Nothing ever is what it seems. In many respects this could be said of the United States in the 1950's as it proffered a lineament, on the one hand, of a society beset by overwhelming problems wrought by an escalating Cold War that moved from harsh rhetoric to bloody violence in Korea, contention over internal security that led to loyalty oaths and witch-hunting, and work stoppages in major industries as organized labor exercised its considerable clout. On the other hand the same nation projected an image of wholesomeness as typified by preoccupation with traditional, if otherwise stultifying, values of education, homemaking, religion, private home ownership and security. It was a time, critics charged, when Americans wallowed in sterile, balsamic, selfish pursuits that found concern over crabgrass in manicured front lawns of new suburban developments of greater moment than the fragility of the United Nations. These were the years of pursuit of the American dream as typified in the exodus from the central cities to the sanitized developments on the outskirts, where old-fashioned American ideals characterized interrelationships and when American television households, now approximating two thirds of the public, were attracted like unerring magnets to the adventures of "Ozzie and Harriet," "Life With Father," and most especially, "I Love Lucy." Yet change was discernible. From Hollywood there emerged a new breed of actors such as Marlon Brando, Montgomery Clift and the short-lived James Dean, young, moody, introspective personalities whose existential, unconventional approach defied the mythical "Jack Armstrong" all-American, wholesome boy image. Indeed the nation was experiencing a more profound dualism than most observers acknowledged.

New York City, of course, mirrored these varying

currents so markedly that in the face of many
positive trends, by the fall of 1951 problems of
municipal workers discontent, a serious dock strike
and work stoppages in other areas of the private
sector as well as smothering traffic congestion
clamored for attention. If there was ever an
Impellitteri "honeymoon" period, it clearly was
over. For city employees, the need for higher wages
and shorter hours led the list of grievances. The
mayor's record of sympathy toward city workers'
requirements was estimable and of long-standing;
years before becoming mayor, he was outspoken on
behalf of the necessity to increase their wages in
keeping with the spiraling cost of living. Indeed
earlier in 1951, Impellitteri had approved a $250
across the board annual increase for city workers,
a move that, while well-intentioned, was hardly
adequate to keep up with inflation. The result was
intensified agitation especially from the line
organizations within the police, fire and
sanitation departments. The city administration
readily acknowledged that its employees were
underpaid, estimating, however, that it would
require a prohibitive cost of $100 million to
adjust wages. It likewise endorsed the propriety of
the forty hour work week concept, which had become
standard in American industry but which had thus
far eluded attainment by numerous city workers
because of the realization that it would cost
additional tens of millions dollars. Thus,
acknowledged desirable goals had to be matched with
budgetary realities. With financial constraints
precluding instant implementation, at long last on
July 10, 1952, the mayor announced the initiation
of the forty hour work week for 55,000 city
employees to be installed in stages. Working with
budget director and the future first mayor of
Jewish background, Abraham D. Beame, Impellitteri
ordered a gradual reduction of hours uniformly
throughout city departments to the end that a
maximum work week of forty-two hours be effective
by July 1, 1953 and that full implementation be
accomplished in the 1953-1954 fiscal year.

Although movement was in the right direction, the
gradualist approach was not appreciated by the
affected city employees, largely policemen, firemen
and sanitation workers, who insisted on an
accelerated schedule of implementation of a reduced

work week with an advanced starting date at
variance with the city administrations. To
emphasize their demands some of the line
organizations undertook aggressive actions
including strike threats, a march of 5,000
protesting firemen on City Hall and the
organization of militant unionism, even
contemplating the potential benefits of
establishing a policemen's union under the aegis of
Transport Workers Union (TWU) President Michael
Quill, the bete noire of management, who frequently
resorted to threats, bombasts and strike actions in
efforts to cow city administrations into
submission. One consequence of the dispute was a
bitter clash between Impellitteri and the ambitious
new city council President Rudolph Halley, who had
encouraged firemen and policemen to engage in mass
demonstrations. At one point this encouragement
found angry policemen on the verge of trekking to
the Mayor's residence at Gracie Mansion. These
deplorable actions led to a severe Impellitteri
animadversion.

As Mayor, and with the approval of the Board, I intend to
present to the State Legislature a program designed to give
all City employees financial relief . . . .
After receiving Mr. Halley's letter, I consulted with all
the other members of the Board of Estimate and they are in
agreement that no useful purpose would be served by
encouraging mass demonstrations of police and firemen, or by
affording their representatives an opportunity to give further
expression to their desires for salary increases. This can
only lead to similar requests by other groups of City
employees, all of whom deserve the same consideration as the
police and firemen. The conditions which they would present
have been aired before the Board of Estimate at public
hearings.
I deplore the coincidence in timing between Mr. Halley's
letter and the call for a mass demonstration of police and
firemen. I would admonish the new member of the Board that
encouragement of mass demonstrations by those charged with
maintaining law and order in our City is fraught with serious
danger to the public welfare.[1]

Although police unionization under Quill's auspices
did not ensue, just the thought of it was enough to
send shivers up the spine of city officials who
only too well-remembered instances in which TWU
city transit workers did in fact strike. Not
surprisingly both the mayor and police
commissioner, although acknowledging the

correctness of the stand of the Policemens' Benefit
Association (PBA), the main police line
organization, were, nevertheless, extremely
unsympathetic to the unionization proposition and
repeatedly referred to the Condon-Wadlin law that
forbade strikes by public employees. For some time,
a degree of tension between city policemen and the
Impellitteri administration persisted, although the
situation was not significantly exacerbated, in
part because Impellitteri tried to support some of
the policeman's desires. For example, at the risk
of serious criticism and in contradistinction to
many leaders, including Police Commissioner Murphy
himself, Impellitteri delighted the PBA by voting
against delaying a policeman's pension on
retirement. The mayor also pledged himself fully in
favor of expanding the size of the police force and
was likewise supportive of Murphy's successor,
George P. Monaghan, when the police department was
the subject of a federal investigation over police
brutality charges in March 1953.

For their part city sanitation department workers
applied pressure via the "slowdown" technique, that
is a procedure short of outright work cessation but
one marked by a decided deceleration of normal work
activity. Believing that the use of this tactic
earlier in the year had helped them obtain a cost
of living increase, sanitation workers once again
resorted to the slowdown maneuver in an effort to
wrest concessions from the city administration
during Impellitteri's fall 1951 absence from City
Hall due to his tour of Italy. The leadership of
Sanitation Men's Local 111A of the Building Service
Employees Union sought to pressure Acting Mayor
Joseph Sharkey into giving in to its demands,
otherwise it would greet the returning mayor with
mounds of uncollected garbage. At issue was not so
much the merits of the sanitation workers' case,
that is wage increases and reduction of hours,
matters on which virtually all critics were agreed,
but the illegal manner by which they sought to
obtain them. What the union was engaged in was
considered in violation of law as well as an
endangerment of public health. Given Impellitteri's
stand, it was a gamble that did not succeed.

Here is a matter of policy on which Mayor Impellitteri's
stand is known. He made it perfectly clear when the union

pulled a similar stunt last July . . . . Faced with a previous slowdown Commissioner Mulrain shelved the rules on which it was predicated and suspended the ringleaders. This had the approval of the Mayor and won the applause of the public.[2]

As if that were not enough, the returning mayor and his wife witnessed still another case of labor discontent in an instance of a wildcat longshoremen's strike that threatened to put him in an embarrassing situation over the handling of his own luggage. The potentially serious problem was dexterously handled by the Impellitteris as they personally carried off their own baggage with assistance from the mayor's staff. In sum, proliferating labor headaches were principal issues by the end of 1951 and would remain dominant for the remainder of his term.

The most difficult labor headache of all revolved around the actions of the city's transit workers. Uninhibited by state labor laws to the contrary, in order to obtain their demands transit workers conducted strikes, slowdowns and other actions that impaired the transit system, and thereby proved to be a thorn in the side of all New York City mayors. The reason for the TWU success was inherent in the formation of the organization and in its leadership. Organized largely by Communists in the 1930s at a time when there were two private subway lines that subsequently were purchased and operated by the city, the TWU perceived the value of being the exclusive bargainer for transit workers as well as the importance of a formal labor contract. Thus, even after it severed its relations with Communists, the TWU comprehended that one way to circumvent the somewhat unsympathetic, semiautonomous New York City Transit Authority, was to apply direct pressure on the mayor. Skillful in the exercise of political power, the union accordingly exerted greater influence than other normally less militant line organizations with the consequence frequently being the attainment of generous concessions as, for example, in the LaGuardia and O'Dwyer administrations.[3] Once again displaying militancy, the transit union sought further concessions from Impellitteri.

While Quill had enjoyed considerable success for his union under the two previous mayors, he would be required to extend his Irish charms to the

fullest to gain a hearing with newly elected
Impellitteri whom he had openly opposed in favor of
Pecora in the 1950 election. With considerable
effort Quill seemed to have achieved some success
in improving relations with the Sicilian immigrant
chief executive, however, the Irish immigrant
continuously applied pressure on City Hall on
behalf of transit workers. Denounced for his
demands, in reality, Quill's outrageous posturing
was by design as he masterfully manipulated the
transit systems that were divided between public
and private ownership. This stance enabled him to
use a hedge-hopping process whereby gains in wage
and work conditions achieved on city lines were
used to jack up standards on private routes and
vice versa. Accordingly, in violation of state law,
and a no-strike understanding, in June 1951 Quill
launched a half day work stoppage on the city
transit system in order to pressure the city to
accelerate adoption of a shorter work week.
Although criticized for not immediately invoking
the Condon-Wadlin Law that prohibited strikes by
public employees, Impellitteri's threat to use it
infuriated Quill, who in reality was testing the
mayor to determine whether or not he could achieve
his ends through threat and bluster as he had done
previously. The situation was well described by
labor writer A. H. Raskin,

Mr. Quill, who built up his union on strike threats that
almost never had to be carried through, is up against a new
kind of adversary in Mayor Impellitteri, and there is real
worry in union and official circles that the customary rabbit
will not pop out of the Mayor's hat in time to head off a tie-
up this year.
    This would be a marked departure from the tradition
established in the regimes of Mr. Impellitteri's predecessors,
Fiorello H. LaGuardia and William O'Dwyer. The sulphurous
exchanges of insults that went on between the mayors and the
blustery leader of the transit workers were usually part of
a carefully devised script that worked its torturous way to an
amicable settlement before any serious damage was done to the
riding public. Mr. O'Dwyer developed a particular zest for his
jousts with Mr. Quill, and the contrived crisis with its preordained end became a hallmark of his administration.
    Mr. Impellitteri lacks that appetite for corny drama that
characterized both of his forerunners. Mr. LaGuardia was the
only man in New York who could outshout Mr. Quill; Mr. O'Dwyer
was the only man who could match him in blarney.[4]

By the fall of 1951, the forty hour work week had

become a major issue for the transit employees not only on city lines but also those working for private bus firms. For the moment the emphasis was on the latter who claimed they could adjust wages only with a fare boost. In keeping with his enfant terrible reputation and in violation of a signed contract, in November 1951 TWU president Quill threatened the city with a bus strike of private bus lines. Under a semantic shield, the Irish American labor leader then asserted that the walkout would force such massive numbers on to subways so that employees in the latter transport system might have to quit also. Impellitteri saw this for what it was--a strike threat to be resisted. Unlike other mayors before and after him, who swiftly submitted to outrageous TWU demands, Impellitteri courageously spurned Quill's proposed solutions by rejecting any notion of a rise in bus fares; he likewise categorically refused to become involved in negotiations between private bus operators and Quill, aside from enforcement of the existent and binding "no-strike" contract feature.

With regard to city-owned bus lines, Impellitteri seemed to have sensed the inherent detriment to the city in operating a public transportation system as opposed to private enterprise. Whereas the lodestar of private enterprise in a competitive market atmosphere is a profit and loss statement, the same is untrue of public ownership where, because service, not profit is the guide, the result frequently was operating losses. Accordingly Impellitteri proposed that the city sell the affected bus lines to private firms, carefully conditioning his recommendation on a labor agreement between the companies and the union--a proposition that did not come to fruition because of an impasse over pension funds, which consequently led to a retraction of the divestiture proposition.

In an effort to force Impellitteri to speed up plans for creation of a seven member Transit Authority and direct it to consider the strike threat, in November 1951, Quill's transit workers conducted a one day wildcat strike. Resisting the pressure to impetuous acquiescence, Impellitteri reiterated his position that the existing contract be obeyed. Subsequently he moved to the creation of a Transit Commission that would study the matter

but that was not to become involved in labor
negotiations. In the interim, when it became
evident that a link existed not only between wages,
hours adjustments and a fare increase, but also
that a fare augmentation impacted the financial
stability of the whole transit system, many close
to him in his administration such as Robert Moses,
supported a fare rise as the only way to end
deficits. In a rare display of public disagreement,
even the mayor's own wife favored fare escalation,
a position the mayor dismissed by inferring that
she was misquoted and "not in politics."
Nevertheless, once again succumbing to a latent
stubborn streak, Impellitteri became adamant, for
months he unilaterally opposed a fare rise. That
the pressures on Impellitteri were enormous was
reflected in the plaintive plea of a Baptist
minister before the City Council, who prayed that
the body reject the fare increase notion. "May they
remember the common man who stands with his family
at the subway entrances and looks at the distance
with less than a dime in his pocket."[5] Finally,
when it became evident that the unbending antifare
rise stand rendered the city's case before the
state legislature more vulnerable, in June 1952
Impellitteri relented and signed a bill that
indirectly raised the fare by ending the 15 cent
combination ride. Beyond that he reiterated his
opposition to proposals for fare increases.

As 1952 wore on the determined transit workers
continued to apply pressure, including a threat to
strike the private bus lines early in 1953, in an
effort to wrest concessions from the Impellitteri
administration. Undoubtedly union politics also
played a role. As a Quill biographer stated, "The
first ten months of 1952 were decisively
unproductive insofar as bus drivers were
concerned." They had suffered layoffs, been under
management pressure to speed up activity and put up
with poor equipment. Above all the period was
marked by a "lack of substantive victories by the
TWU."[6] On the brink of the bus strike Impellitteri
responded by using television, declaring that the
city could not afford demands for wage increases
and that it would not give in to heavy-handed union
tactics. He pointed out that at $1.91 per hour,
city bus drivers were the highest paid of that
occupational ilk in the nation and that demands of

$2.25 to $2.51 per hour were as "unrealistic as dreamland." At the same time he attempted to develop a thoughtful plan aimed at facilitating an opportunity for private bus companies partially to accommodate their workers. In pursuit of the design he called on the state legislature to approve the Omnibus Redevelopment Corporation Law under which qualified bus lines could be exempt from state taxes. In an impressive, albeit losing argument, he showed that there was precedent for this strategy because the state already had made exemption allowances in the case of the Long Island Railroad. Scenting an opportunity for toppling New York City Democrats from power, the Republican dominated state legislature was disinclined to make things easy for the city and summarily rejected the proposal. On January 1, 1953 private bus lines drivers walked out in a major test of power with the Impellitteri administration, which refused to approve a fare rise that private entrepreneurs insisted was a prerequisite for their acceptance of union demands for a forty hour week. The union did not dispute the companies' claim, leading Impellitteri to conclude that both the line operators and the union favored a fair increase--an action deemed highly unpopular, especially in a mayoral election year. The union strategy clearly was to so inconvenience city commuters in the midst of inhospitable winter weather, that the administration would yield. There was indeed enormous stress on Impellitteri to approve the fare hike from groups like the Chamber of Commerce, and workers on city-owned transit systems who observed a ban imposed by the union on working overtime. Some of the city's most prestigious newspapers lashed out at the mayor unmercifully with editorials charging that the strike reflected a mismanaged city on the part of a public-be-damned city administration.[7] It was not as if the mayor refused to propose viable solutions because two weeks before the strike commenced he offered a tax-relief plan drafted by his Transit Advisory Commission, which would request that the state free bus operators from paying $3,000,000 in taxes and for the city to likewise surrender $844,000 in levies. Rejected as insufficient by both bus line operators and the TWU, the strike commenced.

An estimated one third of the city's

approximately 300,000 daily riders who normally
depended on the privately operated bus lines, were
now forced to find alternate means of going to
work, shop, visit, and so forth. Attention was
riveted on the city because it alone had authority
to raise fares. Evidently more than a typical two
party labor-management dispute, this polemic also
brought up the role of the municipal government and
was further complicated by political maneuvers. At
least one half of the eight members of the powerful
Board of Estimate, whose approval was indispensable
for a fare increase, had their eyes on the upcoming
November 1953 mayoral election. For obvious reasons
none of the mayoral hopefuls craved to be perceived
as   approving   an   unpopular   fare   increase.
Simultaneously   they   all   jockeyed   for   positions
politically advantageous for themselves and at the
expense of their rivals, especially the incumbent
mayor. A tricky situation at best, it was made even
more tenuous due to Impellitteri's circumscribed
view   of   the   power   of   his   office,   namely   that
because he was only one of eight board members each
of whom had an equal vote, he could not dictate
policy.   It   was   on   the   one   hand,   an   admirable
gesture   of   participatory   democratic   government
recognizing   full   participation   by   all   elected
officials, yet on the other hand impractical in a
situation   where   erstwhile   colleagues   were   also
competitors for his job. Less democratic, LaGuardia
and   O'Dwyer   were   more   inclined   to   charter   the
course of action, habitually ignoring the views of
other elected city officials. In a sense it was
analogous   to   strong   presidents   clearly   leading
Congress or bypassing it when it suited them, as
opposed to weak presidents who accepted a major
role   on   the   part   of   Congress   in   designing
government   policy.   Each   has   its   merits   and
drawbacks.
      Surprising almost everyone, especially Quill, who
thought the inconveniences attending the strike
would so demoralize city officials that they would
succumb, New Yorkers bore up admirably even as
freezing   rain   and   snow   worsened   conditions.
Improvisation was the order of the day as plucky
New Yorkers used subways, city-owned bus lines,
taxis and private car pools in order to cope with
the   dislocation.   Daily   the   strain   increased.
Looking toward next November's election, political

opportunists within the city administration such as Council President Halley, launched moves to undercut the mayor's resolve, actions that so irked Impellitteri, who was so anxious to maintain administration solidarity, that he responded with vehement denunciation. Even Impellitteri's critics acknowledged that a united front of city officials was essential if the city was to prevail against Quill. For his part the labor leader threatened to close the subways in a sympathy strike action. Despite enormous hardships the city refused to bog down as vital services were sustained and an expected decline in business failed to materialize. Even before the strike began Impellitteri proposed that the union and the companies select an arbitration panel to decide the main issue of a forty hour work week with no loss in prestrike take-home pay. "It was a good plan the Mayor came up with," opined one editorial.[8] Originally resistant, the union continued the strike until January 29, when the TWU, faced with a rebellion within its ranks and virtually admitting that the strike was not succeeding, agreed to return to work in favor of laying its case before the board of arbitration. The reality was that Quill ended the strike on the mayor's terms, namely that a fair arbitration be promulgated between the bus companies and the union and that the ten cents fare remain intact. Although some interpreted this as a victory for Quill's tactics in view of the arbitration board's subsequent awards on November 18, 1953, to grant drivers the forty hour work week at a high wage, it also was a victory for Impellitteri in effecting concessions from bus companies and convincing strikers to return to work. The evaluation was well described by an interesting and unusual turn-of-phrase Daily Mirror, editorial.

The bus strike limps toward an end, and, as usual, there is no victory for anybody . . . .
No victory for anybody? Lets amend that. Quill started out with a strike threat and fully expected that the Mayor and the City Government would fold up like cardboard figurines and grant his every demand even if it meant an end to the 10-cent fare.
Hadn't that always happened before?
But somebody changed the script. A stubborn little guy named Impellitteri, his head bloodied, perhaps, but unbowed by

editorial brickbats, called Quill's bluff . . . .
The Mayor has warned, however, that no settlement will be
allowed to jeopardize the 10-cent fare. In that, there is a
victory for the innocent bystander, ordinarily the first
victim of a strike, the public--in this instance more than
3,000,000 [sic] daily bus riders.[9]

Comparisons with how other mayors dealt with the
TWU is instructive. During his mayoralty,
LaGuardia, who was every bit as forceful and
pugnacious as Quill, and who was convinced that a
strike against the city was unlawful, nevertheless
succumbed under the threat of a transit work
stoppage when he "was virtually coerced into
accepting the contracts until the following
year."[10] When confronted with the issue of
avoiding a strike with the transport workers in
1948, O'Dwyer agreed to grant a very substantial
raise even if it meant ending the traditional five
cents ride and doubling subway fares to ten cents.
Whereas O'Dwyer saw fare increases as workable
solutions, Impellitteri was much more adamant and
determined to resist the formula. The record also
shows that because Robert Wagner was indebted to
Quill for his union's financial support in winning
the 1953 mayoral Democratic nomination as well as
for ongoing TWU support as mayor, he too succumbed
to Quill persuasion on a number of occasions. In
1956, for example, Wagner rebuffed the appeals of
disgruntled motormen who had defied Quill as they
sought to obtain recognition from the city
administration. When one considers the concessions
of mayoral successor John Lindsay to Quill's
demands for a generous wage increase and an even
more beneficent supplementary pension feature that
"set a precedent for other city employees that
would make all other bargaining difficult," and
thereby bequeath the city with a permanent heavy
financial burden, it becomes even clearer that
mild-mannered Impellitteri exercised admirable
strength in resisting Quill's pressure on behalf of
the city and its future.[11]

The record demonstrates that under Impellitteri's
guidance, a number of labor problems were
satisfactorily resolved. The issue of a forty hour
work week that simultaneously consumed much of
private industry in the city, also wreaked havoc on
city life and accordingly taxed Impellitteri's

mediating talents. For example, when a strike launched by bread truck drivers of four striking locals of International Brotherhood of Teamsters, A.F.L., in July 1951 led to an extreme shortage of white bread, the result was widespread price-gouging and violence throughout the metropolitan area. Housewives complained that bread, which normally sold for eighteen cents a loaf, was now selling for thirty-five cents and within a couple of days was disappearing from shelves altogether. Independent company truck drivers not involved in the strike reported personal assaults, vehicles damaged and threats of further harm. When "cooling off" efforts proved unavailing, Impellitteri was called in to name a fact-finding committee that quickly produced a five day work week plan, albeit with provisions for the possibility of higher bread prices. Nevertheless, the incontrovertible result was that the dispute was resolved fairly expeditiously only after Impellitteri stepped in. Notwithstanding the favorable conclusion, the New York _Times_ could not resist carping even on the flimsiest grounds, as it engaged in unwarranted specious argument by inferring that bread company officials welcomed City Hall intervention in order to be able to raise prices. The fact of the matter was--and it was even reported in the same newspaper--that before bread prices could be raised, the approval of the federal Office of Price Stabilization was required. Moreover, federal officials specifically indicated that the city-sponsored settlement would have no weight in the agency's decision.

Impellitteri also had a hand in resolving grievances on the part of city teachers. In pursuit of a pay raise for a year and a half, the educators resorted to the technique of refusing to conduct extra curricular programs, activities prized as rich sources of educational enrichment. When an accord was reached via a pay raise in August 1951, the mayor was congratulated for the role he played in bringing an end to the unhappy situation and thereby helping to promote the community's esteem for its teachers.

In December 1951, after being informed by his labor troubleshooter Daniel Kornblum, that contract talks were making no progress, Mayor Impellitteri stepped in to head off a threatened strike by coal

and fuel delivery men. He appointed a three man
citizens committee to promote a settlement and
alerted affected city departments to prepare
emergency measures should a strike ensue. The
resolution of the discord which came on December 28
with an agreement of a $2 a day pay raise and other
benefits, averted a strike that would have caused
undoubted hardship.

Another serious problem afflicting the city
occurred in January 1953, when, after postponements
and futile efforts to resolve the dispute on the
part of state mediators, 11,400 cemetery workers
went out on strike. That this brought pain and
anguish to grieving families who were forced to
carry coffins and dig graves for their dear
departed ones can readily be imagined. Against a
background of 472 unburied corpses, which left an
intolerable situation not only for the affected
bereaved families but also for the general public
health of the city, Impellitteri stepped in to try
to resolve the situation. Employing every effort to
bring both cemetery management administrators and
cemetery workers union leaders together, finally,
on February 17, he was able to report a
satisfactory settlement that caused strikers to
return to work.

In addition to strikes and other instances of
labor unrest, New York, along with the rest of the
nation in mid-century, was compelled to deal with a
number of scandals. On a national scale, there was
an instance of federal civil servants who were
forced to resign over implications of improprieties
in the tax office. In 1951, West Point, the famed
United States Military Academy, was tainted with a
major headache in the wake of revelations of
wholesale cheating that ultimately led to the
ouster of ninety cadets. Within the city there were
exposures of scandals that were a reflection of
this sorry state of affairs in many walks of life,
however, they were traceable basically to the pre-
Impellitteri mayoralty. One of these embarrassments
rocked the world of amateur sports with revelations
that over a dozen players on leading college city
basketball teams received money from a convicted
gambler in return for agreeing to "fix" scores in a
number of major college games. The end result was
that several individuals with promising
professional careers received jail sentences, while

big-time basketball at Long Island University, New York University and City College went into decline.

During the Impellitteri mayoralty New Yorkers read about the unearthing of instances of "official corruption," virtually all of which predated his administration by years. One of the most notorious and publicized instances concerned a bookmaker named Harry Gross, who wore flashy, custom-made suits and silk monographed shirts, who patronized a barbershop daily and whose pockets bulged with hundred dollar bills, and whose style of living was said to be an imitation of the big-time underworld "big shot" of Hollywood perception. Gross's high living habits were supported by millions of dollars earned via illegal activities, aided and abetted by dozens of Brooklyn policemen, extending back to 1942. Thus, beginning in the LaGuardia mayoralty and growing extensively under the O'Dwyer regime, the Gross bookmaking operation was estimated to have taken in $20,000,000 a year with payoffs to policemen approximating $3,000,000 annually. Gross also was said to give clothing and television sets and other favors to cooperating law enforcement officials, including the use of his influence to try to get a police captain's daughter admitted to college. In an extraordinary display of rectitude while serving as city council president, Impellitteri proved the main supporter of Brooklyn District Attorney Miles McDonald, who faced opposition from the O'Dwyer-dominated Board of Estimate, when he sought city funding to conduct an investigation into the matter. The probe, which began in 1949, revealed that those implicated included high officials in the police department, twenty-one of whom were indicted with fifty-six others being named as co-conspirators. McDonald had apparently built up quite a strong case, only to see it destroyed when Gross refused to testify against the accused, thereby accepting a long prison term for himself. Nevertheless, police departmental hearings resulted in forty-five discharges from the police force, including twenty three in February 1951, the largest mass dismissal of policemen in recent history. The Gross scandal proved to be a damaging indictment of the predominant Democratic party and prompted Pecora to consider it a major cause for his defeat.

Another scandal concerned James J. Moran who, as

Mayor O'Dwyer's appointee as first deputy fire
commissioner, used that position to enrich himself
through extortion. Specifically, Moran supervised a
scheme whereby oil burner contractors were required
to pay gratuities to inspectors before their
applications to proceed were approved. Determined
not to tolerate corruption in government, on March
22, 1951, after Deputy Fire Commissioner John Crane
admitted that he had paid off Moran, Impellitteri
immediately demanded and received the fire
commissioner's resignation. "Politics had nothing
whatsoever to do with my decision," he informed
Moran, explaining it was "based solely on the
ethics and morality of good public policy, and I am
positive that the people of this City will support
it."[12] Moran would be convicted of perjury for
false testimony before the Senate Crime Committee
and sentenced to a five year prison term.

One of the few scandals actually to occur while
Impellitteri was mayor and that he was resolutely
determined not to tolerate, revolved around sewer
installations in the Laurelton section of Queens.
In keeping with his determination to provide an
upright administration, Impellitteri, personally
visited the Queens site and was most supportive of
proposals to allocate city funds to conduct an
investigation into charges that sewer contractor
Victor Clemente had defrauded the city of $74,000
by deliberately installing faulty sewers not up to
city specifications. Despite denials and delays by
the accused, in 1955, a record 202 day trial
concluded with conviction of Clemente and three
Queens County employees for fraud and conspiracy.

The most spectacular scandal to unfold in this
period was the one unearthed by the Special Senate
Committee to Investigate Organized Crime in
Interstate Commerce, commonly known as the Kefauver
Committee, named after the committee chairman,
Senator Estes Kefauver. In May 1950, virtually at
the same moment that Senator Joseph McCarthy was
beginning his crusade against the threat of
communism, other senators on the Kefauver Committee
left Washington to conduct hearings on organized
crime in various cities; nowhere, however, did the
Committee attract attention as it did in New York.
Aided by perhaps the first extensive use of
television for public hearings, the deliberations
made enthralled American viewers aware for the

first time of a national syndicate with an array of intriguing personalities. Daytime television viewing audiences grew to phenomenal new heights as the media technique provided a prominent example of its impact by enabling the committee to throw a powerful searchlight into the role of crime in politics. Here, before millions of people who eschewed their usual fare of inane programs and watched with fascination in eerie half-light, the frosty screens that depicted the stream of individuals taking part, unfolded a kind of morality play. Among the cast of characters was Senator Kefauver, the Tennessean who was quick to see the unfolding spectacle as a vehicle that could propel him to the White House (he did in fact make a strong but losing bid to gain the Democratic nomination for president in 1952 and eventually became the party's vice-presidential nominee). There was also Senator Charles W. Tobey, a straight-laced teetotaler from New Hampshire whose latent animus toward the city now found ready grist for his mill. There was also William O'Dwyer, former mayor, who in spite of illness, returned to testify while sporting a suntan that was in sharp contrast to the predominant New York pale faces and that likewise revealed his current job as ambassador to Mexico. There was Rudolph Halley, committee chief counsel, whose relentless questioning gained a considerable following, which he parlayed to election as New York City Council president in 1951 and then as a serious mayoral candidate in 1953. There was also a string of notorious underworld figures such as Meyer Lansky, Joe (Doto) Adonis, Thomas (Three Finger Brown) Lucchese, Willie Moretti and statuesque Virginia Hill, the actress woman friend of many gangland personalities. Among this company was Frank Costello, who as the acknowledged "prime minister" of racketeers, was the "star" of the hearings, and who, because his avid covetousness of respectability, refused to plead the Fifth Amendment in a futile effort to proclaim his innocence. As the most famous and best-connected underworld figure of his time, the always immaculately attired Costello, parried questions of his interrogators in the hopes of being exonerated of charges of undue political influence, only to betray himself as a consequence of his fidgeting,

nervous hands and buffed fingernails, which became
the center of attention and served to convince many
of his guilt.

The avowed purpose of the investigation was to
shed light into the tie-up between organized crime
and politics. On May 1, 1951 the committee
completed its formal report identifying New York
City as a major center of organized crime and the
headquarters of the Costello-Lansky-Adonis "crime
syndicate." It scathingly assailed O'Dwyer for
directly and indirectly contributing to the rise of
crime in the city by his actions as a city
official. The committee charged O'Dwyer with laxity
against top gangster echelons in the matters of
gambling, narcotics, bookmaking, murder and
waterfront activities, and, in addition, accused
him of impeding promising investigations into these
rackets. Costello was said to have perjured himself
by denying that he was a factor in city politics
throughout the 1940's and thus earned a jail
sentence. It is important to note that none of this
reflected on Impellitteri who not only had no role
in the deplorable affair, but actually had called
attention to the unwholesome connection between
Tammany Hall and Costello during the 1950 mayoral
campaign. Although the committee never actually
proved the existence of an organized crime
syndicate, it established the notion so credibly
that it was constantly referred to by subsequent
government inquiries into the subject. As a
consequence the myth was perpetuated that organized
crime was an alien import brought to the United
States by Italian immigrants, especially Sicilians,
in the form of the Mafia, a highly centralized,
secret entity whose criminal ways preyed on the
weaknesses and vices of the public.

In 1952 the New York State Crime Commission
conducted an extensive investigation into criminal
activity in the New York waterfront that also
sought to uncover actions that predated the
Impellitteri administration. While the Mayor
appeared before the commission voluntarily and
apparently without negative implications, hundreds
of individuals, including some Impellitteri
associates such as Frank Sampson, testified under
the coercion of subpoenas. The only point at which
Impellitteri's name came up was in the testimony of
Thomas (Three Finger Brown) Lucchese, who

acknowledged knowing the mayor and appearing at certain political and charitable functions. Aside from these specific instances, Lucchese testified that no other meaningful meetings or understandings were involved.[13]

Whether it is organized crime or individual criminal activity on the street, there is hardly an issue of more concern to city residents. From the first to the final decade of the twentieth century one finds persistent demands to control crime rending the air and posing almost insuperable challenges for New York City mayors. As is typical with virtually all mayors, Impellitteri was reluctant to acknowledge a crime rise during his tenure, however, an August 11, 1952 police department report documenting an acceleration of crime could not be easily dismissed. Despite explanations from the mayor and police department officials that the perceived increase was really attributable to a basic change in the reporting procedure that now included instances that previously were regarded as trivial, the public was not assuaged. Indeed the slaying of a patrolman the very day the report was issued only served to give further credence to belief in a crime wave. By the fall of 1952 the problem had become so acute that residents of the West Side were said to fear to leave their homes at night, prompting prominent clergymen representing the main religious persuasions to appeal to Impellitteri to bring the police department to full strength. This was a reference to the fact that the police department was 1,454 men short of the allowable quota of 19,847. Even the allowable quota figure was said to be too low because it was based on assumptions of a city population smaller by a million people. When it became clear that Impellitteri's effort to becalm people's fear by announcing the addition of hundreds of new policemen within the next several months proved unacceptable, the mayor bit the bullet and accelerated the process even if it might mean cutting some less essential services. Eight hundred new policemen were appointed by the beginning of October, and 200 civilians were added to relieve police personnel engaged in clerical duties for deployment as foot patrolmen. This was the kind of action that evoked ready, positive response. Vigorous congratulations were extended to

Impellitteri for strengthening the police force. "More than that he has made it clear beyond any doubt that he subscribes to the belief which has long and incessantly been expounded upon in these columns and elsewhere that what counts most is putting more cops on the beat."[14]

Given conditions that are endemic with city life in industrial societies replete with congestion, overcrowding, space limitation, filth, poor air quality, transportation difficulties, and so forth, it was evident that post-World War II urban mayors were required to give increased attention to manifold problems of an environmental nature. In collaboration with Commissioner Robert Moses, Mayor Impellitteri moved for the adoption of municipal policies designed to control pollution and purify sewage. Imbued with the conviction that such programs were necessary, Impellitteri demonstrated his resolve on the occasion of the dedication of a six million dollar Rockaway pollution control plant, even at seemingly staggering costs to the city. Proudly declaring that "the health and welfare of our people" came before dollars, his stance was applauded as forward-looking and in the best tradition of good government. He was praised

for the dignity of public service, which deserves appreciation when it is well done . . . . Mayor Impellitteri deserves the support of the public in leadership that fulfills that aim. Every New Yorker has a self-interest in seeing such a purpose boldly carried out.[15]

Noise abatement and smoke control were additional environmental problems that had long plagued the city and that had prompted former Mayor LaGuardia to have enacted antinoise ordinances aimed at prohibiting unnecessary horn blowing and loud radio playing. During Impellitteri's tenure as President of the city council, that body had expanded such programs by distributing pamphlets which demonstrated the adverse impact of excessive noise. As mayor, Impellitteri reorganized smoke control by taking the matter out of the Department of Health and Housing where smoke control was subordinate to other concerns and not energetically pursued. Under Impellitteri's prodding, in August 1952, the New York City Council and Board of Estimate approved a new Department of Air Pollution

Control to be headed by Dr. Leonard Greenburg, an expert in the field. Impellitteri also called on the governors of New York, New Jersey and Connecticut to cooperate in coordinating efforts on the matter. Using statistics that showed increases in summons and fines in his first six months in office, Greenburg was able to report that his agency was making significant progress in enforcing the city's antismoke laws.

Improvement of traffic and transportation, both of which had direct impact on the city's economy and environment, merited high priority on the Impellitteri administration agenda. The evidence is that he gave it significant attention, although it was also an area for which he was severely criticized. One New York <u>Times</u> analysis of the situation inferred that because of municipal indifference and a lack of enlightened business leadership, New York City lagged behind other major cities with respect to traffic management and safety. Not surprisingly this led to lacerating editorial sarcasm. "Surely Mayor Impellitteri is not going to take much credit for relief of traffic congestion . . . . The Mayor has had to be prodded every step of the way in the minor gains made."[16]

The rebuke notwithstanding, the record shows that he was cognizant of its importance early in his tenure. Accordingly, he summed up his perspective succinctly in his annual message to the city council.

> The problem of traffic congestion which plagues every large municipality in the country is still with us. Improvement in traffic control, the provision of parking facilities and the improvement of traffic arteries, has lagged far behind the rapid growth of traffic. We are doing all in our power to deal with the situation. The problem is being attacked on many fronts. We are replacing trolleys with buses and removing the tracks from the streets. Little used and run-down elevated structures are being removed. We are reconstructing old bridges and building new bridges and arterial highways.[17]

Under Impellitteri's leadership, a significant number of archaic, traffic-impeding trolley car lines operating in the city were phased out. Appropriately, the replacement of ten Brooklyn trolley car lines with buses, left the city with only three remaining such lines. Plans were also

put into place to begin to demolish the Lexington
Avenue Elevated and the Third Avenue Elevated
Structures, both of which hampered a more rapid
flow of arterial traffic. The mayor was well aware
of rampant complaints that the cost of delivering
bulk merchandise in the city had risen 25 percent
in the previous three years because of the city's
failure to end parking abuses. These traffic
violations handicapped the delivery of furniture
and other bulk items because there was inadequate
space for vans and trucks to park at curbs. Indeed
the situation had become so grave that coal and oil
suppliers resorted to sending their own emergency
vehicles equipped with powerful jacks to remove
illegally parked cars. All of these inconveniences
and extra steps tended to increase costs that would
be inevitably passed on to ordinary citizens.

In grappling with the problem Impellitteri
developed a three part plan to untangle the city's
snarled traffic: to bar trucks over thirty feet in
length from the garment district during day
business hours; to require that all city agencies
and utilities companies file in advance requests to
open streets so as to coordinate schedules and
bring minimal dislocation; to convert First and
Second Avenues to one way traffic flows. The last
point resulted in an embroilment among
Impellitteri, Manhattan Borough president Robert F.
Wagner, Jr. and Construction Coordinator Moses,
thereby leading to one of the few open splits
between the latter and the mayor.

The Impellitteri administration's determination
to make a basic attack on arterial congestion due
to problems revolving around automobile parking was
reflected in the promotion of the Merli bill, a
measure designed to engage the municipality
directly in the task of providing and maintaining
adequate parking facilities. Financing was to be
accomplished by a combination of city initiatives
including revenue from parking meters and the
issuing of bonds for capital construction of
offstreet parking spaces. The plan, which required
the approval of the state legislature, called for
the activation of a new Parking Authority to
preside over the city's massive parking problems.
Predictably there was opposition, in part due to
the ongoing feud between Impellitteri and city
council President Halley and his allies who

frequently were thorns in the mayor's side, and in part due to the fear that the measure would grant unwarranted power to a newly activated Parking Authority. The Citizens Union, with the support of Wagner, objected to the city council's approval of the plan in the absence of sufficient information as well as the lack of hearings to allow groups who opposed the plan the opportunity to present their case.[18] As it turned out the state legislature did not approve that bill.

Notwithstanding Impellitteri's earlier unheeded call for sale of certain city bus lines, the Sicilian American Mayor did sponsor some important innovations in the transportation system. In September 1952, the city closed a deal for the purchase of the Far Rockaway line from the bankrupt Long Island Railroad. Within the next few years that line was linked to the city rapid transit system thus effecting an expansion of service to city residents in that far corner of Queens.

Facing strong opposition from within and outside his administration, Impellitteri proved steadfast in his promotion of the new Second Avenue subway. He called for movement of the project despite a warning from Comptroller Lazarus Joseph that the city should reexamine the project in the face of stringent finances. Citing a growing city transit deficit as the city's major financial weakness, the city's banking community also called for a delay of the project. Although construction of this subway line did not come to pass until after Impellitteri's tenure, he deserved credit for his unchangeable support.

By the early 1950's motor traffic congestion caused by to increased vehicular volume and abuses in parking in unrestricted areas by United Nations personnel in midtown Manhattan, had reached such proportions that relief could come only with the building of a third tube of the Lincoln Tunnel. Consistently advocated by Wagner and Howard S. Cullman, chairman of the Port of New York Authority, the project was postponed fifteen months because of opposition by Moses, backed by Impellitteri, over the issue of adequate street connections. In his determination to move the project along, Cullman sought to apply heavy pressure on the mayor, a strategy that backfired as Impellitteri refused to be intimidated. Even though

Cullman was supposedly under Moses's influence, as
Caro infers, this did not deter Impellitteri from
giving him a stinging tongue-lashing.[19] Informing
Cullman that he was well aware of his "grave
responsibility," to the city the chief executive
admonished the Port Authority official.

When I vote on the matter, I shall know what it is about and
shall recommend for or against the plan which the City
Planning Commission submits and as my conscience dictates. I
don't propose to have you stick the city for approaches you
should pay for, or foist on the city a scheme that won't fit
into a sensible plan for solving the crosstown and marginal
traffic problem. The Port Authority will have to do what is
best for this city and not what suits the Commissioner from
New Jersey . . . .
   If protecting the city against additional traffic hazards
and heavy future city expenditures which can be avoided, is
bad business for the city, then we in the Board of Estimate
are guilty of neglect. Meanwhile, we suggest you get yourself
in a frame of mind to cooperate.[20]

Thus, all sides favored the third tube, with one
side more concerned that the others were
overminimizing the additional, if only temporary,
traffic congestion that would result without
properly planned street accesses and egresses. When
the points of dispute were finally resolved, the
project was approved. Notwithstanding his earlier
opposition because of concern over necessary street
connections, by his presence as principal speaker
at ground breaking services for the third tube
connecting New York and New Jersey on September 25,
1952, Impellitteri provided a further demonstration
of his commitment to improving transportation in
New York. At the occasion a beaming mayor asserted
that the project had full city blessing and that it
augured well for the city's traffic future.
   Because of its sheer physical size, which dwarfs
all other cities in the land, its heterogenous and
constantly changing population, its numerous and
confusing overlapping authorities and
jurisdictions, its powerful business leaders
seeking to exercise influence, its fractionalized
politics and its competition with other cities and
states seeking to attract its businesses,
management of New York City has frustrated every
mayor. Administration of the city is complicated
furthermore, by its unique legal status. John
Lindsay summarized the situation succinctly.

A mayor, moreover, is the chief executive of a stepchild form of government. The states are an integral part of our constitutional framework. The United States is, after all, a federal union of states--sovereign states, we are reminded at every political convention. But a city does not exist by constitutional guarantee. It is the creature of a state, subject to its mandate. It cannot raise its resources according to its lights, raise its debt ceiling, change its tax base, or change the way its government works without the approval of the state. It is, in other words, a governmental unit without direct access to power obliged to take direct responsibility for the problems of the people.[21]

Realizing the import of this observation it becomes understandable that successful management of city affairs is highly dependent on the establishment of good relations with the state government in Albany. During the Impellitteri years this meant gaining a hearing with the frequently hostile, Republican-dominated state administration, a task that Impellitteri conducted with skill and some degree of success. Just as he did in 1951, again in 1952 and 1953, the mayor trekked to Albany repeatedly to confer personally with Governor Dewey, Lieutenant Governor Frank Moore and State Comptroller J. Raymond McGovern as he beseeched them on behalf of the city's budget proposals. Just as importantly he also sought to obtain bipartisan support in the state legislature, an effort perhaps humiliating but nevertheless politic. To the detriment of the city, not every mayor has exercised the same skillfulness in cultivating Albany. For example, in November 1990, Mayor David Dinkins was faulted for committing a major blunder in failing to foster legislative support for funds in order to expand the city's police force. "The prospects for financing Mayor David Dinkins' sweeping anti-crime plan have been damaged . . . by his lack of personal diplomacy with politicians whose support is needed to make the plan a reality."[22] Although Impellitteri did not necessarily obtain complete approval of his budget plan in those years, he was partially successful in 1952 and a little less so in 1953.

Assessment of the effectiveness of city management brings up the role of the mayor's management survey committee established in 1950 by Mayor O'Dwyer, whose endorsement guaranteed approval of the somewhat lukewarm Board of

Estimate. The mayor's management survey committee's
was designed to provide a systematic, scientific
review of city administrative functions with an eye
to effecting greater efficiency and economy.
Although the official chairman of the committee was
Comptroller Joseph, the real engine behind the
committee's activity was its Executive Director Dr.
Luther Gulick, eminent Columbia University
political scientist and president of the Institute
of Public Administration. Other members of the
twenty-seven-man committee included a variety of
political viewpoints and strong personalities, a
formula that was bound to result in controversy. As
Gulick recalled, "the stresses and strains within
the committee were based upon these differences of
interest and background." In addition, there were
political considerations that could be attributed
to committee members as in the case of Comptroller
Joseph, for example.

Larry Joseph had political ambitions, though he could never
quite make up his mind whether he wanted to be a candidate or
not. But he didn't want anything to happen in the Committee,
or didn't want to have any surveys made or published, which
might embarrass him in a subsequent electoral situation.[23]

Although good government and reform groups saw this
as a virtual panacea, as the only remedy to bring
rationalism to bear on an otherwise irrational,
archaic form of city government, others were more
cynical. Budget Director and committee member
Abraham Beame termed the cost savings economies
predicted by the committee as exaggerated.
Imperious Robert Moses, another committee member,
was even more caustic in his evaluation of the
committee's value, rejecting the notion that
enforced efficiency and economy could result in
substantial savings in the light of city population
growth and increased public expectations of
services that required expansion of programs and
expenditures. Admitting the possibility of some
cost reductions via elimination of patronage exempt
positions, Moses calculated the potential savings
as minimal, and in a further rebuke, maintained
that they were approximately equivalent to the cost
incurred to conduct the management survey. Moses
furthermore, regarded Gulick and his associate

reformers to be engaging in hypocrisy in as much as they simultaneously called for drastic economies yet vociferously insisted on additional expenditures for their pet projects. Consequently, he resigned. The offended Gulick could not resist commenting to the Construction Coordinator, "God never designed you to work with any committee or board."

In actuality Impellitteri's record vis à vis the Mayor's Committee on Management Survey should be evaluated as moderately successful: neither implementing numerous far-reaching changes yet incorporating many committee suggestions. He rejected committee recommendations that were in fact drastic and revolutionary, as, for example, a reorganization plan which rested on the principle of autonomous city departments under a Director of Administration appointed by the mayor. This was in reality akin to the city manager plan that Impellitteri emphatically denounced as unworkable in a large and complex city. Predictably this stand earned Impellitteri the castigation of Gulick who was a leading advocate of the city manager form of municipal government to replace the mayor's committee plan; although the truth of the matter was that hardly any of the nation's big cities had adopted the city manager idea. Rather impressed with a sense of his own importance, Gulick tended to step on many toes, even as he viewed himself above the game of grimy politics. Thus, he alienated many people in the administration by charging the police department with poor management and calling for a reduced role for the city comptroller. Gulick saw himself a tireless advocate of seemingly fundamental municipal governmental changes that were "as original as was the constitution of the government of the United States when it was proposed in 1789." Accordingly, he was inclined to judge Impellitteri's administration on the basis of how closely it conformed to his views--and he usually found the city wanting.

Nevertheless Impellitteri took some steps in keeping with committee recommendations such as his concurrence with the committee's thinking in opposing a fare increase, namely that it would result in such a drastic reduction in the use of transit facilities as to constitute a serious economic loss. In other matters there existed

honest professional differences between different
sets of experts. For example, while Fire Department
Commissioner Grumet and his advisors felt it unwise
to eliminate certain fire companies, as advocated
by the committee, yet Grumet readily acknowledged
the value of other committee recommendations that
his department almost immediately implemented.
Heeding the advice of the committee as well as his
Board of Management Improvement, in November 1952
Impellitteri created an interdepartmental Health
Council to coordinate the jurisdictions, policies
and programs of the Health, Hospitals and Welfare
Departments in the field of health services. Acting
in conformity with committee recommendations,
Impellitteri moved to create a Civil Service
Classification Bureau in a restructuring of the
machinery that articulated relations between the
city administration and civil service employees. In
the matter of the city budget Impellitteri not only
deliberately awaited completion of the committee
report early in 1953, in order to incorporate
department calls for economies into his new budget
proposals, but he also asserted that steps toward
economy compliance had already resulted in a $30
million budget reduction. The 1953 city budget,
furthermore, reflected the committee's suggestion
that a program budget system be substituted for the
line-by-line itemization method of expenditures,
wages, salaries, materials and supplies. The mayor
also directed department heads to determine where
surplus positions could be found and abolished.
Finally, before he left office, Impellitteri
approved the Gulick plan to establish the office of
City Administrator answerable to the mayor, to
oversee the work of city departments. This was done
to accommodate Wagner, the incoming mayor, who,
belatedly endorsing the idea of a city
administrator position, reversed an earlier stand.
Political expediency rather than confidence that
the new post would actually cut city spending by a
predicted $75 million was evidently at work in
Wagner's decision. In view of the favorable press
Gulick's committee was receiving in the press, it
was desirable to look good. "Neither Wagner nor
DeSapio believed anyone could cut city spending by
$75 million, for what might be saved in one area
would always be needed in another." But there was
nothing to lose, for if Gulick could not bring

about the savings, it would be proof that no one could, and if he did the credit would go to Wagner anyway. When Gulick was named city administrator in 1954, he undoubtedly saw it as an approximation of the city manager idea, yet its role in positively effecting city administration was questionable. Nor, it might be added parenthetically, was Gulick above using despised pressure politics to advance his agenda.

Calls for changes in the city's government were part of an old scenario wherein reformers periodically proposed sweeping new ways of dealing with problems. As to whether or not the highly touted modifications did result in substantial improvements is debateable. More clear is the realization that the summons for changes reflected the constantly changing make-up of the city--a subject to be further explored in the succeeding chapter.

NOTES

1. Release in response to President of the City Council, December 12, 1951, Box 51, file: Mayor's Annual Messages to the City Council, 1951-1953, VRI.

2. New York World Telegram & Sun, October 2, 1951.

3. Sayre and Kaufman, Governing New York, 435-38.

4. New York Times, June 10, 1951.

5. New York Times, March 2, 1953.

6. L. H. Whittemore, The Man Who Ran The Subways. The Story of Mike Quill (New York: Holt, Rinehart and Winston, 1968), 180-81.

7. New York Times, December 30, 1952.

8. New York Journal American, January 26, 1953.

9. New York Daily Mirror, January 30, 1953.

10. Whittemore, The Man Who Ran The Subways, 85.

11. Whittemore, The Man Who Ran The Subways, 285.

12. Letter from Impellitteri to James J. Moran, March 22, 1951, Box 7, VRI.

13. New York Times, November 15, 1952.

14. Brooklyn Eagle, September 26, 1952.

15. New York Times, August 11, 1952.

16. New York Times, May 5, 1953.

17. Mayor's Annual Message to the City Council, March 9, 1951, Box 51, file: Mayor's Annual Messages to the City Council, 1951-1953, VRI.

18. "Across From City Hall," Citizens Union News 7, no. 3 (April 1952).

19. Robert Caro, <u>The Power Broker: Robert Moses and the Fall of New York</u> (New York: Vintage Books, 1975), 692-93.

20. Letter from Impellitteri to Howard S. Cullman, December 12, 1951, Box 73, file: New Expressway Construction, <u>VRI</u>.

21. John V. Lindsay, <u>The City</u> (New York: New American Library, 1970), 14-15.

22. New York <u>Times,</u> November 17, 1950.

23. <u>Gulick Memoirs</u>, Oral History Collection, Columbia University.

8

A City in a State of Flux

Incorporated in 1653, New York City celebrated its tricentennial anniversary with appropriate commemoration of its Dutch and English origins and its phenomenal growth into the premier city in the United States if not the world. It was evident that the small, struggling and barely solvent seventeenth century community had undergone spectacular expansion and change in the interim and that the 1953 tricentennial offered a unique opportunity to assess the city in mid-century. Included in the yearlong festivities was a special Metropolitan Museum of Art exhibit of paintings by Rembrandt and other masters of Dutch art, a parade replete with the police department band, horses, a "Pony Express" rider and a television play on religious freedom. Although their absence from the city precluded renowned songwriters Richard Rodgers and Oscar Hammerstein from orchestrating an otherwise ambitious gala, there were, nevertheless, many city functions that revolved around the tercentenary theme. Mayor Impellitteri played his part well by presiding over the John Wanamaker Department Store lighting of a 300 candle-bedecked special birthday cake, by representing the city at public ceremonies honoring 300 New York City men who had enlisted in the Marine Corps for the tercentenary occasion, and by hosting the mayor of Amsterdam and other Dutch dignitaries who paid an official visit.

Given its unique status as the nation's foremost city, the metropolis has always had its share of critics prepared to document With asperity its imperfections: corruption, mismanagement, uncleanliness, and so on. Yet even these customary critics admitted that with all its defects, New Yorkers took too much for granted, namely that the city was a good place to live, that it possessed much beauty and culture, that its arts, music, dance, and drama centers were suffused with a creative spirit. The city could rightly boast of the energizing enrichment brought about by its world-famous museums, libraries, institutions of learning and spiritual centers. As home to the most notable wholesale and retail centers, the largest banking firms and the nation's greatest corporations, New York not only was a stimulating place in which to live but also in which to work.

New York as a work center was one positive attribute that was taken for granted in mid-century, however, a review of its role in this regard could provide meaningful insight. Thus, in 1953 New York soared to a record high of nearly four million persons earning wages, with approximately one third engaged in manufacturing, one fourth in retail and wholesale trade and the largest group in services. The last cluster was the more typical as it engaged in the type of activity that set New York apart from other cities. One perceptive analysis described the group this way:

The average city toiler rents either his brain or a special skill to entrepreneurs dedicated to satisfying a small fraction of a particular (and a frequently unvoiced) desire shared by many persons, by the week, month, or year, on a piecework basis.

It is this factor which may be responsible for the special New York brand of insecurity, and its compensatory attitudes, aggressiveness and cynicism which critics of the city constantly complain about.[1]

This was a city that never slept. Whether it was during the dark of a winter night as half-empty busses prowled the avenues or on board the underground subway trains that provided nocturnal service every twenty minutes before dawn's paroxysm of movement, New Yorkers were on the job. As the marketplace of the world, as the international world headquarters in consequence of the United Nations headquarters location, daytime New York was indeed an incredibly busy place. Visitors could not fail to be impressed by the concentration of so many people performing their work in so small an area. Six hundred thousand people worked in the garment industry, one of the city's major industries; 250,000 were employed by banks, brokerages, insurance firms and exchanges; 119,000 worked in the real estate field, while 125,000 earned their living in the city's extensive printing and shipping trades. In mid-century, as almost always, the city gave the appearance that it was ever-building; indeed with 103,000 employed in this field, construction was a major employer. As one of the world's greatest cargo and passenger ports, its import and export industry was legendary, as was the New York waterfront-generated business that was said to encompass up to 10% of the city's work force. It was estimated that in 1953 of the 4,000,000 employed in the city, 2,600,000 working New Yorkers were men and 1,400,000 were women. Some revealing average salaries were $65 per week in the garment industry, $78 for brokerage employees, and $107 for fur workers. The average New Yorker earned $1,869 annually against a national average of $1,436.

Depending on one's perspective the social, economic, physical and political changes that characterized New York City in the early 1950's could be deemed auguries of impending doom or heralds of a better tomorrow. While some critics decried the sad state of the city's position, others confidently prognosticated its ascent to greater heights predicting that its population would total nine million by 1970. Whatever the future might bring, the reality was a portrait of a mid-century cosmopolitan metropolis of nearly eight million people living in 2,433,465 dwellings. Although most residences compared favorably with the rest of the nation, there was the disturbing fact that a minority lived in 112,117 subpar dwellings, most lacking private baths, and in general considered to be so dilapidated as to be unfit for human habitation. Despite this negative dimension, on the other hand, there was a positive aspect of 450,185 single family homes occupied by their owners, whose average value of $12,149 was significantly higher than the national average. Thus, when joined with the extremely expensive dwellings on Fifth or Madison Avenues, this gave credence to the image of a wealthy city. Next to Manhattan, Queens had the highest real estate values. Brooklyn had the most dwellings as befit the most populous city borough, while Richmond had the fewest homes. At $5,109 a year the average New York family income was considerably higher than the national average income of $4,350.

The city was undergoing sweeping physical changes
as old structures were replaced by newer and more
daring architectural forms. Those that impressed
the most were the United Nations General Assembly
Hall and the predominantly glass enclosed sheath of
the dashing Lever Building, that monument to the
glass and soap industry. Although more and more
people were resorting to airplane travel, newly
built attractive luxury super liners like the
gleaming white USS United States, aroused
excitement. That transportation movement within the
city was undergoing transformation was illustrated
by the recent opening of the Brooklyn-Battery
Tunnel, following the closing of the Aquarium in
lower Manhattan and a dozen years of digging. By
1953 the growing number of television households
marveled at Bishop Fulton J. Sheen's inspirational
program that was able to compete favorably with
veteran professional entertainment shows like that
of Milton Berle. Although the great Joe DiMaggio
had retired, New Yorkers could cheer the New York
Yankees new center fielder, Mickey Mantle, who was
on his way to becoming a star in his own right.
That inflation was an irrepressible fact of life
was brought home to New Yorkers who now had to pay
one penny more for a total of four cents for the
New York Daily News.
    As it was in its beginning, but even more in mid-
twentieth century, the city was the home of many
peoples and tongues from all over the world. The
classic catch-basin for newcomers to this land, the
dynamics of migration made its indelible impact on
city   social,   economic   and   political
interrelationships. The ever-changing demographic
makeup of the city once again underwent radical
alteration as tens of thousands left their old
ethnic neighborhoods for suburban life. Italian
Americans,   perhaps   the   archetypical   rural
immigrants now city dwellers, just like other
ethnic groups, were caught up in the dynamics of
the changes and exiting traditional neighborhoods
of parents and grandparents even while newly
arriving immigrants supplanted them. While most
were still encompassed in the proletarian category,
there was notable emergence from that background
into the realm of minor entrepreneurs who were
increasingly breaking with aspects of their ethnic
past. This point was illuminated within ethnic

neighborhoods as realistically revealed in the movie classic, <u>Marty</u>. A remarkable slice of Italian Americana, the film struck poignant, responsive chords among the second generation of that era as it articulated the juxtaposition of a beefy bachelor butcher from the Little Italy of the Bronx struggling with the demands of his ethnic subculture, and his joy at finding happiness with a homely but understanding young non-Italian woman.

Demographic analysis demonstrated that the significant loss of city population was more than offset by both increased birth rates among city dwellers and an equally important annual inpouring of newcomers (which together added 260,000 a year) to occupy the flats and apartments recently vacated, and to augment the labor force with its voracious appetite. The verity was that large numbers of the influx were members of minority ethnic groups--blacks from rural southern settings and nonEnglish-speaking Puerto Ricans from America's Caribbean possession--which tended to exacerbate intergroup friction. It was of course an old story: The newcomers satiated many of the low-paying jobs yet those longer in residence in city neighborhoods regarded them as poorly educated, low income racial types, whose exotic religions and customs were not only decidedly different, but also threatening to their own recently achieved positions of relative comfortableness. For their part the newcomers naturally resented blatant discrimination that relegated them to an inferior status on the job and in residential housing.

City race relations during the Impellitteri mayoralty were typical of the postwar period in so far as proffering an articulated vision of toleration albeit against a condition of defacto segregation of black people. While recent years had been characterized by important strides in locating jobs in the general work force, particularly in the civil service category and while there had occurred discernible political emergence, the major gains--those associated with the 1960's civil rights movement--were still to come. Impellitteri was personally free of outlandish and even subtle prejudices in matters of race, a point confirmed by those acquainted with him for many years. Ruth Whitehead Whaley, the first female African American graduate of the Fordham University Law School and

the first of her race and sex to practice law in
New York and North Carolina, had been a law school
classmate of Vincent and came to know him quite
well. Subsequently, during the Impellitteri
administration, she attained the highest ranking
post of all black women to that date within city
government as secretary of the Board of Estimate.
She readily attested to Impellitteri's refreshingly
open way when dealing with blacks by contrasting
his attitude with that of many whites who, upon
meeting a black person whom they had not seen in
many years, revealed their self-consciousness by
asking only about other black classmates. Not so
with Vincent with whom she could converse on any
subject minus the racial content and who did not
stoop to a pseudoliberal patronizing posture by
commenting on how much he liked blacks. She
regarded him as an honest, sincere man who dealt
with people on the basis of equality.[2] More than
once the mayor visited black areas where he
reiterated his view of toleration. "We have no
place in the educational institutions in this City
for anything which nurtures or gives comfort to the
methods of intolerance," said Impellitteri on the
occasion of his visit to a Harlem Church in 1952.
He asserted, furthermore, a commitment to
toleration for the city and a "determination to
wipe out the forces of bigotry and bias wherever
they exist; and that job properly starts in our own
City, in our own neighborhood, and with our
children."

This favorable disposition notwithstanding, as
mayor Impellitteri was subject to a degree of
coercion in hopes that he would become more active
in speaking out against racial discrimination. In
one instance in 1952 he was exhorted to take
explicit action in condemning the brutal killing of
a black NAACP man and wife in a house bombing in
Florida. Understandably embittered, New York
African American leaders applied persuasion on city
officials to demonstrate their outrage by refusing
to take vacations in the sunshine state. The
Impellitteris did in fact refrain from taking a
Florida winter vacation that year, however, it is
doubtful their decision was due to the pressure;
indeed in April of that year they journeyed to one
of their favorite Palm Beach settings, explaining
it was suggested by the mayor's doctor who had

ordered a rest. This did not mean, however, that Impellitteri ignored the black leaders' appeal, a plea to which he responded vigorously by denouncing the dastardly bombing deed, "I most heartily subscribe to the protest rally that is planned against the Florida outrage."

Within the city there were at least a couple of instances of race-related problems with which Impellitteri had to deal. A 1951 racial riot between whites and blacks in Franklin Lane High School in Queens saw Impellitteri respond by directing the Mayor's Committee on Unity to investigate the riot and monitor racial relations at the school. The committee did in fact conduct an investigation that permitted it to issue a report of improved relations a year later. The Mayor's Committee on Unity proved to be one of Impellitteri's more important steps to promote interfaith and interracial understanding. Designed to investigate immediately charges of bigotry, it won repeated citation as a valuable resource to combat discrimination. Moreover, Impellitteri's promise to give the committee full support was duly hailed as a positive step. Nonetheless, racial problems emerged as charges of police brutality within the police department provided yet another example of the struggle over racial tolerance. Specifically, there were accusations that police department officials were covering up instances of brutal treatment of blacks. The furor over these charges took on national significance as flashy Harlem Representative Adam C. Powell attacked the New York City Police Department in the halls of Congress and as the Department of Justice investigated the matter. The announcement that the charges proved unfounded led to further accusations of a "secret deal" between the city and the federal agency; it also led to demands that the mayor dismiss Police Commissioner Monaghan. Against this substantial pressure Impellitteri showed his mettle by an emphatic denial of the existence of collusion, a stalwart defense of the police department and, in a demonstration of true loyalty, a refusal to oust the Police Commissioner. It is no small matter to note that it was under Impellitteri's mayoralty that a black man was appointed a deputy police commissioner, the first of his race to reach that rank in city history.

Impellitteri projected his civil rights stance beyond the city as, for example, his telegrams supporting a civil rights plank to House Speaker John McCormack, Senator Herbert H. Lehman and Democratic National Chairman Frank McKinney, who were conferring on the matter at the 1952 Democratic National Convention in Chicago. It must be remembered that over the years the Democratic party had split over the sensitive issue. Indeed Harry S Truman faced an uphill battle for the presidency in 1948 because of the defection of Southern Democrats who supported a candidate who favored segregation. Once again Impellitteri, who subsequently attended the convention as a delegate, proved a forceful advocate on behalf of equal treatment of the races by referring to his pride, intermingled with understandable hyperbole, over intergroup relations in New York City where people enjoyed civil rights regardless of race, color or creed.

Puerto Ricans, who were one of the largest ethnic groups to migrate to the city during the Impellitteri years, duplicated the experience of previous groups who had sought out the city as a Mecca of hope for better housing, jobs, opportunities, family life and education. Predictably they encountered similar problems as, for example, acceptance only in inferior dwellings, obtaining the most menial and poorest paying jobs, being provided with service in crowded community resource centers and schools, a difficult language handicap and a misunderstanding of their culture. To better understand this population in 1949 the city created a permanent body called the Mayor's Advisory Committee on Puerto Rican Affairs in New York City. From its beginnings sensitive Italian American leaders such as renowned educator Leonard Covello were active in promoting the work of the committee. For his part both as council president and even more so as mayor, Impellitteri, who likened their problems as newcomers to those faced by his own parents after their arrival in a new country, was sympathetic to their plight and supportive of steps to alleviate living conditions in Puerto Rican neighborhoods. In March 1951, he personally visited Puerto Rico in an effort to solidify relations between the inhabitants of the island and the United States. Echoing a liberal

hope, Impellitteri predicted that it would merely
be a matter of time before they became "familiar
with our language and customs" and thereby make
their contributions and become assimilated. He
sought to promote services to Puerto Rican
newcomers in neighborhoods like East Harlem, which
was then undergoing a transition from the city's
largest Little Italy to El Barrio. Thus, on the
occasion of the opening of a new East Harlem health
center that was designed to bring high levels of
proper health aid to neighborhood residents,
Impellitteri obtained the support of popular Puerto
Rican Governor Luis Munoz Marin, in urging Puerto
Rican migrants to cooperate with the city and make
use of the facility. Relations between Puerto
Ricans and Impellitteri were rather positive and
were additionally reflected in the frequency of
correspondence between Puerto Rican organizations
and the mayor, in his support of many of their
functions by personal appearance or official
communication and in his backing of measures
designed to encourage ethnic pride and recognition.
In November 1952 he proclaimed Discovery of Puerto
Rico Day, and in June 1953 he lent his
administration's endorsement to official
recognition of St. John The Baptist Day as a time
to be set aside to honor those of Puerto Rican
heritage. Accordingly, he successfully encouraged
the city council to allow Puerto Rican civil
service employees paid time off to join with him in
attending the St. John The Baptist celebration, as
well as in an effort to help establish the feast as
a New York tradition comparable to Columbus Day or
St. Patrick's Day.
    In June 1952, Impellitteri ordered a thorough
investigation of a disastrous Brooklyn fire that
had taken the lives of several recent arrivals from
Puerto Rico. The investigation subsequently
revealed that migrants from the United States
island possession in the postwar era were subject
to discrimination and exploitation in New York as
slum landlords crowded them into old and unsafe
apartments that rendered them vulnerable to
accidents and fire disasters such as the
aforementioned Brooklyn inferno. In the wake of
this tragedy the New York mayor intensified his
calls for Congressional hearings in support of
providing additional funds for public housing in

Puerto Rico and New York.

In a further demonstration of his regard for the city's Puerto Rican population, beginning in 1951 Impellitteri incurred the wrath of establishment New Yorkers by his appointment of Puerto Rican Emilio Nunez, rather than an incumbent favorite, to the temporary post of judge of the special sessions--a designation which eventually led to a permanent bench seat. This appointment served to demonstrate that Impellitteri's pro-Puerto Rican stance was more than mere rhetoric, it was something that resulted in meaningful action. Indeed Impellitteri was willing to withstand importuning from friendly elements within the Democratic party, namely James Roe's Queens organization that offered its own nominees for the post. Needless to say while the Nunez appointment resulted in criticism from establishment sources, it also elicited favorable reaction within the New York Puerto Rican community. One Spanish American newspaper noted the Nunez selection as a welcome turn of events of an independent mayor who, in naming a Puerto Rican jurist and political supporter, not only spurned political pressures but also thereby acknowledged his debt to an ethnic community that had played so meaningful a role in his election.[3]

With respect to his relationship to the city's largest nationality element, Italian Americans, Impellitteri remained unyielding in his role of championing their cause, especially when it came to discrimination and defamation issues. Along with other leaders he railed at the discrimination inherent in the nation's immigration law that based immigration on national origin rather than on individual worth. He likewise postulated the view that the recently passed McCarren-Walter Act served to heap "insult upon injury" due to its intolerant assumption, and supported actions of the Italian Committee on Italian Migration to change the law. On numerous occasions he chastised indiscriminate defamation of Italian Americans in the media with compelling lucidity.

Over the years many novelists, screen writers, creators of radio scripts and now playwrights who contribute their questionable talents to television crime have regularly--far too regularly--adopted the literary habit of depicting

Italians as thugs. The knife-wielder, the murderer or the peddler of narcotics all too often bear Latin names in this fiction that pours into millions of homes. It is insidiously indicated that Italians and Americans of Italian origin have a monopoly on criminality. Now, I do not say and I have never said that we do not have our criminals. But we do not have them all. Every other national strain and every section of the nation and the world has its share. Crime has no special national origins or boundaries.

How, then, do we explain this vicious bias. The reason is not ill-will alone. Our own responsibility is even greater for we have done nothing to protect ourselves. We have allowed the fiction to grow until it has penetrated newspapers, magazines, radio and television.

Let us take definite and aggressive action to halt the libels against us. Let us organize to tell the nation that the contribution of Italy to the United States only started with Columbus. Let us remind our fellow Americans of patriots of Italian descent who fought and died for this country in every war from the revolution on. Let us call attention to Italian pioneers who helped open up the west; to explorers who opened areas of wealth and freedom to future generations. Let us tell of contributions to science and medicine, law and public service, religion and commerce, that have been made by Americans of Italian origin.[4]

Impellitteri's unfeigned pride in his heritage was reflected in other ways such as regularly lending his name to Italian American social and fraternal organizational fund-raising functions. In 1952, for example, he and prizefighter Rocky Marciano, heavyweight champion of the world, helped launch the Budget Fund Drive of The Italian Charities of America Inc. Along with Metropolitan basso great Ezio Pinza, he was guest of honor at an October 1952 fund-raising benefit dinner in honor of St. Frances Xavier Cabrini sponsored by the American Committee on Italian Migration. Always concerned with the plight of orphans, some of whom he would greet at City Hall, he was a regular supporter of Boy's Town of Italy, an Italian counterpart of the famous United States facility.

A spokesman for Italian Americans, he remained a steadfast defender of Italian democracy continually denouncing Communist efforts to gain political ascendancy in that country. Although Italian Communists had been defeated in the critical elections of 1948, the issue was far from resolved and would continue to be a source of anxiety for years to come. The defeat of the Christian Democrat Italian Premier Alcide DeGasperi on August 1, 1953, that was attributed to Communists and which was regarded as a blow to the West, underscores the importance that still attached to the topic. Therefore it was meaningful for prominent Italian American anti-Communists to continue to oppose them on behalf of furthering Italy's democratic cause. Impellitteri's Italian connection rendered him the dubious recipient of numerous letters from Italy from parents and children who appealed for his intercession in arranging marriages with Americans. In her missive, in which she enclosed a flattering studio photograph of her dark-haired son, a Sicilian mother beseeched Impellitteri's aid in finding an American girl of Sicilian descent for him to marry. In another instance the mayor received a supplication from an imploring Neapolitan young woman who wrote with a "heart full of hope" that he could save her and her piteous family from poverty and starvation. Citing as a precedent help given to a poor Italian family by the late Mayor LaGuardia, she hoped that Impellitteri likewise could save her desperate family by facilitating her marriage to an American for whom she promised to be a devoted and affectionate wife. There is no direct evidence that Impellitteri responded to these appeals, however, they are indicative of the desperateness of Italians in the demanding immediate postwar years.

New York's 1953 celebratory atmosphere was marred partially by the disquieting execution of Ethel and Julius Rosenberg. A cause celebre in the staunchly anti-Communist climate that characterized the period, the Rosenberg case attracted world attention because it involved the first instance of peacetime execution for espionage in this country. It evoked sympathy also because it involved a husband and wife whose death would leave two small boys orphans. The fact that Rosenberg adherents adamantly rejected the evidence against them and that the principal damaging evidence was introduced by a member of the family, exacerbated the issue. When all appeal routes, including those to the Pope himself were exhausted, the couple were in fact executed. Although an anti-Communist stance was the prevailing posture on the part of major players in New York City politics, there is little indication that city political leaders were directly involved in the matter. Their concern was the arena of practical politics.

As 1953 unfolded New York was caught up in the vortex of politics that annually surrounded the creation of a city budget. Not surprisingly a replica of the previous two years ensued as the city promulgated a financial budget only to find state officials rejecting it and thereby once again underscoring the limitations of city home rule. It was, furthermore, a minor miracle merely to reach a budget accord within the Impellitteri administration when one realizes that many of the individuals within it were in fact jockeying for advantageous political positions in order to challenge and topple the mayor in the upcoming November elections. The situation was further burdened by the debilitating consequences of trying to continue operation of the city's deficit-running transit system.

Citing his intention to terminate the past practice of patchwork financing, Impellitteri energetically directed his fiscal experts to meet with state officials prior to enactment of the city budget in order to apprise them of the city's needs. An innovation in city history, the effort involved numerous hours and days of meetings, undertakings which did not, however, bring about the desired result because state officials failed to respond with offers, opinions or suggestions to the city's proposals. Impellitteri stated that as distasteful as it was to relinquish city operation of its transit system to a state-created Transit Authority, it was necessary to acquiesce in order to surrender the major financial liabilities or otherwise face the unhappy prospects of major layoffs of city personnel. Impellitteri's budget proposal for fiscal 1953-1954 called for expenditures of $1.5 million, including a shortfall of $218 million that would be raised by a series of measures. The state, however, rejected almost the entire list of city proposals thus precluding acceptance and implementation of the city budget. In view of his repeated trips to Albany and his strong messages to the governor, it was ironic that Impellitteri's critics charged him with not doing enough to advance the city's position. Thus, on March 26, 1953, Impellitteri denounced state action in siphoning off millions of dollars in pari-mutuel taxes from races conducted in the city and to which "the City is morally and logically entitled." Again

on May 21, he sent Governor Dewey a message
deploring the state's obfuscation and inconsistency
in rejecting as an iniquitous burden, the city's
call for a raise in real estate taxes so that the
latter could pay its fair share. "Your Committee's
effort to support the position that real estate is
already paying its fair share of the tax burden is
contrary to the report of the state's own
committee on Constitutional Debt and Tax Limits."[5]
Although citation of the state's own study, which
indicated that New York City's real estate rate was
the fifth lowest among sixty-two cities of the
state, meant Impellitteri had logic on his side, it
was to no avail in the face of an implacably
unsympathetic Republican Dewey administration. The
end result was that Impellitteri had to accept
inexpedient state-directed limitations on his
budget, although he did have some success in
gaining state concessions. Criticized by some for
his performance in this regard, others complimented
him for coming out of the fiscal crisis in a fairly
positive position and for his openness in listening
to other Board of Estimate members who wished to
supplant him as mayor, rather than "playing
politics" and blindly refusing to consider their
worth.[6]
There was to be no surcease of political
animation in New York City during the last half of
the Impellitteri administration as attested to by a
bevy of activity. There were the customary efforts
of politicians to ingratiate themselves with
influential leaders, the endless round of fund-
raising affairs so essential to maintaining a
viable political presence, the necessary display of
partisan campaigning within and without the city,
the constant juggling for favorable positions on
the part of major protagonists, the enlistment of
allies or potential allies in preparation for
future political bouts and other collateral actions
designed to insure prominence in party councils. In
other words, it was politics as usual as
Impellitteri approached the culmination of his
abbreviated term and as he prepared for reelection.
Despite a denial that he had come to a decision to
once again run for mayor, as 1952 gave way to 1953,
it was clear that the Sicilian-born official
intended to do just that by attempting the
difficult feat of balancing opposites. That is, he

projected himself as being a true Democrat even while he continued to spar openly with the city Democratic leaders of Tammany Hall. The nearly impossible position of straddling political identification that worked for him so well in 1950 was now put to a further test as he persisted in a political vendetta with DeSapio. Try as he might he could not oust the crafty Greenwich Village leader who was equally averse to reconciliation. "The only way out seemed unconditional surrender by one party to the other. But who wanted to buy peace at that price?" was the way one insider described the situation.[7] Although in his post mayoralty years Impellitteri came to view DeSapio with equanimity, this was not the case in the 1950-1953 period. The animosity was such that the mayor was greatly disconcerted to learn that his seat at the 1952 Democratic National Convention was next to the Tammany leader. A voluntary change of seats by John Lyons, a Bronx Democrat, spared Impellitteri the embarrassment. In retrospect one is tempted to conclude that having failed to defeat his political antagonist even by a mere single vote of the executive committee in 1951 when the mayor was at the height of his political power, Impellitteri should have calculated that with diminished power in 1953, he could do no better against the Tammany boss.

Having failed to knock DeSapio off his political pedestal and further eschewing prospects for rapprochement with the Tammany leader, Impellitteri tried a flanking maneuver, namely reconciliation with Edward Flynn, as a means of being welcomed into the bosom of the regular Democratic organization. Following the 1950 election and much to the chagrin of critics, a degree of cooperation, born of self-interest, existed between Impellitteri and Flynn. The Bronx leader left open lines of communication to City Hall for patronage reasons, while the mayor appointed Flynn men to the Bronx judiciary in the hopes of gaining favor with the powerful party leader. Forsaking a repentant profile but nevertheless swallowing his pride and putting behind him prior differences, in 1952 and 1953 Impellitteri conducted an approximation of a "journey to Canossa" by traveling to the Bronx where, in hopes of gaining the veteran leader's blessings for the mayoralty nomination, he briefly

acknowledged nary a single past difference, as he
endeavored to link himself with the Democratic
Party.

> I have not always agreed with Mr. Flynn on political
> matters. Indeed, we had one major difference. But since then
> he has offered me his friendship and cooperation.
> Ed Flynn and I have also many points of agreement. One of
> the fundamental points on which we agree is that I join him in
> the very firm and very vigorous knowledge that <u>it is not a
> crime to be a Democrat</u>. Some people would have the public
> believe that it is.
> Well despite the assaults, I am proud to be a Democrat and
> I look ahead to continued victories for this party. Opponents
> in all parties are trying to make the voters forget the
> advances that Democratic leadership has brought over the years
> to our nation, our State and to the City of New York. They are
> trying to make voters forget that times are good. They are
> trying to make them forget that their government- and I mean
> their government right here in the City of New York- is giving
> them more services vital to their welfare than ever before in
> the history of this community.[8]

In his 1953 overture to the Bronx leader,
Impellitteri once again hailed Flynn as one who
"will be high on the list of Democratic stalwarts
who have been responsible for the social and
economic progress of the past decades." A pragmatic
necessity, the effort elicited expected ridicule
with one newspaper sarcastically predicting that
the next move would find the mayor "sending his
right arm to Flynn."[9] Unfortunately the elaborate
efforts were not sufficient to alter the equation
coming as they did at a time also when the
physically ailing Flynn not only gave no evidence
of a shift toward Impellitteri but indeed indicated
support for Robert F. Wagner instead. The
reconciliation effort unraveled completely when
Flynn passed away in August 1953, just before the
Primary Day of reckoning, to be succeeded by
Charles Buckley with whom Impellitteri did not have
close ties. With the Democratic party divided as
nominations for the 1953 mayoralty were underway,
Flynn's death had the effect of strengthening the
position of Impellitteri's arch rival, DeSapio, who
now saw a Wagner victory as an opportunity to be
cast as the number one Democratic leader.

Impellitteri's loyalty claims toward the
Democratic party, in other respects was based on
fairly solid substance. In 1952 he joined visiting

President Truman in a New York campaign swing on
behalf of Adlai Stevenson against Dwight
Eisenhower. During the same year he was conspicuous
in the campaign for future president John F.
Kennedy, then running for senator in Massachusetts,
a state in which Italian Americans represented a
sizeable and perhaps even decisive segment.
Realizing the desirability that would accrue to
Kennedy by enlisting the active backing of the
Italian American who held the most prestigious
elected position in the country, Kennedy
strategists obtained Impellitteri's direct and
personal participation by convincing the New York
City mayor to come to Boston to promote the Irish
American candidate. Possessing a sturdy knowledge
of immigration history, the visiting mayor used the
occasion to attack the McCarren-Walter Law for
flouting American democratic traditions. He
reminded his listeners that the law was passed by
the same kinds of conservatives who had previously
dominated the 1907 Dillingham Committee, which had
issued a report prejudicial to southern and eastern
Europeans and which justified the passage of the
detrimental Literacy Test and National Origins
Quota Act. The result of these laws was to limit
Italian immigration to a miserly quota of 5,645
annually, thereby robbing the nation of honest,
hard-working immigrants. He boldly denounced these
laws as injurious and personally gave "thanks every
day of my life that there was no McCarren Act in
1900 to keep my mother and father out of the United
States of America." Citing Kennedy as a friend of
Italy and Italian Americans, he urged his election
to the Senate.[10]

Political pundits had a field day in the early
part of 1953 as they speculated on who might run
for New York City mayor. The field of potential
candidates ran the gamut from the eccentric health
faddist proponent Bernarr MacFadden, self-styled
"Father of Physical Culture," who proposed to run
on the "Honesty Party," only to find his petitions
voided thereby ending his whimsical political
ambition, to the persistent Democratic maverick
Robert Blaikie, who had previously backed
Impellitteri. In addition, there were traditional
party regulars. Among the many names advanced in
Republican circles were those of Robert Moses,
Jacob Javits and Harold Riegelman. Although the

preference of the establishment press like the New
York _Times_, Moses, whose only previous electoral
venture for governor ended disastrously, showed no
interest in running for the office, secure perhaps
in the knowledge, that no matter who became mayor,
he would maintain his influential posts and have a
vital say in city development. Although he did
little active campaigning, Moses remained a
faithful Impellitteri backer. At one point he even
ridiculed as a "manifest absurdity" Republican
Riegelman's claim that as postmaster of New York he
had completely reorganized the New York postal
system. The articulate Congressman Javits, on the
other hand, was definitely interested in the race,
officially declaring his candidacy in February
1953. This did not come to fruition, however,
because in the end the Republican party selected as
the official mayoral standard-bearer, a sacrificial
lamb, Riegelman, described as "honorable,
respectable, decent and dull." The expected
Republican defeat was based on the assessment that
the strongest candidate in the race might be City
Council President Rudolph Halley.

Surging to the forefront originally on the basis
of his role as chief counsel for the Kefauver Crime
Committee that brought him into the national
limelight, by 1951 the dark-haired monotonous-
voiced young prosecutor had emerged as a crime
buster, matinee idol and a New York City
protagonist. Riding on the crest of a television-
generated popularity wave, he was elected city
council president and then proceeded to invoke his
flair for showmanship, to use that medium to
promote his views and career, all the while
competing with the mayor. A political maverick,
Halley lacked commitment and identification with
either of the two major parties thereby becoming
the darling of the city's Liberal party, which, in
nominating Halley, eschewed a decision to ally with
Republicans.

Division and factionalism characterized
developments within the Democratic party as 1953
unfolded. Franklin D. Roosevelt, Jr., Averell
Harriman, Sam Leibowitz, Lazarus Joseph, Frank S.
Hogan and Robert F. Wagner were among the names
that circulated as possible challengers to
Impellitteri. With the inherent advantages of name
familiarity and a powerful pulpit to espouse his

views, incumbency would seem to give Vincent
Impellitteri an edge over his many rivals. And
indeed the city's chief executive did have much
going for him that he sought to exploit. Thus, in
the spring of 1953 he launched a television series
of talks in which he explicated the current state
of the city, taking the opportunity to portray his
stewardship as productive and highlighted by
significant gains and progress. Properly he
emphasized construction of city hospitals and
schools as areas of accomplishment. "The record of
the present City administration demonstrates that,
step by step, a tremendous job was done and is
being done," he intoned before the convention of
the Affiliated Young Democrats, as he proudly cited
his building and rehabilitation program. "We are
carrying forward the greatest hospital building
program ever undertaken by any city in the world."
He also mentioned renovation, rehabilitation and
expansion of the park system, the building of new
bridges and tunnels, the improvement of city piers,
as other achievements that warranted endorsement.

Another Impellitteri advantage lay in the support
given him by the three Democratic county leaders of
Staten Island, Brooklyn and Queens. Of all city
county leaders the most vigorous backing came from
Queens Democratic leader James Roe whose strong
support of Impellitteri in 1950 remained
undiminished and who was conspicuous in actively
seeking to line up additional support. Dismissing
Halley as a pawn of the Liberal party, Roe also
lashed out at Democrats DeSapio and Flynn for
reneging on an agreement to abide by the decision
of the majority of the five county chairmen
regarding the mayoral candidate.

If the Liberals, pinks, political mixbreeds, un-American
opportunists and friends of Alger Hiss seize New York City as
they plan to in this Election, it will be one of the darkest
and saddest eras in the history of our Nation. Unfortunately,
the Leaders of two of our Democratic counties have fallen into
this scheme of seizure. "Rule or Ruin" Flynn's alignment with
Carmine (the sap) DeSapio and unscrupulous segments of Tammany
are selling their constituents, business and labor, "down the
river" . . . .
Impy was offered a Supreme Court Judgeship (14 years at
$28,000 per year) but he would not sell out the people who
elected him. Two weeks ago he was again "offered" the same
bait but his interest is really in the people. He has been a
good Mayor under trying circumstances when every effort has

been made to destroy him.[11]

Because it was the least populous of all the boroughs, the benefit of Staten Island Democratic leader Jeremiah Sullivan's endorsement was primarily of psychological value. For exactly the opposite reason Brooklyn Democratic leader Kenneth Sutherland's support was highly important because it ostensibly could bring the most populous county into the Impellitteri camp. Although there was some initial uncertainty as to where Sutherland stood, in the end he joined up with the Impellitteri people. Consequently, the incumbent mayor had the advantage of endorsement from three of the city's five county leaders. Important as that was, he was conspicuously unsuccessful with respect to the Bronx and met especially adamant and damaging opposition from DeSapio's Manhattan Democratic organization, a crack in Democratic unity that would prove fatal to his reelection chances.

Impellitteri also received the hearty endorsement of popular nonpolitical figures such as Joe Louis whose telegraphed support, while couched in pugilistic terms, was nevertheless insightful regarding the nature of the political contest confronting Impellitteri. "Most people are wise enough to watch the fighter whose always yelling foul because they know he's the one throwing the low blows and is the real dirty fighter. Wish you luck in the coming primary so that comes election a real honest clean fighting champion of all people will remain in City Hall."[12]

Determined not to give Impellitteri his backing, DeSapio first put forth Franklin D. Roosevelt, Jr. as a potential mayoralty candidate. Apparently seriously considering the notion, the late president's son and namesake joined in the Impellitteri-bashing ritual by chiming in with his own criticism of the mayor accompanied by an announcement that he was ready for a draft. When this failed to materialize and when Roosevelt expressed a change of heart regarding a run for the post, DeSapio turned to other names. The viability of Lazarus Joseph's candidacy rested on the fact that he had been a major figure in city Democratic politics for years, had been repeatedly mentioned as a mayoral candidate in 1949 and 1950 and that his long service rendered him favorable to the

large city Jewish vote. As city controller, for
months Joseph had spoken out on various issues
sometimes differing with Impellitteri, although not
consistently. As 1953 unfolded it was evident that
he was seriously considering challenging the mayor,
only to change his mind and not throw his hat in
the ring (indeed by late spring 1953 he declared
his refusal to run for any public office). These
developments caused DeSapio to conclude that Robert
Wagner, Jr. would be the best choice. Determined to
spurn Impellitteri, DeSapio proceeded to conduct a
poll of registered Democrats to obtain a sense of
the feelings of typical party members. The first
results of the poll in May were actually heartening
to the incumbent mayor as the James J. Mahoney
Democratic Association of Manhattan revealed that
he had received 1,435 or 41 percent of the straw
vote--a total 8 percent greater than the combined
vote of his two closest rivals, Joseph at 18
percent and Wagner at 15 percent. More good news
came from the highly respected New York Daily News-
sponsored poll in June that indicated that even
though he was not the number one choice, a
substantial number of New Yorkers polled had
confidence in him. As journalist Frank Conniff put
it,

Despite years of vilification and the added burden of
resentment that traditionally accrues to an incumbent, the
Mayor ran a strong and convincing third in the newspaper poll
finishing behind Council President Halley and Rep. Franklin D.
Roosevelt Jr.[13]

Indeed his showing was so impressive that Conniff
was prompted to draw a parallel between
Impellitteri and President Truman, who had lost the
confidence of the press and party elements who did
not expect him to win in 1948. "Even more than
Harry Truman, Vincent Impellitteri lacked
influential press support," commented Conniff, who
stated that "Columnists adopted him as a clay
pigeon whenever they needed target practice, just
as they did the Democratic standard-bearer in the
dear dead days of 1948." Like Truman, Impellitteri
"lacks support everywhere--except among the
people."
     Unfortunately for the Sicilian American political
figure, when DeSapio's poll was completed on June

16, it saw the mayor winning only one heavily
Italian district, however, otherwise garnering only
21 percent compared to the winner Wagner whom he
trailed badly. Predictably the results saw the
Manhattan and Bronx County Democratic organizations
nominate Wagner for mayor in a direct primary
contest with the other county leaders. The first
Democratic primary contest for that office since
1925 when, in an exciting contest James Walker
defeated John F. Hylan, it was expected that the
Impellitteri-Wagner race would also attract huge
audiences--a development that failed to
materialize.

James Farley, former postmaster and Democratic
national committeeman, Bernard Baruch, erstwhile
presidential advisor and Miles MacDonald, Brooklyn
district attorney were among the other important
Democratic Impellitteri boosters. Farley's
involvement was interpreted as part of an
intraparty fight for control between the Farley
(conservative) and Flynn (liberal) camps. Just as
he did in 1950 Farley exhorted fellow Democrats to
vote for Impellitteri in the primary, asserting
that the mayor had done a creditable job. Calling
Impellitteri's mayoral tenure a good one, the
respected confidant of presidents, Baruch also
called for his reelection. To the extent that an
extreme partisanship dimension was not involved in
MacDonald's support of Impellitteri, it was perhaps
most revealing, resting as it did on an
anticorruption theme. Simply put, MacDonald
provided an illuminating account of a profile of
political courage as Impellitteri put municipal
integrity before personal political aggrandizement
when it came to fighting noxious behavior in
municipal government, a fact that rendered ironic
anti-Impellitteri criticism on the grounds of
iniquity. Having made a career as an anticorruption
district attorney, MacDonald reminded people that
it was Impellitteri who, as city council president
and in direct opposition to Mayor O'Dwyer, was the
mainstay support of efforts to eliminate
corruption.

He well knew of Mayor O'Dwyer's opposition to our proposed
investigation. He knew that if he voted for the resolution and
secured its passage he would incur the disapproval and enmity
of the city's most powerful official. He realized too that his

action in voting to authorize our investigation could well mean the end of his own political career. Yet when the resolution was called for adoption, he voted for its passage.[14]

In the light of this testimony, Wagner's insinuations that Impellitteri was connected with organized crime figures deserve to be labeled as a cheap shot.

Notwithstanding critics who charged Impellitteri with placing the city in a precarious financial position, responsible bankers actually concluded that the opposite was true. On August 31, 1952, John S. Linen, vice president of Chase National Bank vouchsafed that the city's financial situation was indeed very favorable. A review of the city's finances, found Linen asserting that its tax rate compared favorably with any of the larger cities in the state, that its realty tax collections were excellent and that in fact the city was not facing a financial crisis. As a member of the Mayor's Management Survey Committee, Linen's report was equally important as he positively evaluated Impellitteri's record of cooperation and compliance with committee recommendations, affirming that a goodly number of them had already been put into effect and that there was every reason to believe progress would be made on others.[15]

There was an ethnic dimension to the 1953 municipal election. Almost as if to contradict otherwise astute analysis that adumbrated that the cynical acceptance of a "balanced ticket" that had characterized local elections for years was coming under serious attack, the 1953 lineups of the major party tickets were in fact very much in the old tradition of candidate inclusion designed to appeal to numerically large ethnic and racial segments of the electorate. In New York City this meant giving prominence to candidates for mayor, controller and city council president who could appeal to Jewish, Irish, Italian and African American voters. Accordingly, with Impellitteri, a Catholic and an Italian American for mayor, the rest of his ticket included Julius Helfand, a Jew, for controller and Charles Keegan of Irish extraction for council president. German Catholic Wagner was joined by Jewish Abe Stark for council president and Lawrence Gerosa, an Italian American for controller. Harold

Riegelman, the Republican choice was a Jew, while
his running mates were Henry J. Latham, a
Protestant for council president and Congressman
Paul Fino of Italian stock for controller. Jewish
Rudolph Halley, Liberal party mayoral candidate,
was running with Italian American Eugene Canudo for
council president and Protestant Chase Mellon, Jr.
for controller. With one exception every major
candidate for Manhattan Borough President was an
African American thus assuring that the post would
go to a member of that ethnic group. Although there
was much evidence that economic factors had become
more important than ethnicity and that recent
elections had disproved the "balanced ticket"
theory, there was still that realization that in a
city where voters were divided into 35 percent
Jewish, 15 percent Irish, 12 percent Italian and 6
percent black, ethnicity would continue to be a
major factor in the political equation.

With Italian Americans Impellitteri and DeSapio
at opposite ends of the intraparty fight, the issue
of attracting the Italian American vote received
its share of attention. Taking advantage of growing
anti-Communist sentiment, Gerosa, a prominent
member of the ethnic group as well as the Wagner
ticket, dutifully assailed Impellitteri, by
attempting to impugn his character with charges
that left-wing support engineered by Vito
Marcantonio and the American Labor party first
promoted him in 1945. The plausibility of the
association needs to be juxtaposed to a strong
Impellitteri record of opposing communism over the
years, this record was in large part the basis for
a major attack against him by the Daily _Worker_ in
October 1953, which declared that an Impellitteri
victory would be a victory "for extreme
reactionaries." This denunciation would seem to
render ludicrous the charge of being the recipient
of left-wing support. Indeed Impellitteri proudly
pointed to that very rebuke by the Communist daily
as proof of his Americanism. He further proudly
proclaimed that he was the first mayor with "guts
enough" to deny Communists permission to march on
May Day. The mayor assiduously cultivated the
Italian ethnic vote in the belief that to garner
that support was critical in winning the primary.
Thus, in rallies and campaign stops at Democratic
political clubs in Italian enclaves and in

greetings before the people at the sites of feast
day celebrations in Italian American parishes
throughout the city, he called on the ethnic group
for support. Moreover, he obtained favorable
cooperation from the Italian press such as Il
Progresso Italo-Americano, that provided extensive
coverage of his campaign activities including
columns which asked for support on ethnic grounds.
One example of this coverage emphasized the
significance of Impellitteri's tenure to the city's
Italian American community by stating that "In fact
the Italian Americans occupy more positions under
his, than whatever previous administration." Citing
his own humble immigrant beginnings, the article
declared that Impellitteri was committed to furnish
an opportunity for advancement to influential
political positions to those young, intelligent and
deserving people of his own ethnic background.
"Americans of Italian descent must never forget and
must never cease to be grateful for the great works
undertaken by the Impellitteri mayoralty and the
benefits for our New York Italian Americans and for
Italy and the Italian people."[16] It then proceeded
to provide names of six department or assistant
department heads, twelve city judges, and two
members of the Mayor's personal staff as Italian
Americans currently holding important posts.
Americans of Italian descent were exhorted to
demonstrate their gratitude by voting for him in
the forthcoming primary. That this was a matter of
concern for Italian American politicians was
illustrated by the recollections of Assemblyman
Joseph Corso of the twentieth assembly district,
Brooklyn. While the heavily Italian Democratic
district endorsed Impellitteri in the primary, it
was only by a disappointing small margin, causing
Corso to lament, "How can an Italian American vote
for Wagner."[17] In an understandable but perhaps
unwise appeal for the ethnic vote during a Harlem
campaign rally for black candidate Chauncey M.
Hooper for Manhattan borough president,
Impellitteri's eagerness found him inferring that
in opposing him, DeSapio was anti-Italian. "DeSapio
is from my own stock and he is against me. As soon
as a man gets away up his own people try to knock
him down." Not surprisingly the mayor was rebuked
by DeSapio and Gerosa as well as the city press for
the blatant ethnic appeal. Despite the intraparty

fighting, the Democratic primary contest
deteriorated into a bland affair. It was not a case
of failing to commit oneself to the arduous task of
campaigning because Impellitteri electioneered as
hard as ever. As a matter of fact his campaign
schedule was so grueling that veteran reporters
could barely maintain pace with it. A newspaperman
who accompanied the mayor in his cadillac limousine
that followed behind a siren-wailing motorcycle
police escort to "pep rallies" at eight Brooklyn
clubhouses, confessed that he had a hard time
keeping up with Impellitteri. "Campaigning with
Mayor Impy is no cinch. He leaves you pooped. But
the Mayor shows little sign of the strain and
fatigue as he keeps one speaking schedule after
another."[18] Typical rallies saw Impellitteri give
essentially the same message adjusting it only
slightly in order to satisfy the ego of groups he
was addressing. Speaking before Italian Americans
he stressed his Sicilian birth, whereas before
Jewish groups he emphasized the many honors heaped
on him by Jewish civic and philanthropic
organizations and then he proudly boasted, "I was
made honorary Mayor of Haifa, Israel." He usually
received the biggest applause when he referred to
the fact that there had not been a single scandal
in his administration. However, neither
Impellitteri's strenuous efforts nor Wagner's
campaign served to excite the voting public.
Possessing neither the charisma of a crusading
spirit nor the charm or excitement of the rogue
Jimmy Walker, both Impellitteri and Wagner failed
to generate excitement or large crowds (most
numbered a few hundred).

As to viable campaign issues, the incumbent mayor
sought to point to a historic record of
accomplishment in the construction field, such as
the building of hospitals, schools and parks, and
he also stressed progress in the fields of health,
antipollution, anticorruption and anticommunism,
defining them as follows:

We've developed, and you've approved, a $150,000,000 hospital
building program, which has put up new hospitals at a speed
never before equalled, or even approached, in the history of
this city.
    We've ninety-seven school building projects under way, the
most extensive program in any three-year period since the city
was founded.

Venereal diseases have been licked as a public health problem. Our work on venereal diseases has been so effective that we've been able to close down nine of our social hygiene clinics.

We've gone more than two-thirds of the way in cleaning up the dirty, polluted water of our harbor and seashore recreational areas in the most comprehensive attack on water pollution ever made anywhere.

We've increased park, playground and beach acreage and begun a network of recreation centers in a continually expanding program. We've opened eighty-four additional vacation and after school playground and community centers. Almost 100 additional parks and playgrounds have been completed or are under way.

We've carried forward a low-rent housing program which already provides decent living space for 32,000 low-income families. What's more, families of all races and religions live together in harmony in these projects in the spirit of democracy . . . .

Does anyone have the nerve or the stupidity to say that these are not sound contributions to good, decent government, contributions which make New York a better place to live in?[19]

Although there were some legitimate questions as to the excessiveness of construction costs at the expense of expenditures for repairs and maintenance, nevertheless, the Impellitteri hospital construction record in particular, was impressive. Covering all sections of the city, it included additions to existing hospitals as, for example, the erection of a new Bellevue Nurses Residence and School, and a six-story addition to the Queens General Hospital. Other construction involved building totally new hospitals such as East Harlem General Hospital, Elmhurst General Hospital and the Bronx Municipal Hospital Center.

For his part the phlegmatic Wagner hammered away at the debacle over the transportation situation that had recently plagued the city and had compelled it to succumb to a humiliating state takeover and to a hated fare increase. In an effort to paint Impellitteri into a conservative corner, he accused the mayor of having formed a coalition with Governor Dewey akin to that created by the Dixiecrats and Republicans in Congress. Wagner also attributed an increase in rent ceilings to weakness in the Impellitteri administration even as he conveniently overlooked the fact that he himself had been a member of that administration. Politics, it has been said, makes strange bedfellows.

Individuals who for years functioned as members of
the same team, can, because of political
expediency, such as in a primary, portray
themselves as in fact having been in opposition to
the administration in which they served. Jumping at
the opportunity to expose the hypocrisy, the New
York _Times_ found it startling to hear the barrage
of Wagner reform proposals "when one recalls how
well he kept such ideas under restraint in the
forum of the Board of Estimate. How little the
public dreamed," the paper further chided, "of Mr.
Wagner's scorn for the Mayor through those years of
association . . . in which he was a leading actor."
Nor was this the only area in which Wagner was
vulnerable as once again the newspaper rebuked him
(along with Halley) for resorting to political
expediency rather than to give primacy to the
welfare of the city on a vote to lease city-owned
subways and bus lines to the Transit Authority.[20]
Using the most scanty evidence Wagner tried to
smear Impellitteri with "government by terror" and
association with criminal figures "that is odious
to decency," a stance that in the light of his
subsequent appointment of Impellitteri to the city
court, becomes even more incomprehensible. The
Wagner camp tried to gain political mileage by
reporting that there had been a physical threat on
DeSapio's family, attributable to Impellitteri
supporters but subsequently discounted as baseless.
Extreme opportunism bordering on hypocrisy was not
absent in this campaign as both Wagner and Halley
took issue with the administration slum clearance
program by demanding that slum clearance be
accomplished by concentrating on empty lots rather
than occupied older residences. This stand elicited
the most ringing denouncement from Impellitteri
supporters such as Moses. To the near legendary
construction coordinator, Robert Wagner and Rudolph
Halley were "sob sisters" who had previously rent
the air with calls for slum clearance as the answer
to urban rot, yet now compromised their positions
by joining forces with "the phoneys, stooges and
fake uplifters" who derided slum clearance programs
for providing living quarters for fewer people than
were living in designated areas before.

However, the strongest asset Wagner had going for
him was his name. The son of one of the most
respected United States senators in history, a man

whose name was forever enshrined in the annals of progressive champions, and whose appellation was synonymous with the National Labor Relations Act, considered labor's "Magna Carta," Robert Wagner, Jr. was bound to be the beneficiary of New York's powerful labor vote. Thus, even though Impellitteri's prolabor record was itself outstanding, it was destined to suffer substantially by comparison. Indeed with the largest organized labor elements supporting Wagner and with a significant minority backing Halley because of the ties between labor leaders and the Liberal party, formal union endorsement of Impellitteri was drastically reduced.

The results of the primary had to be particularly galling to the Italian-born mayor whose total of 181,295 was little more than half of Wagner's 350,474. Swamped by the Wagner plurality in all boroughs except Richmond, the only question that remained was whether Impellitteri was prepared to withdraw or to run as an independent, much as he had in 1950. All the signs pointed to the latter as Impellitteri people circulated an Experience party nominating petition, apparently having little difficulty in obtaining the requisite number of signatures. Furthermore, the days following the primary defeat saw him display a vigorousness not in keeping with one about to exit the active political arena. Thus, on September 25, 1953 he sharply rebuked the president of the New York Automobile Club of New York for attempting to pressure him regarding an auto use tax. "It has never been and never will be my policy to resort to political demagoguery to explain or to justify my position with respect to the City's important problems," he advised. Further, "I can assure you that threats of political reprisal will not be a factor in my decisions."[21] He also visited Cardinal Francis Spellman, ostensibly to gain his cooperation in urging people to turn out to register but in reality undoubtedly sensing the public visit as a means of strengthening his own appeal. The virtual certainty that Impellitteri would run as an independent caused Democrats uneasy moments as they nervously recalled his 1950 victory under an independent label. Apprehension reigned until October 20, 1953 when, on a technicality, a court decision disqualified many Impellitteri petition signatories rendering it virtually impossible to mount a meaningful campaign. His decision to forego a challenge and to retire from the campaign elicited many sympathetic messages with perhaps that from William R. Hearst, a former mayoralty aspirant himself, who commended him for his "courageous fight," registering the most appropriate comment. Impellitteri's response is indicative of his feelings. "It is a pleasant reminder that brings encouragement during an unpleasant period."

Observers cite his failure to stand up to and resist Governor Dewey as among the major reasons for Impellitteri's defeat. "Mayor Impy actually lost the primary runoff last March and April on Albany's Capitol Hill," was the way one reporter analyzed it. According to this view, instead of fighting back against Dewey's harsh denunciation of city policies, Impellitteri remained silent thereby giving the impression of supine acquiescence. In actuality he did not remain altogether compliant. As demonstrated previously, repeatedly he and members of his administration met with state officials, (on March 2, 1953, Impellitteri held a seven and one half hour marathon meeting with Lieutenant Governor Moore in a futile effort to obtain an equitable city budget and stave off the state's Transit Authority Plan which included a fare rise, until at last it became a fait accompli).

Rewarding twelve Tammany chieftains, some with unsavory reputations, was considered another error. Other factors involved a number of Democratic leaders in Brooklyn who, in a rift with the Brooklyn Democratic leader Sutherland, did not apply themselves on behalf of the candidate. One also has to wonder whether or not Impellitteri made the correct decision regarding the deployment of resources. With the Italian element fairly well committed to him, (he had received almost half of their votes in 1950 against two other Italian American candidates and there was every indication that Italian districts would provide his largest primary vote totals) it might have been wiser to concentrate his personal appeals to other groups such as the Jews whose voting strength could make the difference. Indeed he had received only 21.2

percent of the Jewish vote in 1950 and since they were the largest single ethnic group within the Democratic party, their electoral endorsement was critical. This is not to convey the impression that he ignored them entirely. He visited Israel in 1951, appointed almost as many Jews to positions as he did Italians and lent his support to numerous fund-raising efforts on the part of the New York Jewish community. Although impossible to prove what the final consequences might have been, the impression is he probably would have been well advised to spend more time trying to win their backing.

Thus, the first mayor elected as an independent was now in the closing weeks of his three year term. Still relatively young at fifty-three and only two years shy of sufficient municipal service to warrant a pension, he now used whatever political muscle remained to continue in municipal employment. Accordingly, he stunned political observers with one of his last mayoral acts when he appointed two avid DeSapio supporters to significant positions in city government in what was interpreted as a friendly gesture to the incoming party leadership. Relieved that he would not run an independent race and win as he had done in 1950, indeed some astute observers saw that as a genuine possibility, an agreement was reached between Impellitteri and the incoming administration whereby he was appointed a city special sessions judge. It is interesting to note that at his appointment in January 1954, even his former political enemies were happy for him and joined in his judicial swearing-in ceremonies sharing fond recollections. Nor was this surprising because Impellitteri was perhaps the most personally likeable man to serve as mayor in recent history.

Impellitteri was not one to use his vaunted career as an entitlement for preference. As a magistrate and former mayor he continued for years to ride the subway--much to the surprise and glee of strap-hangers--where he rubbed shoulders with ordinary workaday New Yorkers, many of whom failed to recognize the former chief executive en route to the downtown court house. He remained on the bench until 1965 when he retired to take on a modest private law practice. Childless, the death of his

wife due to Parkinson's disease in 1967 left him
rather lonely; however, as long as he was
physically able, he continued to remain a New
Yorker, residing for years in the New York Athletic
Club and enjoying his favorite hobby, swimming. In
time, as his physical condition deteriorated as he
still persisted in smoking his favorite ivory-
tipped cigars, although consenting to the use of
plastic cigar holders and eventually to pipe
smoking, he went to live with his only remaining
sibling, his sister Rose, in Derby, Connecticut,
the town adjoining Ansonia where he had spent his
childhood. His final year was in the Carolton
Convalescent Hospital, Fairfield, Connecticut,
where he remained until his death on January 29,
1987. A Requiem Mass for the repose of his soul was
celebrated in Ansonia"s Holy Rosary Church and
burial was in St. Peter's Cemetery, Derby,
Connecticut.

NOTES

1. Lawrence Klingman, "New York City of Work," <u>Park East</u>
(February 1953), 6-13.
2. Interview, Ruth Whitehead Whaley, April 6, 1966.
3. <u>El Diario De Nueva York</u>, December 27, 1951.
4. "Remarks of Hon. Vincent R. Impellitteri at the 1952
Meritorious Public Service Awards Dinner of Friends of Sicily
Inc.," Philadelphia, March 1,1953, Box 62, file: Mayor's
Messages, <u>VRI</u>.
5. Letters from Impellitteri to Governor Dewey, March 15,
21, 26, 1953, Box 23, file: Crime, <u>VRI</u>.
6. New York <u>Daily Mirror,</u> March 26, 1953.
7. Eisenstein and Rosenberg, <u>A Stripe of Tammany's Tiger</u>,
198.
8. "Remarks by Mayor Vincent R. Impellitteri at Annual
Dinner Democratic County Committee of Bronx County," May 15,
1952, Box 75, <u>VRI</u>.
9. New York <u>World Telegram,</u> May 18, 1953.
10. "Remarks by Hon. Vincent R. Impellitteri, Mayor of the
City of New York, in Behalf of Congressman John F. Kennedy,"
October 27, 1952, Box 82, <u>VRI</u>.
11. Message of James A. Roe to leaders and Party Workers,
July 24, 1953, Box 49, file: Mayoral Campaign 1953, <u>VRI</u>.
12. Telegram from Joe Louis to Vincent Impellitteri,
September 4, 1953, Box 49, <u>VRI</u>.
13. New York <u>Journal American</u>, June 16, 1953.
14. New York <u>Times,</u> September 10, 1953.

15. Memorandum, Abraham D. Beame to Mayor, August 31, 1953, Box 44, file: Increased Revenue, <u>VRI</u>.

16. <u>Il Progresso Italo-Americano,</u> September 7, 1953.

17. Interview, Joseph Corso, October 17, 1963.

18. Brooklyn <u>Eagle,</u> September 6, 1953.

19. New York <u>Times,</u> September 12, 1953.

20. New York <u>Times</u>, September 10, 14, 1953.

21. Letter from Impellitteri to William J. Gottlieb, September 25, 1953, Box 43, <u>VRI</u>.

9

Giving Credit Its Due

It is time to consider Impellitteri's place in municipal history. It is time to register conclusions as to his legacy in public service and his impact on the city. It is time to ask and to answer questions regarding the competency of his stewardship and the meritocracy of his leadership, that is, whether he deserved to be regarded as a positive leader or merited charges of inadequacy. Was his administration an effective one? In which ways can it considered positive? What were his important accomplishments? What can one point to of lasting effect? What of the criticism leveled against him during his tenure and afterwards? Is it justified? Is it exaggerated? Is it biased? Has he been given a fair evaluation? Was he beyond his element, his abilities? How does he compare with contemporary municipal governments? How does he compare with other New York City mayors? What are the relevant lessons? What was his significance to Italian Americans in political life? Does this have relevance for other ethnic groups?

Assessment of historians, political scientists and the few others of informed opinion who have commented on the Impellitteri mayoralty have, on balance, registered a negative appraisal. Hailed for making political history by his election as mayor on an independent ticket, without the support of a major political party, he was also unceremoniously admonished for not knowing what to do with his office once he attained it. It was argued that the requirements of the office were beyond his talents. Specifically, he was accused of quickly cashing in his "independent" status in favor of tainted, old-line Democratic functionaries, as demonstrated, for instance, by his appointment of Frank Sampson as his patronage dispenser, and thereby lining his pockets with the tarnished coin of the political realm. It was

further declared that procrastination in the face
of serious problems and acquiescence in matters
detrimental to the city characterized his
administration. His public acknowledgement of the
need for more policemen, for example, remained for
too long mere rhetoric with action commencing only
after a public outcry over a perceived increase in
city crime. It was said he cow-towed to Governor
Dewey, whose anti city bias proved costly to the
city with regard to sanctioning increases of rent-
controlled apartments, in the matter of yielding
city interests in budget negotiations and in
surrendering control of the transit system, which
in turn led to a rise in subway fares. He was also
criticized over the caliber of his appointments to
various posts and for his failure to retain
outstanding public servants as illustrated by his
bypassing esteemed members of the Board of Higher
Education when their terms expired. Additionally,
he was rebuked for excessive vacation time.

Before proceeding further on the matter of
assessment, a word must be said about the relative
lack of indepth research into his career. That is,
there is little indication that the critics have
devoted much effort in consulting the extensive
collection of material contained in the
Impellitteri Papers while conversely there is
considerable evidence that successive evaluations
border on the superficial because they are
dependent on a meagerness of sources. Accordingly
judgments based on minuscule research have been
repeatedly and automatically incorporated as
definitive--a process constituting an inherent
basic flaw. The kind of objectivity that precludes
measurements of favored public figures until
extensive research has been completed, is in this
respect, denied to Impellitteri. Based on my own
lengthy research into Impellitteri archival
material, I conclude that while the critics'
charges have some partial validity, they are too
frequently exaggerated even to the point of
misrepresentation.

It must be remembered that one of Impellitteri's
severest critics is Warren Moscow, whose
credentials as a reporter and political writer are
otherwise impressive. However, we must equally be
reminded that Moscow was a very partisan figure
during the Impellitteri period, serving as an aide

to Manhattan Borough President Robert Wagner and also engaged as an energetic campaigner for Wagner against Impellitteri in the 1953 primary. This background seems to render questionable his complete objectivity. So pronounced was Moscow's partisanship that, without genuine proof, he resorted to tawdry character assassination by asserting that Impellitteri was backed by notorious underworld figures. Notwithstanding this fundamental subjectiveness, Moscow's characterization of Impellitteri as a failure, a "perfect Throttlebottom",[1] is almost blindly repeated verbatim by others, apparently attracted more by its literary phrasing appeal than its accuracy. Among those who used the "perfect Throttlebottom" phrase in emulation of Moscow are John Davenport and Robert Caro.[2] Caro is even more devastating in his judgment of Impellitteri, calling him a pathetic figure beyond his element.[3] It is almost as if armed with Moscow's description, it is not necessary to probe more deeply. In depicting Moses as the real power during this period, Caro, it might be added, did consult some of the Impellitteri Papers, although without consulting the detailed bibliographical citations necessary for straightforward corroboration, to buttress his rebuke of the mayor as a spineless, errand-boy for Moses. Because he is intent on proving that Moses was the peerless power broker, Caro's references to Impellitteri, not unexpectedly, are designed to promote his own central theses and, therefore, do not necessarily unmistakably substantiate his conclusions, however remarkable his biography. Making allowances for Moses's expertise and years of municipal administrative experience, much of his communications are interlaced with formalities, language and requests not markedly different from other members of the administration. They frequently represented, moreover, responses to charges that Impellitteri placed on his construction coordinator. For the mayor to have manifold reliance on him is not surprising considering the universally acknowledged belief that in the realm of public administration Moses was a genius--his arrogance notwithstanding. Indeed a perusal of the Impellitteri Papers, can lead one to the conclusion that, although Moses was a major

factor in guiding the course of the Impellitteri
administration, he was not alone, there were other
individuals who played principal roles as the
previous chapters demonstrated.   Unfortunately
completely missing from the Caro account of
Impellitteri, yet amply present in the Impellitteri
Papers, are the numerous instances in which the
mayor made decisions and established policy in
which Moses had no role.

Perhaps the most recent work to deal with
Impellitteri in some detail is Chris McNickle's
1989 dissertation.[4] While rendering useful analysis
of the ascendancy of New York City Jews to
political power, this work is much less helpful
concerning Italian Americans. It attributes Edward
Corsi's loss in 1950 to the fact that his "wealth
and upstate connections made him unfamiliar to his
urban, working class countrymen" and gives the
erroneous impression of socioeconomic elitism that
ignores the fact that for years Corsi lived and
worked in East Harlem, the heart of the largest
Little Italy in the city. McNickle regrettably
places heavy reliance on the works of Moscow and
Caro, for his assessment of Impellitteri and
unsurprisingly regurgitates the old theme of
Impellitteri's inadequacy. The McNickle study
contains numerous categorical statements such as
Impellitteri doing nothing regarding a housing
initiative, a charge that is readily refutable by
the historic record. It can be argued that, in
fairness to McNickle, because his study did not
focus on Italian Americans, it is understandable
that he could err when dealing with them. That may
be, nevertheless, it is important to recognize the
need to continue to strive to unearth new and
untapped material relative to the Italian ethnic
group and thereby be open to the possibilities of
reassessment.

A deeper examination of Moscow's work raises
other questions of accuracy and corroboration.
Moscow's erroneous categorizing of Edward Corsi as
a Protestant is a case in point.[5] His assertion
that Impellitteri's 1945 inclusion on the
Democratic ticket as dictated by Marcantonio in
behalf of Thomas Lucchese, of underworld infamy,
must likewise be placed in the dubious realm. For
Moscow to quote a Charles Buckley story of being
present when Marcantonio phoned a "Billy-O" with

"my own ginzo"[6] (allegedly referring to the designation of Impellitteri as candidate for city council President) may make for colorful reading but is not persuasive enough to prove incontrovertibly the existence of a sinister link between Impellitteri and Lucchese. Although this supposed connection was raised more than once, there were no meaningful revelations to substantiate any wrongdoing. Nor, it might be added, was there any reasonable explanation as to the motive for the supposed connection. The so-called "Green Book" account of Impellitteri's inclusion on the Democratic ticket in 1945 is rationalized on the grounds that an Italian was sought for ethnic balancing purposes. Completely ignored in this account is the fact that before Impellitteri's name surfaced, the original choice of Democratic leaders nominated Italian American Gerosa for comptroller, however, it was at O'Dwyer's insistence that Impellitteri was designated the council president candidate thereby forcing a substitution of Impellitteri for Gerosa.

In an effort to demonstrate Impellitteri's attitude of acquiescence to actions detrimental to city residents, Moscow lays increases in controlled rents at Impellitteri's door, once again overlooking the fact that over the years the mayor spoke out and acted strongly in both State and national forums in favor of maintaining rent controls. One example occurred in June 1951 when Impellitteri forwarded a forceful letter to Senator Herbert H. Lehman, urging reestablishment of federal rent control in New York City in view of the inadequacy of state laws to protect poor tenants. This message was then submitted to the Banking and Currency Committees of the House and Senate. Another example came in March 1953 as Impellitteri addressed letters to every New York City member of the state legislature vigorously opposing relaxation of rent controls.[7]

Another point to be kept in mind is the short duration of Impellitteri's tenure. Given the reality that it customarily requires some time for a new administration to institute its own programs, it would seem that less than a full four year tenure would be a disadvantage. Accordingly, an abbreviated three year period was destined to suffer from invidious comparison with those of

LaGuardia, Wagner, and Koch whose tenures of twelve consecutive years provided more time to develop and implement programs. Longevity alone is, of course, not enough of an excuse if the overall effectiveness is negative, however, it is a valid consideration.

Impellitteri deserves credit for a number of important points. For many city workers the Impellitteri administration meant the establishment of the long sought after forty hour work week. This administration also won respect for exercising reasonable control over organized labor excesses. One example was the determination displayed in standing up to Quill who had been quite successful in holding the city hostage to his demands during the LaGuardia and O'Dwyer administrations and even more dramatically during the Lindsay administration. Impellitteri was willing to risk a transportation strike in order not to surrender to the labor leader's untenable demands. Against similar circumstances, many other mayors caved in. Impellitteri's labor endeavors were in fact quite constructive as he provided the leadership to resolve a number of thorny disputes and thus won commendation from management and labor representatives. In addition to the previously cited labor incidents, mention must be made of the 1953 teamsters strike that interrupted construction operations and that had defied solution until he stepped in. As the mayor's daily and evening log showed Impellitteri exerted himself to the utmost from the beginning of the dispute in early July as he summoned and prodded government mediators to personal conferences, and pointed out the extreme hardships to the city resulting from interruption of essential public works projects like hospital and housing construction. He then appointed a tripartite commission including labor and construction company representatives to recommend solutions and notified national union officials to use their good offices. When this yielded scant results he proceeded to name a Fact Finding Committee to formulate a settlement, which indeed it reported out the following day. It was only Impellitteri's personal intervention that finally obtained union cooperation. Unfortunately newspaper coverage omitted most of details of the mayor's efforts, concentrating instead on costliness of the strike. Averting a strike was apparently less newsworthy than a dispute, observed an experienced city labor mediator who confirmed that 90 percent of labor disputes under Impellitteri were settled amicably, albeit without attracting media attention. "But such omissions should not be allowed to cloak the constant and constructive endeavors of the Mayor to bring about the swiftest possible settlement of the strike."[8] The end of the building trades strike elicited gratitude from the president of the Building and Trades Council for "patient and calm leadership," and from the Teamsters president for his "earnest efforts."[9]

Impellitteri's appointment record is another area in which he is unjustly evaluated as his critics emphasized the negative while virtually ignoring his positive accomplishments in this regard. Thus, although criticized for some nominations, he received deserved praise for many other appointments such as his first Police Commissioner Murphy, Fire Commissioners Monaghan and Grumet, Judge Cooper, and especially Moses. Even those who attacked him for at first not reappointing various individuals to the Board of Higher Education came to praise his appointment of people like Arthur Levitt whose board tenure was considered very beneficial. Moreover, in making selections Impellitteri demonstrated his ability to withstand unusual instances of coercion. Thus, the tact of exerting heavy pressure did not sway Impellitteri with respect to reappointing to the court Roland Sala, a flamboyant Brooklyn judge whose sartorial choices earned him an eccentric reputation and who had further alienated many with intemperate remarks. Notwithstanding appeals from local groups including a nun who reminded the mayor that he and Judge Sala shared ethnic and religious backgrounds, Impellitteri refused to rename the judge to the city court. Impellitteri likewise resisted influence from some of the most prominent political and judiciary leaders to reappoint Judge Northrop, using his vacancy instead to nominate to the city court one of its first Puerto Ricans members, Emilio Nunez. Thus he risked rebuke for not reappointing a seasoned court member in favor of a policy of inclusion of minorities, a policy that could also be regarded as sensitive in meeting the symbolic needs of a pluralistic society. As previously mentioned, the Theodore Lowi analysis of appointments made by New York's chief executives finds that Impellitteri carved out a responsible appointment record in recognizing the need for more professionalism and specialization of appointees, well over half of them had previously served in city cabinets. Moreover, although the percentage of appointees in his cabinet who were functionaries in party affairs was high, fewer top-level nominations went to county and assembly district leaders than most city administrations. Also of note is the fact that upon his elevation to mayor, Wagner retained a large number of Impellitteri appointees.

The Italian-born mayor deserves credit for presiding over a municipal government that helped considerably to rid the city of corruption and one that was in sharp contrast to its predecessor as well as some of its successors. Although he inherited an administration that had gained a negative reputation for unscrupulousness and duplicity that had attracted national attention, with minor exception the Impellitteri years were free of true, verifiable linkage between underworld figures and elected officials. Vulgar efforts by political enemies to attempt to implicate Impellitteri with corruption, significantly came to naught for reason that there were no such connections. Considering the sorry record of many administrations before and after his mayoralty, Impellitteri's leadership in this regard was truly significant.

One of the bright spots in the Impellitteri administration was the promotion of commerce. Virtually ignored by Impellitteri's critics is the rather strong record compiled during his tenure under his appointee, William Shirley. Commerce Commissioner Shirley effected surprising cooperation from business, government and labor representatives that enabled the city to maintain its national business preeminence while preventing substantial amounts of business from being lured away. Further, there were actual trade gains for the city during this period. Impellitteri did his part to attract business and tourism by his personal involvement at trade shows, exhibits and other promotions. Although it was an uneven picture and even conceding the existence of problems in certain fields, on balance "since the depression

Thirties   the   city's   business   has   steadily
increased."[10]

The question arises as to why the public did not
perceive the progress made under Impellitteri and
why the press did not give him his due. Could it be
that at times the establishment press has settled
on   a   view   (Frank   Conniff   maintained   that
"Columnists adopted him as a clay pigeon whenever
they needed target practice") in such a manner that
it becomes the prevailing perception and so fixed
as to be impervious to the possibility of other
opinions?   Interestingly,   Robert   Caro,   when
criticizing the press for failure to see Robert
Moses in anything but a positive light, because it
"was not interested," comes to essentially the same
conclusion.[11]   Whether   the   failure   to   render
Impellitteri his fair share of credit can be
attributed to an unappreciative city press is a
matter of conjecture, however, it is important to
note that all save one city newspaper had opposed
his election in 1950. By 1953 pro-Impellitteri
dailies   had   increased   to   two,   nevertheless,   it
meant that the vast majority of city dailies were
still not in his camp although they did commend him
on numerous occasions. Some, like the New York
Post, which could never bring itself to say much of
an affirmative nature about Impellitteri, almost
from the outset inveighed heavily against him for
inaction, for frequency of appearances at fund-
raising   social   affairs   and   for   succumbing   to
Republican party bosses. In a lengthy series in
1951 and 1952, the _Post_ even asserted that he had
become annoyed at reporters--a basically spurious
charge because Impellitteri generally accepted
reporters' appraisals with grace and repeatedly
maintained that the press had treated him fairly.

One important scholarly study of the interaction
between the municipal chief executive and the press
saw his dealings with the press as professional and
astute. His appointment of William Donaghue as his
original press secretary, for example, reflected
the high regard he had for the press on which he
depended in getting messages out to the public. "I
tried to cultivate and encourage the support of the
press on a particular issue. I would issue press
releases stating my position and the position of my
administration on a particular subject." This did
not mean that Impellitteri was above manipulating

the press for trial balloon purposes as for example, in his selection for city cabinet posts. Accordingly, when contemplating appointing Thomas Murphy police commissioner, "I put out a trial balloon, it was very well received." Likewise his selection of Jewish Republican Jacob Grumet as fire department commissioner to rid the department of scandals was also preceded by a newspaper trail balloon, in which "the feedback was excellent."[12] Impellitteri prepared for press meetings by reviewing possible questions with Donaghue, even though he never knew for certain what questions would be asked and generally welcomed all reporters. Significantly the City Hall press corps presented him with a briefcase as a symbolic gift when his tenure as mayor was over.

Impellitteri was aware of the specific charges against him but differed as to their meaning. For example, what sometimes appeared to be inaction, was in his mind a calculated response to situations wherein he wished to avoid impulsive or even frenetic steps that could exacerbate issues. "I'm a methodical fellow with a methodical mind. I'm not blatant--I'm modest in my approach, but, I get things done." This deliberateness was a position for which he was duly chastised, however, it is to be borne in mind that his successor Robert F. Wagner, was very similar in style in this regard, yet Wagner was praised for exercising wisdom and proper caution when he premeditated at length and allowed problems to resolve themselves. One wonders about a double standard in that essentially the same quality that was judged procrastination in Impellitteri's situation, was touted as a "genius for leaving bad enough alone" in Wagner's case.

Political scientists maintain that Impellitteri undervalued the mayor's power vis-à-vis the Board of Estimate--an estimate with which he would agree. It is to be conceded that Impellitteri's view of the role of the Board of Estimate differed from that of his two predecessors who had to bargain with the same body (prior to LaGuardia's time the Board of Aldermen functioned in a similar capacity). Whereas LaGuardia and O'Dwyer regarded the Board of Estimate as something that the mayor should control completely, that is, to be in effect a rubber stamp of the administration, Impellitteri saw himself as a member of the board, who together

were charged with determining city policies. He saw
board members as elected independently and,
therefore, responsible to the electorate. He was,
furthermore, aware of political reality in that
since his election he was trying to return to the
good graces of the Democratic Party-- which was the
affiliation of most Board members whose respect he
must cultivate. Berating political scientists for
"cruel thrusts" at his inconclusiveness, veteran
professional politician Louis Eisenstein accurately
portrayed the problem Impellitteri faced.

The professors claimed that he neither grasped the potential
of his office nor employed sound administrative measures. From
high, ivory-coated towers, however, they completely ignored a
basic fact that limits definition of the word "science" in
"political science." The mayor did not operate in a vacuum. He
held office under a party system and alongside a powerful
Board of Estimate. Political foes of his own party wanted his
scalp, and the more ambitious on the Board wanted his job.
Impellitteri was certainly not the most effective of Mayors.
But he was undeserving of the damning criticism levelled
against him. I am proud to count him as a friend.
    No taint of scandal attached itself to his name. But
throughout his administration, his position was undermined and
his plans constantly sabatoged. Impellitteri's administration
had as much opportunity for success as did the German Weimer
Republic between the world wars.[13]

Both philosophically and temperamentally
Impellitteri rejected the notion that he ought to
ram his views down the throats of the board. It was
labeled a "weak" mayoral form, but perhaps it would
be more accurate to describe it as a less
dictatorial and a more democratic approach to
municipal government. Interestingly, in 1990 a
change in the New York City Charter that has led to
the growth of power and influence of the city
council, has been hailed as a democratizing step
because it allows for real input on the part of a
larger number of elected city officials. One can
likewise consider Impellitteri's perception of
greater involvement by Board of Estimate members as
pursuing a similar policy of participation. Mayor
Impellitteri's dealings with the city council also
reflected an awareness of a politically
fractionalized situation. Since his victory as
mayor as an independent precipitated such an
internecine struggle within Tammany Hall that he
could not count on automatic support of all members

even though they were basically of the same party, it required the greatest skill and maneuvering to gain endorsement of needed legislation. "When Mayor Impellitteri wanted to insure the passage of his tax proposals, which he needed to balance the city's 1952-1953 budget, Majority Leader Sharkey was obliged to caucus, to threaten and cajole."[14]

It has been observed that the mayor of New York City must be three men: a public relations person, a planner and an administrator. Accordingly, the mayor's functions may be divided into the ceremonial category that encompasses making public appearances at dedication ceremonies, issuing significant and insignificant proclamations and greeting an array of visitors to the big city. He also functions as a planner with respect to his view of the city of the future, and finally he must display a hands-on, day-to-day administration of the municipality to see to it that services and operations are carried out effectively. Of the three categories common consensus concludes that compared to other mayors Impellitteri excelled in the first category (the ceremonial role) and indeed he reveled in that capacity although he too could complain that it was exhausting to attend six functions per night following a full day in the office. He was said to be less effective in the other two areas. A review of his administration supports the view that he saw his job as representing the city in functions ranging from greeting foreign dignitaries to meeting boy scout troops. Unlike other mayors who regarded these activities as annoyances, Impellitteri looked on them as "quasi city business" that he willingly performed during eighteen-hour days. Nor would he agree to substitutes standing in for him. "Try getting the deputy mayor to do it and just see the resentment it stirs." He thought it important for the citizenry to meet with the city's chief executive and for the mayor to expend himself on behalf of beneficial causes. "Ninety percent of the people who come in here for pictures represent worthwhile causes."

The areas of planning and administration are notably less glamorous, however, Impellitteri did not shirk from these responsibilities. His support of numerous recommendations, although not all, of the Mayor's Committee on Management Survey indicate

his concern for the future efficient operation of
the city. Indeed in one report the committee stated
that, "Compared with any other large American city,
New York renders a grade of service and a range of
services of a high order. We may be excelled from
time to time at one point or another, but taken by
and large, over the whole range, no big city meets
the composite standards of New York."[15] The effort
he expended in building hospitals, schools and
parks, in civil defense preparations, sewage
disposal systems and so on were, in effect, actions
in furtherance of planning for the future. Suitably
his frequent trips to Albany (four trips in less
than ten weeks in 1952) represented a willingness
to go the extra mile on behalf of a favorable
financial package for the city. Impellitteri's
dealings with Albany are in marked contrast to
O'Dwyer who, according to Robert Caro, was said to
leave all brokering deliberations with Albany to
Moses abstaining even to travel to meet with the
Governor.[16] Even allowing for Caro's exaggeration
of Moses' role, the record demonstrates that
O'Dwyer ventured to Albany perhaps only once during
his tenure.

Administrative performance is rightly regarded as
an important measurement. How well the city's chief
administrator handles the diverse and frequently
conflicting agencies, how successfully he manages
the army of civil servants and their organized
labor representatives, and what sort of a record he
has compiled regarding future planning and growth
are all important criteria to be evaluated. There
are conflicting opinions as to how well
Impellitteri administered his office. Criticism was
leveled against him for allowing things to drift
when in actuality he was deliberating over the
matter, as was his style. Not one to move swiftly
or impetuously, he preferred to study and review a
situation before responding: a perhaps overly
cautious posture that elicited considerable and
understandable editorial rebuke. Rather than trying
to refute these opinions directly, he purposefully
wrote letters infrequently to editors of city
newspapers because he saw that as "idle gesture,"
opting instead for press releases that would not
"go out without my OK," and that carefully spelled
out his position. Clearly, whatever his critics
maintained, in later postmayoralty years

Impellitteri saw himself as the policy maker of his
administration, whereas, more accurately, he
usually endeavored to obtain a consensus within the
Board of Estimate and thereby strengthen the
administration's position. The results were mixed,
but they were far from negative.

Personality and style always are considered when
evaluating mayoral performances. Although
possessing a warm and friendly disposition and a
strong loyalty that was reminiscent of Truman to
reporters who covered him, he lacked the dynamism
of his predecessors with whom he was inevitably
compared. "In his office he shows little of the
turbulent energy or whimsical humor of the late
Mayor Fiorello H. LaGuardia or former Mayor William
O'Dwyer," was the commentary of a lengthy
observation of his approach to the job. "His speech
is almost devoid of colorful language and his
gestures are limited to pointing a finger, clasping
his hands or twisting a cigar in his mouth."
According to associates the Mayor's failure to
dramatize himself in the LaGuardia manner was
mainly responsible for the lack of public
appreciation of his achievements. "He is not a
headline hunter, and his main reason for attending
so many functions is not because he likes accolades
but because he considers it his duty."[17]

Editorial reaction to the Mayor's performance may
be regarded as a useful means of shedding light on
the subject. Impellitteri attracted his share of
critics of course, however, it was not as lopsided
as it would seem. One inquiry of city newspaper
editorials provided a count of "pro" and "con"
references for each year of his administration, and
it is revealing to note that the "con" number from
September 1950 to December 31, 1951, surpassed the
pro only by a 59 to 52 margin. The "con" margin was
higher for 1952 (35 to 18) and for 1953, however,
many of these were repetitious, consisting of
comments on the same issue as, for example, the
troubled state of city finances during budget
preparations. Moreover, some of the complaints were
satisfied by subsequent action. There is also the
fact that he received criticism and praise for the
same actions, that is judicial appointments that,
while the basis for editorial rebuke, were also the
foundation for some the highest commendations.
Thus, what emerges from editorial review is a

mingled picture rather than universal condemnation.

In evaluating Impellitteri's public career a word is in order about his steadfast championing of Americanism. The son of Sicilian immigrants had accumulated a worthy patriotic record: United States Navy in the First World War, conspicuous involvement in veterans affairs and a singular and extraordinary role in combatting communism. At a time when communism was perceived as a major threat, Impellitteri proudly boasted of his unyielding opposition to the left-wing ideology as manifested by such decisions as supporting laws to prohibit Communists from teaching in city schools and rejecting a Communist application to parade in New York City; stances bound to win no applause among civil libertarians, however, decisions that warmed the cockles of anti-Communist hearts. Most important of all was his active participation in keeping communism out of power in the land of his birth. That he could play a principal role in this endeavor by freely volunteering his services on behalf of the American government rendered his involvement all the more meaningful. Clearly he merits recognition within the Italian ethnic community for exemplifying the highest standards of ardor and commitment to the American cause.

If the absence of vindictiveness is a desirable goal in public officials then Impellitteri qualifies as an unusual representative of the virtue of forbearance. Although he engaged in his share of political battles, he was basically not a vengeful man. Instead he was prepared to let bygones be bygones. Accordingly, albeit his justifiable pride in expanding the city's public housing program to new limits, he was instrumental in urging the housing authority to adopt LaGuardia's name in the title of a major project. That is, despite prior political differences with the late mayor, he thought it especially appropriate to pay tribute to the first New York City Italian American chief executive whose administration launched the first public housing project in the United States. Nor did Impellitteri harbor grudges long against adversaries such as Wagner, whom he had previously excoriated and who had defeated him in 1953. Only a couple of years out of office he could evaluate Wagner as "doing a good job." Even the long vendetta with DeSapio soon

faded as the basis for ongoing vituperation.
Impellitteri's amiability was so genuine that it
had near contagious consequences that saw former
rivals jump at the opportunity to honor him as on
the occasion of his installation as a judge of the
court of special sessions.

Perhaps not in the same company as Mayors
Mitchell and LaGuardia, who were regarded as the
city's greatest twentieth century mayors, Vincent
Impellitteri nevertheless deserves to be considered
as a more than an able mayor. He deserves credit
for raising the moral standards of municipal
government against a background of scandal of major
proportions: for running the city within its
financial means, without horrendous debts, for
curbing the excesses of irresponsible personalities
that would prey on the city's largess, for being
sensitive to the desires of ethnic minorities. He
was, moreover, at the helm of the city during a
pivotal transitional period--post-World War II
America. This was a time of enormous and radical
transformation for the nation's largest
municipality that, because of the United Nations
location, was also making adjustment to its
official status as the international world capital.
Not able to return to the normal pursuits of prewar
city life, it was necessary to gear up to meet new
challenges in constructing medical, educational and
recreational facilities; in instituting innovations
to expedite city traffic flow, in attempting to
improve transportation amid trying monetary
constraints and labor pressures; and in responding
to the growing problems of air and sewage
pollution. These developments were to transpire
within a political environment that required a
delicate balance between working within the
predominant political culture and challenging it.
Not entirely successful in this regard Impellitteri
nevertheless accomplished a great deal without a
genuine hint of personal aggrandizement.
Impellitteri deserves renown as an authentic
representative of the Italian American milieu, an
immigrant from southern Italy, the offspring of a
large, humble, working class, Catholic family, who
willingly grasped the opportunities to rise to
unprecedented heights, which in the land of his
birth would be far beyond his reach.

Never forgetting his heritage, it is worth noting

that the percentages of Italian American appointed to city posts under Impellitteri exceeded all other administrations. In this regard Impellitteri's ascension to high office possessed more tangible significance for the ethnic group than that of many other Italian American political figures who exploited the group's sense of pride in order to gain election but otherwise made little effort for meaningful ethnic inclusion. In other words, if ethnic group efforts succeeded only in election of one of their number to politically important posts with no meaningful follow-up, such success remained little more than a pitiful delusion if they did not lead to group attainment of a greater share in the shaping city policies. As the wise educator Peter Sammartino analyzed it, election to positions of political power can have more than a symbolic meaning when those elected acknowledged a debt of gratitude to their constituency.

At the same time, the payment of the debt, must be consonant with the highest ideals of Americanism. And when you seek to integrate into the present status of American culture, the richness and the grandeur of Italian civilization, then the payment is made in the most valuable specie indeed.[18]

In addition to Italian-Americans, appointments of Jews was extremely high.[19] Impellitteri deserves his share of acclaim for advancing the cause of democracy in his adopted land and for striving to improve city life. An honest, reasonably intelligent and amiable man who administered the nation's greatest city during a significant transitional period, he was representative of the common people of the city he led and served--not a shabby epithet for an immigrant cobbler's son.

NOTES

1. Moscow, <u>The Last of The Big Times Bosses</u> 97.
2. John F. Davenport, "Skinning The Tiger: Carmine DeSapio and The End Of The Tammany Era," <u>New York Affairs</u> 3, no. 1 (1975), 72-93.
3. Caro, <u>Power Broker</u> 787-91.
4. McNickle, "To Be Mayor of New York," Ph. D. Dissertation.
5. Moscow, <u>What Have You Done For Me Lately?</u> 91.
6. Moscow, <u>What Have You Done For Me Lately?</u> 63.

7. Press Release March 9, 1953, Box 62, file: Messages, 1953, <u>VRI</u>.

8. Letter from Daniel Kornblum to Editor of New York <u>Times</u>, August 27, 1953, Box 94, file: Strikes, <u>VRI</u>.

9. Letter from Howard McSpedon to Impellitteri, September 2, 1953 and letter from Dave Beck to Impellitteri, undated, Box 94, Strikes, <u>VRI</u>.

10. New York <u>Times</u>, May 5, 1952.

11. Caro, <u>Power Broker</u>, 966.

12. Caroline Shaffer Westerhof, <u>The Executive Connection</u> (New York: Dunellen, 1974), 100-12.

13. Eisenstein and Rosenberg, <u>A Stripe of Tammany's Tiger</u>, 189.

14. Frederick Shaw, <u>The History of The New York City Legislature</u> (New York: Columbia University Press, 1954), 249.

15. Impellitteri Speech, WCBS, April 13, 1953, Box 52, file: 1953, <u>VRI</u>.

16. Caro, <u>Power Broker</u>, 761.

17. New York <u>Herald Tribune</u>, October 19, 1953.

18. <u>Atlantica</u> (July 1933), 117.

19. Lowi, <u>At The Pleasure Of The Mayor</u>, 198.

Bibliographical Essay

Though not exhaustive, the following bibliography is offered to readers to introduce a selected representation on the subject of Italian Americans and politics. Readers are also referred to works excerpted or cited in notes, not all of which are listed here.

The interaction between immigrants and politics is covered in insightful standard immigration history surveys such as Maldwyn Allen Jones, <u>American Immigration</u> (Chicago: University of Chicago Press, 1960); John Higham, <u>Strangers in the Land</u> (New York: Atheneum, 1971); and Oscar Handlin, <u>Immigration as a Factor in American History</u> (Englewood Cliffs, N.J.: Prentice-Hall, Inc., 1959). The theoretical aspect of ethnic politics is treated in Michael J. Parenti, "Ethnic Politics and the Pesistence of Ethnic Identification," <u>American Political Science Review</u>, 56 (September 1967); and Raymond E. Wolfinger, "The Development and Persistence of Ethnic Voting," <u>American Political Science Review</u>, 59 (December 1965). For perspicacious monographs on ethnic groups and American politics see Harry A. Bailey Jr. and Ellis Katz, ed. <u>Ethnic Group Politics</u> (Columbus, Ohio: Charles E. Merrill, Publishers), a volume containing the views of twenty noted authors on the subject. Edgar Litt, <u>Ethnic Politics in America</u> (Glenview, Illinois: Scott, Foresman and Company, 1970), explores the influence of ethnicity on American politics as does Mark R. Levy and Michael S. Kramer, <u>The Ethnic Factor, How America's Minorities Decide Elections</u> (New York: Simon and Schuster, 1972). In a special issue on "City Bosses and Political Machines," <u>The Annals</u> (May 1964) constitutes another very useful work on the subject. Standard, sturdy overviews on ethnic politics include Robert A. Dahl, <u>Who Governs: Democracy and Power in an American City</u> (New Haven, Conn.: Yale University Press, 1961); Edward C. Banfield and James Q. Wilson, <u>City Politics</u> (Cambridge: Harvard University Press, 1963); V. O. Key, <u>Politics, Parties, and Pressure Groups</u> (New York: Thomas Y. Crowell, 1964); and Samuel Lubell, <u>The Future of American Politics</u> (New York: Harper and Row, Inc., 1952).

For important background on the politics of ethnic acculturation see the following: Salvatore J. LaGumina and Francesco Cordasco, <u>Italians in the United States, A Bibliography of Reports, Texts, Critical Studies and Related Materials</u> (New York: Oriole Editions, 1972); Luciano J. Iorizzo and Salvatore Mondello, <u>Italian Americans</u> (New York, Twayne Publishers, 1971); Richard Gambino, <u>Blood of My Blood</u>

(New York: Anchor Books, 1975); Alexander DeConde, <u>Half
Bitter, Half Sweet: An Excursion into Italian American History</u>
(New York: Charles Scribners & Sons, 1972); Andrew Rolle, <u>The
American Italians: Their History and Culture</u> (Belmont,
California: Wadsworth Publishing Co., 1972); Eric
Amfitheatrof, <u>The Children of Columbus</u> (Boston: Little, Brown
and Company, 1973); Edward Corsi, <u>In the Shadow of Liberty</u>
(New York: Arno Press, 1969); William Foote Whyte, <u>Street
Corner Society</u> (Chicago: University of Chicago Press, 1943);
and Herbert Gans, <u>The Urban Villagers</u> (New York: The Free
Press, 1962). The Fascist impact on Italian American
communities is treated in John Diggins, <u>Mussolini and Fascism:
The View From America</u> (Princeton, Princeton University Press,
1972). Italian language publications such as the newspaper <u>Il
Progresso Italo-Americano</u>, and the periodical <u>Atlantica</u>,
provide immense and indispensable vital details about Italian
American political activity.

The ethnic political situation in New York City is
described in Federal Writers Project, <u>The Italians of New York</u>
(New York: 1938) which provides much concrete information
about the early part twentieth century until late 1930's.
Caroline F. Ware's <u>Greenwich Village, 1920-1930</u> (New York:
Harper and Row Publishers, 1965), and Donald Tricarico,
<u>Greenwich Village</u> (Staten Island, Center For Migration
Studies, 1984), contain meaningful knowledge on politics and
New York City Italian Americans. Likewise Ronald H. Bayor's
<u>Neighbors In Conflict, The Irish, Germans, Jews, and Italians
of New York City, 1929-1941</u> (Baltimore: Johns Hopkins
University Press, 1978), and Salvatore J. LaGumina, ed.,
Ethnicity in "American Political Life: The Italian American
Experience," <u>Proceedings of the First Annual Conference of
the American Italian Historical Association</u> (Staten Island:
American Italian Historical Association, 1968), includes good
background material. Although somewhat dated, Roy V. Peel's
<u>Political Clubs of New York City</u> (Port Washington, New York,
Ira J. Friedman Publishing Co., 1935) is basic to learning
about immigrant/ethnic group political organization in the
city in an earlier period. John H. Mariano, <u>The Second
Generation of Italians in New York City</u> (Boston: The
Christopher Publishing House, 1921), also covers the earlier
period of the century. Nathan Glazer and Daniel P. Moynihan,
<u>Beyond the Melting Pot: The Negroes, Puerto Ricans, Jews,
Italians and Irish of New York City</u> (Cambridge: Harvard
University Press, 1963), is a classic, penetrating analysis of
the application of ethnicity and politics.

Especially informative are biographies on a number of city
Italian American politicians. Accordingly, the East Harlem
radical Vito Marcantonio is the subject of works by Alan
Schaffer, <u>Caucus in a Phone Booth, The Congressional Career of
Vito Marcantonio</u> (Syracuse: Syracuse University Press, 1966);
Salvatore J. LaGumina, <u>Vito Marcantonio, The People's
Politician</u> (Dubuque: 1969); and Gerald Meyer, <u>Vito
Marcantonio, Radical Politician 1902-1954</u> (Albany: State
University of New York Press, 1989). The extensive literature
covering Fiorello H. LaGuardia include Arthur Mann's excellent
<u>LaGuardia: A Fighter Against His Times: 1882-1933</u>
(Philadelphia: Lippincott, 1959) and <u>LaGuardia Comes to Power:</u>

1933 (Philadelphia: Lippincott, 1965), both of which reflect the professional historian's deft touch for sifting out significant causes and effects of LaGuardia's rise to power. Charles Garrett in The LaGuardia Years: Machine and Reform Politics in New York City (New Brunswick, N.J.: Rutgers University Press, 1961) is equally informative as is journalist Ernest Cuneo's Life With Fiorello (New York: The Macmillan Co., 1955). Thomas Kessner, LaGuardia's most recent and most complete biographer provides profound insight. Dorothy Gallagher's All The Right Enemies, The Life and Murder of Carlo Tresca (New York: Penguin Books, 1988), is worthwhile as is Simon W. Gerson's Pete (New York: International Publishers Co. Inc., 1976). The vital role played by Carmine DeSapio in city politics is the subject of Warren Moscow's The Last of the Big-Time Bosses (New York: Stein and day, 1971). Readers should be aware, however, that Moscow is not impartial when discussing Impellitteri.

Biographies on non-Italian American politicians can be perused for profit on the subject. Among these are William O'Dwyer, Beyond The Golden Door (New York: St. John's University Press, 1987). Robert A. Caro's tome The Power Broker: Robert Moses and the Fall of New York (New York: Viking Books, 1975), although exceptionally comprehensive, is skewed to demonstrate the centrality of Moses' role, at the expense of other political figures.

Selected Bibliography

<u>NYMA</u>, New York City Municipal Archives, Impellitteri Papers.

<u>VIFP</u>, Vincent Impellitteri Family Papers are in possession of Rose Comcowich, Derby, Connecticut.

<u>ECP</u>, Edward Corsi Papers are housed in the George Arents Research Library for Special Collections at Syracuse University.

Victor Anfuso Papers are housed in Center for Migration Studies, Staten Island, New York.

Interviews were conducted with the following: Joseph Carlino, August 8, 1963; Eugene Canudo, October 24, 1963; Vincent Caso, August 19, 1963; Rose Impellitteri Comcowich, July 7, 1989; Edward Corsi, October 18, 1963; Joseph Corso, October 17, 1963; Dominic Florio, August 12, 1963; Vincent Impellitteri, August 12, 1963; Ferdinand Pecora, October 9, 31, 1963;, Ruth Whaley; April 6, 1966; Betty Santangelo, December 7, 1990.

Adamic, Louis. <u>Two-Way Passage</u>. New York: Harper Brothers, 1941.

Asbury, Herbert. "America's Number One Mystery Man." <u>Collier's</u> (April 12, 1947): 16-17+ and (April 19, 1947): 33-44.

Bailey, Harry A., and Katz, Eliis, Jr. <u>Ethnic Group Politics</u>. Columbus, Ohio: Charles E. Merrill Publishing Co., 1988.

Bendiner, Robert. "Racketeers and Reformers in City Hall." <u>Park East</u>. Part I, (September 1951), pp. 6-1, 55, Part II, (October 1951), pp. 43-50, Part III, (November 1951), pp. 27-35 .

Bowers, David. <u>Foreign Influences in American Life</u>. Princeton, N. J.: Princeton University Press, 1944.

Caro, Robert A. <u>The Power Broker: Robert Moses and the Fall of New York</u>. New York: Vintage Books, 1975.

Childs, Richard S. "New York's Mayor Must Be Three Men." The New York Times Magazine (April 3, 1953): 12-13, 27.

Costikyan, Edward N. Behind Closed Doors, Politics in the Public Interest. New York: Harcourt, Brace and World Inc., 1966.

DeNinno, Mary L. "Ethnic and Political Consciousness in the Italian Community of New York, 1940-1944." Master's Thesis, San Diego State University, 1980.

Diggins, John P. The Proud Decades American in War and Peace, 1941-1960. New York: W.W. Norton., 1988.

Eisenstein, Louis, and Rosenberg, Elliot. A Stripe of Tammany's Tiger. New York: Robert Speller and Sons, 1966.

Femminella, Francis X. The Italians and the Irish in America. New York: American Italian Historical Association, 1985.

Foerster, Robert F. The Italian Emigration of Our Times. Cambridge: Harvard University Press, 1919.

Fox, Stephen R. Blood and Power. New York: William Morrow and Co. Inc., 1989.

Gallagher, Dorothy. All The Right Enemies, The Life and Times of Carlo Tresca. New York: Penguin Books, 1988.

Gallo, Patrick J. Ethnic Alienation. The Italian American. Cranbury, N.J: Fairleigh Dickinson University Press, 1974.

Goldman, Eric F. The Crucial Decade--And After. New York: Alfred A. Knopf, Inc., 1965.

Halberstam, David. Summer of '49. New York: William Morrow and Co. Inc., 1989.

Iorizzo, Luciano, and Mondello, Salvatore. The Italian Americans. New York: Twayne, 1971.

Katz, Leonard. Uncle Frank, The Biography of Frank Costello. New York: Farrar, Straus, and Cudahy, 1973.

Kaufman, Herbert, and Sayre, Wallace S. Governing New York. New York: W.W. Norton and Co., 1965.

Kessner, Thomas. Fiorello H. LaGuardia and the Making of Modern New York. New York: McGraw-Hill, 1989.

Lait, Jack, and Lee Mortimer. New York Confidential. New York: Crown Publishers, 1952.

Levi, Carlo. Words Are Stone. New York: Farrar, Straus and Cudahy, 1958.

Lindsay, John. The City. New York: New American Library, 1970.

Lowi, Theodore. <u>At the Pleasure of the Mayor</u>. Glencoe, Ill.:
Free Press, 1964.

Mann, Arthur. <u>LaGuardia Comes to Power</u>. Philadelphia:
Lippincott, 1965.

Mitgang, Herbert. <u>The Man Who Rode The Tiger: The Life and
Times of Judge Samuel Seabury</u>. Philadelphia: Lippincott, 1963.

Montalto, Nicholas, V. "The Influence of Ethnicity Upon the
Political Behavior of the New York City Italian American
Community Since World War II." Master's Thesis, Georgetown
University, 1969.

Moorhouse, Geoffrey. <u>Imperial City: New York</u>. New York: Holt,
1988.

Moquin, Wayne, ed. <u>A Documentary History of the Italian
Americans</u>. New York: Praeger, 1974.

Morris, Jan. <u>Manhattan '45</u>. New York: Oxford University Press,
1987.

Moscow, Warren. <u>The Last of the Big-Time Bosses, The Life and
Times of Carmine DeSapio and the Rise and Fall of Tammany
Hall</u>. New York: Stein and Day, 1971.

--. <u>What Have You Done For Me lately? The Ins and Outs of New
York City Politics</u>. Englewood Cliffs, N.J.: Prentice-Hall,
1967.

--. <u>Politics in the Empire State</u>. New York: A.A. Knopf, 1948.

Musmanno, Michael. <u>The Story of the Italians in America</u>.
Garden City, N.Y.: Doubleday, 1965.

Newfield, Jack, and DuBrul, Paul. <u>The Abuse of Power, The
Permanent Government and the Fall of New York</u>. New York:
Penguin Books, 1978.

--. <u>New Yorker</u>. (April 3, 1948): 22-23; (October 28, 1950):
23-25; and (November 4, 1950): 38.

O'Dwyer, William. <u>Beyond The Golden Door,</u> Paul O'Dwyer, ed.
New York: St. John's University Press, 1987.

Orsi, Robert. <u>The Madonna of 115th Street</u>. New Haven, Conn.:
Yale University Press, 1985.

Peel, Roy V. <u>Political Clubs of New York City</u>. Port
Washington, N. Y.: I.J. Friedman Publishing Co., 1935.

Polenberg, Ronald. <u>One Nation Divisible.</u> New York: Penguin
Books, 1980.

Sayre, Wallace S., and Kaufman, Herbert. <u>Governing New York
City: Politics in the Metropolis</u>.New York: W.W. Norton Inc.,

1965.

Schriftgieser, Karl. " A Frantic Day With Our Next Mayor," The New York Times Magazine (October 22, 1950): 15, 50-53.

Shaw, Frederick. The History of the New York City Legislature. New York: Columbia University Press, 1954.

Starr, Roger. The Rise and Fall of New York City. New York: Basic Books, 1985.

Tomasi, Lydio F., ed. The Italians in America: The Progressive View. New York: Center For Migration Studies, 1972.

Truman, Harry S. Memoirs by Harry S. Truman, Years of Trial and Hope. New York: Signet Books, 1956.

United States Federal Writers Project. The Italians of New York. New York: Random House, 1938.

Walsh, George. Public Enemies, The Mayor, the Mob and the Crime That Was. New York: W.W. Norton, 1980.

Walter, John. The Harlem Fox, J. Raymond Jones, 1920-1970. Albany: State University of New York Press, 1989.

Westerhof, Caroline Shaffer. The Executive Connection. New York: Dunellen, 1974.

Whittemore, L. H. The Man Who Ran The Subways. New York: Holt, Rinehart and Winston, 1968.

Whyte, William F. Street Corner Society: The Social Structure of an Italian Slum. Chicago: University of Chicago Press, 1955.

Wolf, George. Frank Costello, Prime Minister of the Underworld. New York: William Morrow and Co., 1974.

Index

About the Author

SALVATORE J. LAGUMINA is professor of history and political science at Nassau Community College and the author of several books, including *From Steerage to Suburb: Long Island Italians* (1988) and *Ethnicity in Suburbia: The Long Island Experience* (1980).